A New Economics of Population, Pollution & Poverty Vs Peace & Prosperity

A New Economics of Population, Pollution & Poverty Vs Peace & Prosperity

R. K. SRIVASTAVA (SASHAKT)

PARTRIDGE
A Penguin Random House Company

To order additional copies of this book, contact
Partridge India
000 800 10062 62
orders.india@partridgepublishing.com

www.partridgepublishing.com/india

CONTENTS

'THE COMMAND OF NATURE

HAS BEEN PUT INTO MAN'S HANDS

BEFORE HE KNOWS

HOW TO COMMAND HIMSELF'

ACKNOWLEDGEMENTS

I am highly grateful to Mr. Rajesh Kumar Dwivedi (Sr.Manager & Faculty) of Allahabad Bank Staff College Lucknow who helped me in getting my access to its Library. I am also grateful to the Librarian of the College Library. I express my sincere thanks to the incharge of the NABARD Library, Lucknow Mr. M.K. Pathak (AGM) who too helped me alot through the NABARD Library. I acknowledge with thanks the valuable help and cooperation rendered by Mr O.P. Chaurasia of the Literacy House Kanpur Road, Lucknow. The facts and figures collected through the above mentioned three institutions became the corner stone of the Book, its props & pillars.

I dedicate this book to my wife Mrs. Rekha Rani and my daughters Pragya and Pragati whose close cooperation and help emboldened my spirits and gave me strength for its successful completion.

LIST OF GRAPHICAL REPRESENTATIONS/CARTOONS

Fig. 2

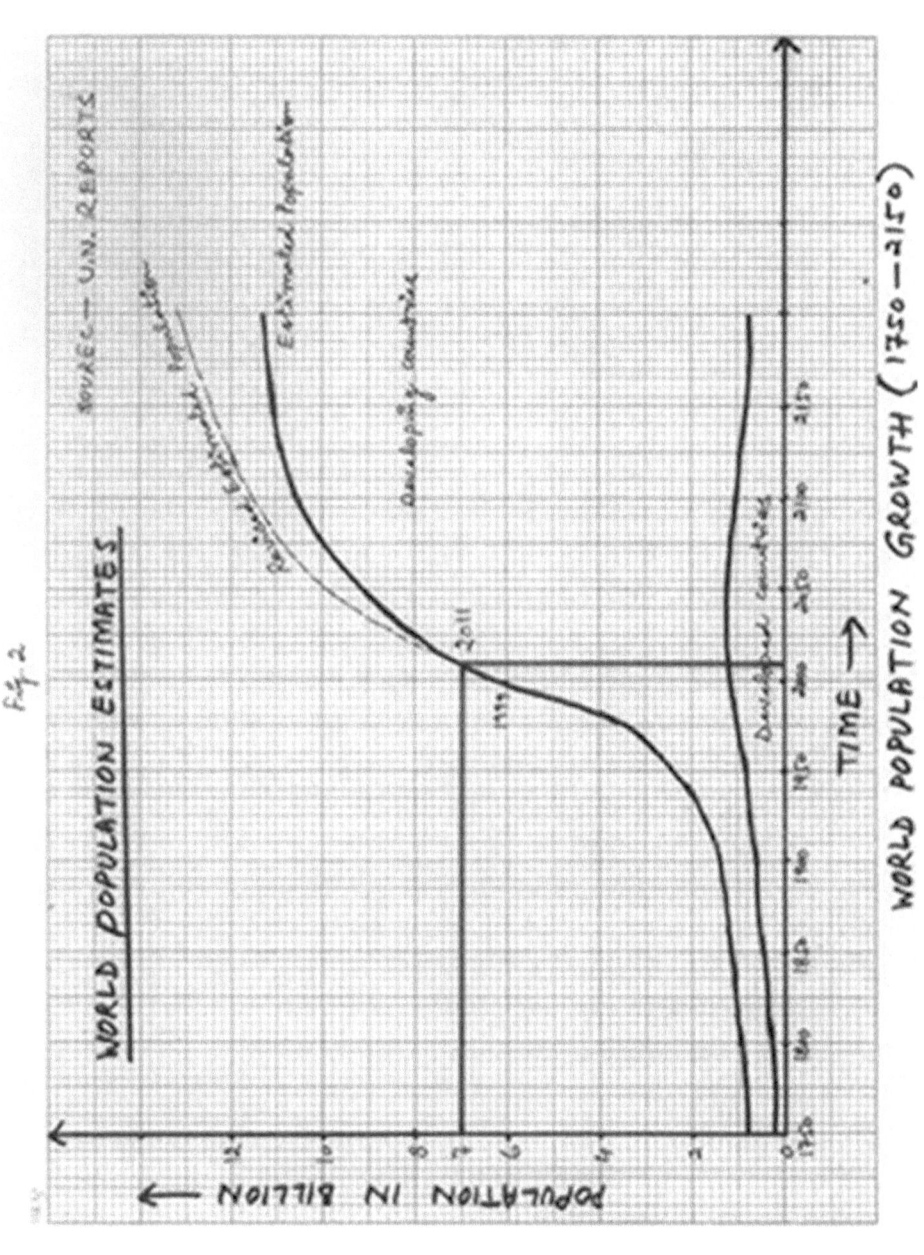

WORLD POPULATION ESTIMATES

SOURCE — U.N. REPORTS

WORLD POPULATION GROWTH (1750—2150)

INTRODUCTION

At the very outset of the book, I would like to mention a theme from a Hindi movie 'Mujhe Jine Do' (Let me survive) wherein wife of a dreaded robber casts doubts and fears regarding her three year old boy's future fate as she eagerly blesses him to attain young age rapidly. This is so, because her boy happens to be a son of a dreaded and rapacious robber who earns a bitter enmity from various corners of society and these enemies of his want to take revenge on this innocent boy. The movie was produced just after the Independence in 1947 and was depicting the menace and problem of robberies in Central India during those days.

The author wishes to draw a parallel between the newly born Indian nation in 1947 and the above story of the robber's son, as this young nation now faces a great threat to her survival from the disguised enemies of mass poverty, widespread unemployment and underemployment, rampant corruption in the entire system, rising inflation and price-rise, increasing attacks on women's modesty and above all failure of our entire political system to tackle the same. People of India, especially the youths are fast losing their confidence in the present political & economic set-up.

Today, on January 26, 2014, we, the people of India, are celebrating our 65th Republic Day, amidst a great political uncertainty. General elections for the new Lok Sabha (16th), (India's lower house of Parliament) are to be held in the coming months of April/May and the prospects of gaining a majority by the United Progressive Alliance (UPA) led by the grand Congress Party are very poor. (UPA lost the election very poorly and NDA came to power with a big majority.) Uncontrolled price-rise of all essential commodities and services for the people coupled with a very low economic growth rate (below 5 percent P.A), generating nil or very thinner employment opportunities for the youth,

1

created a very grave situation before the Indian people as well as the planners of Indian economy. Apart from it, the alleged high degree of corruption in government machinery and political big wigs has been like rubbing the salt over the wounds of the Indian people. Very big scams like 2 G spectrum scam, Coal scam, Common Wealth Games scam and several others involving lakhs of crores of rupees have been exposed none other than Government's own agency, the CAG (Comptroller & Accountant General of India).

India got her independence in August 1947 from the colonial yoke and then adopted a parliamentary democratic system as a means of governance. But, after a lapse of around 67 years, which is not a very big period in the life of a nation, though not worth ignoring, India's 81 crore (810 million) people do not have even the basic need of food security to survive, which demonstrates the hollowness of the policy makers and deplorable state of the economy. There appeared an advertisement in the Times of India, dt. January 18, 2014 issued by the Central Government wherein it was very proudly said that 81 crore (810 million) Indians got 'right to food' through its Right to Food Security Act 2013'.This clearly demonstrates that even after a lapse of 67 years of Independence, our leaders and planners could not secure the basic need of 'food security' to our 67 percent of population which is considered first and foremost security for any civilized society in the whole world. This implies that 810 million people of India are living under abject poverty and those fortunate who have food security but no security of medical health, education, housing and sanitation and adequate clothing would be much more. **By any calculation, the total number of poor who do not have the above mentioned securities including food security is not less than 90 crore (900 million) or 75% of the total population of India. This clearly indicates that poverty in India enormously increased with the passage of years since Independence.** This further manifests that nearly 20 crore (200 million) working-age group people do not have gainful employment and, either are unemployed or underemployed, not generating sufficient incomes to have access to all the above essential securities in India. This is the greatest threat to the survival of our young nation which creates deep concern in the mind of the author.

Fig. 3

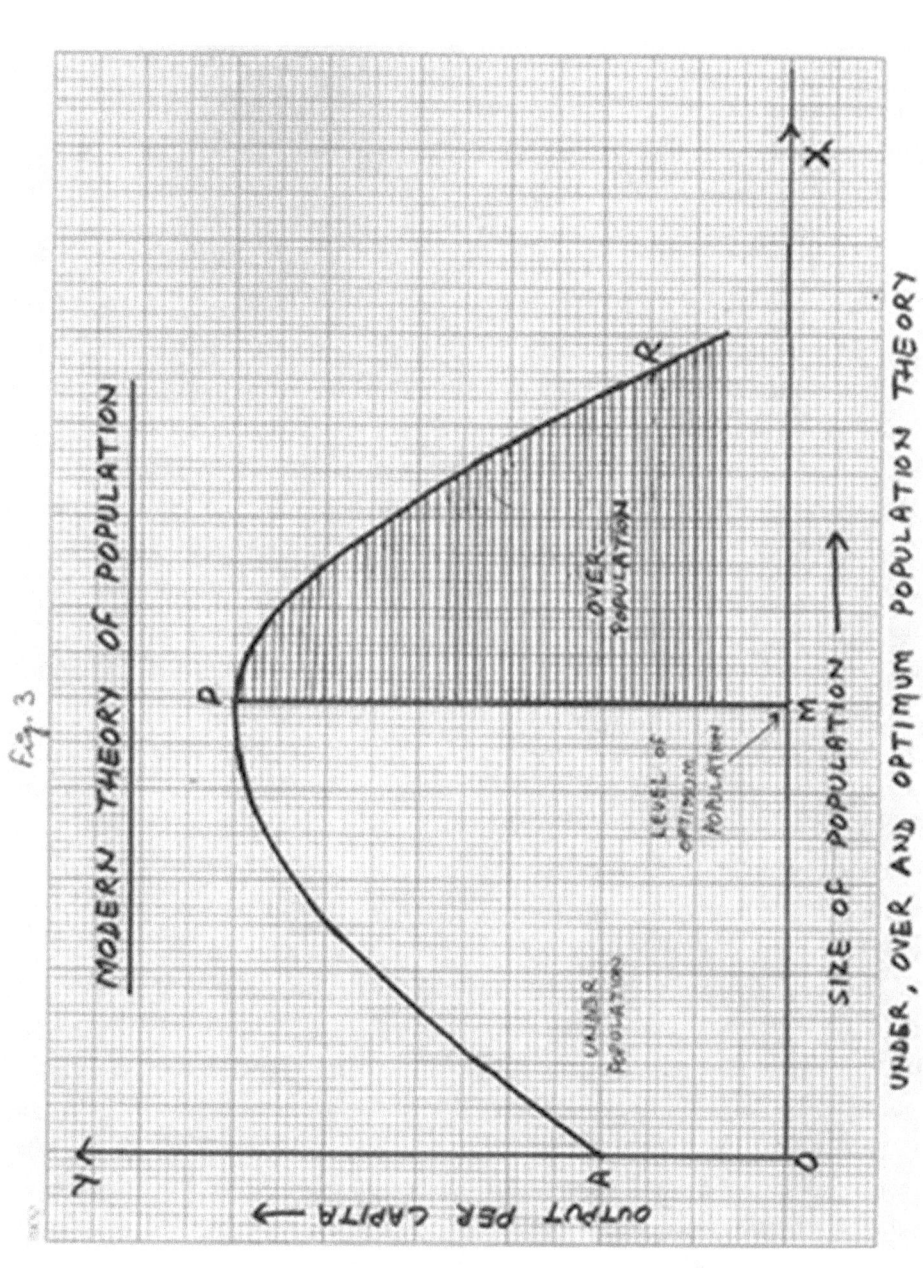

MODERN THEORY OF POPULATION

OUTPUT PER CAPITA ⟶

SIZE OF POPULATION ⟶

UNDER, OVER AND OPTIMUM POPULATION THEORY

The Indian polity has crossed the age of childhood and now acquired the age of a grown-up, matured youth. As it grows younger, the dangers and threats from all around looms large, appearing strong and tough. They are so much strong and sturdy as if it seems that the economy and polity will collapse in the near future, as the author foresees.

This book is a humble attempt to analyze and discover these looming dangers and seeks a viable solution for attaining a sustainable and healthy growth of the Indian economy wherein a pollution-free 'green growth' is envisaged. The author has a book in hand, entitled 'India's Economy in the 21st Century' edited by Raj Kapila and Uma Kapila, wherein India's 14 top ranked economists have contributed their articles, dealing deeply with the various economic sectors of India including Banking and Finance, Agriculture, Industry, Infrastructure and External sectors. These articles are very useful and enlightening, but none of these even tried to touch (with the exception of Mr. K.C. Pant) the gigantic and perilous population problem of India in the 21st century. They even did not discuss the environmental threats and damages to bio-diversity looming large over the sky of India owing to over-population needs. How can an economist remain oblivious of and unconcerned with the dangers of unbridled population growth over and above the **optimum level** in India, and its unchecked and irreparable damaging consequences on India's environment and biodiversity, apart from the existence of abject poverty? Should not the existence of abject poverty in the world, including India, be blamed on the thoughtless, mad expansion of human population beyond the level of 'optimum' one? Do the problems of over population and its consequential damaging impacts on earth's limited resources as well as on the environment and biodiversity not cover the scope of modern day Economics? Is Economics isolated from and unconcerned with the harmful effects of mad-raced 'physical growth' not only on humans but other co-habiting species on this earth also? Has not the high time arrived when Economists should ponder over 'Green Growth' or pollution-free growth? Is there any relevancy in economic growth along with growth of dreaded diseases and other serious death problems simultaneously? Does optimum population concept have any relation with the avoidance or limitation of wars and conflicts within a country and among the countries?

These are the pertinent questions to be put before the economists of India and the United Nations. Almost all the wars and conflicts in the world history have had their genesis in cornering and capturing the limited natural resources at that very point of time by the powerful and organized groups, massacring and subjugating the weak and unorganized. This is nothing but conflicts between the availability of limited/scarce natural resources and a relatively expanding demand for the same. But in ancient and medieval times, the development levels of technology was so low as to provide adequate vital resources to humans had been an impossibility; whereas in modern times, we are in a better placed position to satisfy the needs of all the humans adequately by increasing the supply of goods and services owing to the achievement of a very high level of technological knowhow and various scientific inventions and discoveries, provided we limit our numbers to an optimum level. In this way, we humans may be able to obliterate or mitigate the dangers of wars and conflicts substantially and concentrate our energy and resources towards all round development, including conservation of our environment. Mountainous military expenditures on men and materials (which include arms and ammunitions, atom bombs etc. for mass destruction) by the countries of the world may be reduced to a minimum thereby sparing the funds for more beneficial uses, problems of law and order and crimes shall, to a very great extent, get solved *ipso-facto* as unemployment, underemployment and poverty vanish from the surface of the earth and a relative prosperity steps in, rendering policing redundant. Small family norms (two children or replacement norms) would certainly lead to women empowerment, as women constitute 50 percent of the human race, in addition to raising literacy rate to 100 percent, shall improve the level of mass consciousness and general awareness to an unprecedented level. Society would be disease-free and healthy.

But, the author of this book is at a loss to see that no concrete efforts have been in sight either by the United Nations' experts or by the individual economists of repute to ponder over the need to calculate an **optimum level** of population for all countries of the world separately and then arriving at the world optimum population, which our earth could bear with. Similarly, our Indian economists too failed to ascertain India's optimum level of population; in real terms, they never tried it. The book 'India's Economy in the 21st Century' mentioned above amply proves this point as there are 14 top level Indian economists deliberated upon various economic problems of India, sans population problem, as if there exists no such problem in India or it does not come under the scope of Economics.

Here, I would like to remember reverently a great pioneering economist of the eighteenth century, **Thomus Malthus,** who put forward, for the first time, a theory of relationship between population growth and economic development, which is still valid in the 21st century. His 'Essays' on the 'Principle of Population' published in 1798, Malthus postulated a universal tendency for the population of a country to grow at a geometric rate, unless checked by dwindling food supplies, doubling in every 30 to 40 years. At the same time, food supplies could only expand roughly at an arithmetical rate, because of the principle of diminishing returns to the fixed factor, land. In this way, according to Malthus, after a lapse of definite time, gap between demand for food grains and its supply gets widened and an 'absolute poverty' starts to prevail unless a war or a famine breaks out to maintain the equilibrium between the two. He advised the people to engage in "moral restraint" and limit the numbers of their progeny. Though the theory of Malthus has been subject to ridicule for many modern economists, yet his message is loud and clear and holds good even in today's world. Now the time has come for us to evaluate correctly and honestly the contribution of Malthus in the field of population control. The author of this book pays his great tribute to Malthus and considers him as father of the demographic science who pioneered a close relationship between the availability of natural resources and human population. His message is clear. He necessitated to maintain an optimum level of human population vis-à-vis the availability of natural recourses and thus paved the way for an ecological preservation with a rich bio-diversity to be envisaged. The author has endeavored to bring home this point in this book enthusiastically.

India's population density increased from 163 persons per sq. km. in 1966 to 325 persons per sq. km. in 2001 and further to 382 persons per sq. km. in 2011 Census. The pressure on land and other natural resources is increasing day by day. The high population density generates great pressure on the carrying capacity of the land mass, which is just 2.4% of the world but has to bear the burden of 17.5% of the entire world population. The funny thing about statistical averages is that it masks a lot of harsh realities. While the population density of the country at 382 in itself is very high, the population density of Bihar, West Bengal and Uttar Pradesh is 1102, 1029 and 828 respectively. India's population is now expected to stabilize around 2060. According to the U.N. projections, India's population will surpass that of China by 2030 and make us the most populous nation.

Now the time has come when Economics, Ecology and Demography should be roped in together to attain a pollution free economic growth (or green growth) by maintaining an optimum level of human population, helpful in preserving rich biodiversity and ecology. While green growth or pollution free growth is necessary for a healthy, disease free, and prosperous life for humans, rich biodiversity is *sine qua non* for the very existence of the human race. This is possible only when our planners visualize the necessity and urgency of sticking to maintaining an optimum level of human population not only in India, but also for the whole world. Here the question arises as to how to arrive at the optimum level or how to calculate it? Economists have tried to give a theory of optimum population emphasizing on the level at which maximum output is achieved in any economy, popularly known as 'Modern Theory of Population'. According to it, the level of population at which per capita output or real income is at the maximum, then the population is considered to be optimum. If population further goes on increasing, i.e. crosses the optimum level, output per capita will begin to decline and the country would then become over-populated. (Fig.3) This theory of optimum population takes into account only the level of per capita output or real income and does not take into account the level of environmental degradation or loss of biodiversity within its orbit. Merely pursuing output or GDP growth without ascertaining its consequences on environment and bio-diversity is virtually a self-defeating exercise as what we gain by increasing output blindly might result into an increased level of harmful diseases and a wild destruction of biodiversity; **then we shall be spending a substantial chunk of our national income on medical research, medicines and hospital maintenance on the one hand and on preservation of environment and biodiversity on the other.**

Suppose, we continue to increase our agricultural and industrial output by regularly occupying and cutting down forests, it may increase our GDP in the short run, but ultimately we would be axing our own foot by destroying environment and biodiversity, inviting unbearable pollution and dreadful diseases not only for ourselves but for future generations also which may be irreversible. Similarly if we generate sufficient thermal electricity by burning coal and providing 24 x 7 electric supply to our citizens, neglecting the level of air pollution, it would prove hazardous for health. **These types of development are nominal, not real and are self-defeating. Hence the author puts forward a new theory of optimum population for humans which takes into its orbit** a concept of maintaining a proper balance between output, real income and healthy environment along with a proper care for rich biodiversity. The author termed it as 'green growth'. He emphasizes on maintaining a rational distribution of land area (which is constant) into agriculture, industry, forests, grass land and meadows, water bodies, residential accommodation and infrastructure development etc. In this way we may be able to ascertain a definite land area available for agricultural and allied activities with the simple reason that a healthy food security is the first and foremost priority to be provided to the human population as well as to the livestock. Dairy products and eggs, fish and meat are as essential as food grains for a healthy and wholesome diet, **hence healthy livestock is as important as healthy humans.**

Similarly, minimum 33% of the total land area is to be maintained as dense forests to preserve our environment and rich biodiversity. The 33% shall have to be extended to 40% to neutralize future industrial pollution (air, water and noise pollution). As of now, we have only 12% of real forests in India which are totally inadequate to neutralize the present level of pollution as well as to preserve a rich biodiversity. Factually, our biodiversity is on the decline and we are losing species regularly. A large chunk of forest land has been and is being occupied and cleared to satisfy the needs of regularly expanding human population in the form of agriculture, industrial, residential and other needs. Since the forest land is now impossible to occupy due to public and media attention, agricultural land has become a target of occupation for non-agricultural needs. This is all due to constantly growing needs of human population which is also on the increase. **It seems that a large army of humans has invaded this good earth and destroying its land, water, air and other natural resources in the name of development, consumerism and other tomfoolery actions, and is totally ignorant of jeopardizing their own existence in the end.** If we humans continue to increase ourselves like this and continue to occupy every space for our immediate needs by destroying forests, polluting air and water bodies and occupying agricultural land for non-agricultural uses, then that era is not very far when we shall destroy not only ourselves but all the life on this planet too. We humans have completely ignored and overlooked our future by pursuing a mad rat-race of 'physical growth' only, blind consumerism and foolish multiplying actions. This does not imply that we humans should give up growth efforts and begin to live a primitive life of medieval era, but should march very prudently and cautiously on the path of economic growth and development by limiting our numbers at an optimum level so that our scarce natural resources can be preserved/conserved for our coming generations along with maintenance of earth's environment and its biodiversity. **Mankind's present and future both should be healthy and prosperous.**

To think that humans can ever gain a victory over mother Nature through their scientific discoveries and technological inventions, is our greatest folly. Since they themselves are the creations of that very Nature, they can only discover its laws and mysteries, but can never master it. Whenever they try to meddle in or distort the laws of nature, shall not only they destroy themselves, but the whole of life on the earth too. Humans shall have to accept 'mother nature' as their master and regulator and they themselves are mere its gracious beneficiaries, servants and preservers. The whole ecology, wherein the humans constitute a small segment, is maintained and sustained only by the good natured mercy of the mother earth. **The Nature has had a peculiar system of 'checks and balances' through which it maintains life's sustainability on the earth all through the ages.** In the process of development of species, there appeared 'prudent humans' who had had a 'conceptual brain', with the help of which they began to disturb this system of natural checks and balances through their ignorant, arrogant and childish acts, thereby leading to a path of self-destruction. They are out to destroy the ecology of the Nature by their imprudent acts, threatening the whole biological world, including themselves. They are like cutting the very branch of the Nature-tree where upon they themselves are resting and thriving.

This book is a humble attempt to focus on the present distortions of development and growth concepts and a new approach to pollution free growth or 'green growth' has been put forward by the author before the economists as well as nature-lovers by integrating economics, ecology and demography to bring forth a prosperous, healthy and peaceful human existence, harmonious with the environment and biodiversity. Now the time has come when 'Economics' shall have to be transformed into 'Eco-economics' and profit-hungry 'Capitalism' to be transformed into 'Social-capitalism' to bring about a green, prosperous, peaceful world. **Mass poverty in India and in many other parts of the world has a direct relationship with the over population of humans vis-à-vis their respective deposits of natural resources.** If all the countries of the world prefer to maintain a level of optimum population in their respective domain, then the most of their problems would get solved in a peaceful manner and world peace might descend on the earth. This book may throw a new light in the darkened sky of economics and ecology wherein our good earth is stifling and suffocating today and heading towards an 'evil day'.

Famous economist, Professor Marshal had said;

"The evil day can only be postponed; it cannot be permanently exiled from the economic world."

Professor Marshal's economic world in the 20th century had always been confronting the 'evil day' but in 21st century, we shall be able to exile this evil day forever, provided we humans awake from slumber. I have full faith and a firm conviction in the ability and prudence of modern day humans who have not lost vision.

Lucknow (India)
R.K. Srivastava (Sashakt)
January 26, 2014
e-mail: shashakt07021951@gmail.com

CHAPTER – 1

Population Factor in History

At the dawn of human civilization, man survived his life by securing his food through 'foraging and hunting'- that is, through getting hold of natural produce (fruits and nuts, roots, wild animals, fish and shellfish) and processing them for feeding. This was about 10,000 years hence according to historians. This aboriginal man lived in groups or small societies to which historians called 'hunting & gathering societies' or 'foraging societies'. These groups or societies operated within an area of around 10-15 miles, subject to the availability of plant food or animals. Within that area, the individual members were continuously moving from one source of plant food to another or in pursuit of animals, while the band or group as a whole had had to move on every source of food so often as the food availabilities in a particular locality got used up. As the number of humans grew, the groups got divided and moved to other areas where food was then available. This expansion of human population continued with the passage of time and then there arose a situation where a large number of human groups had been foraging for food within a limited area of land and water. This created a shortage of food which compelled them to come into conflicts with each other. These conflicts and wars brought their male numbers down on the one hand and compelled them to move to new far off places on the virgin land. Early settlements on the banks of rivers and forests are the testimony of these movements.

Gradually these human groups learned the art of cultivating crops instead of relying upon nature to provide them with vegetable foodstuffs, and began to domesticate animals instead of simply hunting them daily. It was an innovation in the sphere of food security which transformed their whole way of living. This settled life activities led them towards agriculture and village life. People settled in one fertile place where water was available easily and began to use their knowledge of plantation gathered through generations for a guaranteed food supplies by planting the seeds of wild plants. Experience taught them that the seeds of certain plants were more fruitful than others and they began to breed such seeds. The regular harvests thus obtained, which enabled them to tether and feed more tame varieties of wild sheep, goats, cattle and donkeys. This settled and relatively peaceful life paved the way for population increase and their number grew at a higher speed which necessitated the search for more fertile land area to be occupied. In this way, first the existing village boundaries expanded and then some groups went away to form other new villages to accommodate extra population. Now land and animals have become the most important source of livelihood, specially the fertile land. Since this fertile land had been obtained by cutting down and clearing the dense forests with much difficulty, agriculture land became very precious and dear. At the same time, the villagers now faced a new problem which hunter-gatherers did not. The stored stocks of food, cattle and implements provided a motive for attacks by armed raiders from outside. **Now war, which was unknown among hunter gatherers, became a regular feature among villagers**. The group, strong enough in numbers and muscle power emerged victorious in conflicts and wars. This paved the way for capturing of women folk of the vauquished tribe after killing their men folk. This type of conflicts and wars continued for several hundred years to capture larger areas of fertile land, women for number increase, stored stocks of food grains, domestic animals and other implements. This was necessary for the existence on the one hand and for maintaining a balance between growing demands for food on the other, for supply of the same was limited and scarce. **Though there had been abundance of land area at that time, yet clear fertile land fit for agriculture with adequate water supply was certainly a scarce resource.**

Emergence of Slave Society

Gradually it was felt by the victorious groups that instead of killing the captured male enemies, they should be accepted as slaves to be used as free labourers in the agriculture and animal husbandry in lieu of their lives. In this way, the victorious party freed itself from the drudgery of labour in agriculture fields, up keep of their animals and other hard manual labour. Slaves had had no rights and their masters were free to use them as per their wishes, even to kill them at will. Later, these slaves were also used as ordinary soldiers in the battle fields. Till this time, small states began to emerge with petty kings and their armies possessing a sizeable area of land. Exploitation of slave labour was so intense that it often gave rise to slave revolts in history. Slaves were used as private property of the masters. There had occurred a number of wars among these small states for land, cattle, women, slaves and other assets. Some vanqished small states vanished from the scene during these wars and a large number of people killed. The victorious states incorporated the smaller vanquished states to emerge as medium-sized states.

Feudal Society

After the lapse of several hundred years, the slave system collapsed owing to large number of slave revolts and internecine wars among slave states. On the emergence of medium size states, the form of slavery too changed. Now the slaves had had more freedoms and transformed themselves into 'serfs'. A serf now had been allowed to have a piece of land to cultivate for himself and his family, but at the same time, he had had to work in the fields of his feudal lord under whose protection he was to live. They had had no liberty to leave their land and area. This may be termed as refined slavery. Exploitation of serfs continued unabated and we find several peasant and serf revolts in medieval history. Now wars among these feudal states became more intense and large scale armies fully equipped with lethal iron weapons became a regular feature which further gave boost to internal exploitation of the weak and external plunder. **Here again we find a naked loot and plunder of limited natural resources to satisfy the growing physical needs of the increasing population along with added greed and lust of the autocratic feudal lords and kings.** During this period, large number of castles, forts, tombs and mausoleums, large and beautiful palaces, magnificent temples, churches and mosques and other magnificent buildings had been built on the forced labour of serfs and war-captives.

Thus feudal society transformed itself into two antagonistic classes. One was a class of feudal lords, knights and the clergy whose way of life centered around luxury consumption, preparation for wars and notions of military honor, which over-time became a drain on the scarce natural resources and hard-earned wealth created by serfs and artisans. A wealthy merchant coterie too emerged during these days. The other class was the oppressed section of the pauperized peasants and serfs, humble artisans and emerging merchant class.

A society based on the oppression and naked exploitation of a large mass of people could not survive too long and gave birth to revolts and revolutions all over the world within these societies. Europe was the hotbed of bourgeois revolutions because bourgeoisie or the middle class came into existence by this time and was enlightened with the new ideas of renaissance and reformation on the one hand and new inventions and discoveries in the field of science on the other, which loosened the hold of church on people's minds. These two factors facilitated for an organized movement of all the oppressed classes under the leadership of the bourgeoisie (middle class) which put an end to the feudal system and a new system took birth from its womb which was later termed as 'Capitalist System' of society.

Birth of Capitalist Society

Renaissance, reformation and scientific advancement preceded the advent of capitalism in Europe. Renaissance implies the rebirth of learning. Reformation stands for cleaning of the Catholic Church of its corruption and putting an end to its high handedness towards the general followers. The flower of renaissance bloomed from Italy and later it spread to Greece. It was an urban growth and the cities of northern Italy gave shelter to it. The city of Florence was the original centre of early renaissance. Names like Leonardo da Vinci, Michelangelo and Raphael were the pioneers and they inspired the people of Italy by their great paintings and wonderful sculpture. Leonardo was not only a great painter and sculptor, but a great thinker and a scientific genius too. He always emphasized on experiment and reasoning and brought the science to a sound foundation. He was always asking questions and trying to find answers to them by experiments.

Renaissance flowered in Italy and Greece from fifteenth century and gradually reached to other parts of Western Europe. Some more names of the renaissance were Copernicus, Giordano Bruno, Galilio, Socreties, Harvey, Newton, Milton and Machiavelli. From fifteenth to the seventeenth centuries, science gradually forged ahead and established itself among the enlightened masses. It came into conflict with the orthodox Roman Catholic Church, for the Church did not like in making people think and experiment. Science told that the earth revolves round the sun and not vice versa, as preached by the Church. It also repudiated the belief of the Church that the earth was the centre of the universe and sun went round it. Science also repudiated the Church's teaching that the stars were fixed points in the heavens. Catholic Church declared science-men as heretics and severely punished them by the Inquisition and burning alive.

Prior to the coming of renaissance and reformation in Europe, there emerged another revolutionary event in Europe and this was the emergence of printing press at the end of the fifteenth century. This printing press brought an intellectual transformation of society. Year by year, the printing press sent forth more books for readers and this made an enormous change on the mindset of the people. Very soon, there were many people who could read and write. The more they read, the more they thought. Then appeared newspapers in Europe. The first newspaper published in England was with the onset of Industrial Revolution. The circulation and sale of newspaper grew as they were cheap and could be purchased by men of ordinary means. This further increased the awareness level among the masses greatly and with it sprouted the thinking process among the common people. This gave a great fillip to renaissance, reformation and spread of science and rational thinking in Europe which produced Industrial Revolution in England during the mid-eighteenth century. This was a turning point in England and Europe as it produced a capitalist system of production wherein production of goods was done with the help of machines on a mass scale. Earlier, the production of goods was done manually by individual artisans and this was need based. Now the production was done on mass scale to earn more and more profits.

Thus Industrial Revolution gave rise to capitalist system of production where all farms, factories and other means of production were either the property of the private individuals or of the joint stock companies. They were free to use them with a view to making profits. The desire for profits was the sole consideration with the capitalists in the use of their capital or property. This system needed a free social & political order where no restriction was to be imposed on production, its sale and movement to markets. Feudal lords and kings were autocrats and whimsical and did not allow a free market or production mode to develop and placed several restrictions thereupon. In few years, there arose a conflict between the emerging capitalist class and the feudal monarch. Ordinary people and peasants were already too much oppressed and exploited by the feudal lords. Hence, all these oppressed classes organized themselves under the leadership of this emerging capitalist class which gave rise to capitalist revolutions all over Europe during the eighteenth and nineteenth centuries. These revolutions turned the table in favor of capitalism and feudalism became history.

Under capitalism, the machine based large scale production turned into mass production and to sell the produced goods into the markets was a big challenge as there were several capitalists who were in competition with one another. This gave rise to capturing of markets all over the world and various capitalist governments in Europe fought with each other for capture of markets in Asia, Africa, Latin America and in Europe itself. Bitter wars were fought during the eighteenth and nineteenth centuries to achieve this end. This gave rise to imperialism and colonialism all over the world and imperialist powers divided the whole world among themselves to boost profits by capturing their markets.

Imperialist Era

Capitalism created a fertile ground for the expansion of imperialism all over the world. New inventions and discoveries with the help of science created a new horizon for machine making and its commercial use to earn more and more profits. With the combination of new machines, new metallurgy and new energy source increased the production immeasurably high which was unprecedented. With the invention of steam engine, engineers applied it to powering ships, the rail vehicles and the factories. The first passenger train ran from Manchester to Liverpool in 1830. Now people could move at a speed they never imagined before. Goods made in one city could be found in another in a couple of hours instead of in a couple of days. Now armies could be moved from one end of a country to the other overnight.

Inventions of gaslights and electric bulbs made night work possible and factories worked from sunrise to late midnight producing goods on enormous scale. Industrial Revolution first transformed England into an industrial society and soon followed other European countries the same British mode and slowly industrialized themselves. The capitalist class of Europe was in the run for markets all over the world to sell its cheap products and earn more and more profits. This mad pursuit for markets produced conditions for imperialism. As Marx wrote in his 'Communist Manifesto';

"The need of a constantly expanding markets for its products chases the bourgeoisie over the whole surface of the globe. It must nestle everywhere, settle everywhere...... The bourgeoisie through its exploitation of the world market gives a cosmopolitan character to production and consumption in every country. To the great chagrin of reactionaries it has drawn from under the feet of industry the national ground on which it stood...... In place of the old local and national seclusion and self sufficiency, we have intercourse in every direction, universal interdependence of nations.... The bourgeoisie by its rapid improvement of all the investments of production, by the immensely facilitated means of communication, draws all nations into civilization. The cheap price of its commodities are the heavy artillery with which it batters down all Chinese walls...... It compels all nations, on the pain of extinction, to adopt the bourgeois mode of production...... In other words, it creates a world after its own image."

What Marx wrote in 1847 completely portrays the present world scenario – of what today we call 'globalization' of the economy. Soon, the whole world was under the domination of European and Japanese imperialist powers with the exception of the Ottoman Empire, Thailand, Ethiopia and Afghanistan. By 1900 AD, almost all Africa was colonized. Britain, France and Belgium had divided the African continent among themselves, leaving small countries for Germany and Italy. Whole of Indian subcontinent was already under the British occupation. During the same period, France, Russia and Germany established wide spheres of influence all over China, and Japan took over Korea and Taiwan. France occupied all of Indo-China and the U.S. seized Puerto Rico and the Philipines from Spain. Britain and Russia agreed to an informal partition of Iran. Even the smaller islands of the Pacific and Indian Oceans were under the control of Britain and France.

This occupation of the world did not happen peacefully, rather large scale wars took place all over the world in which millions of people had been killed and maimed.

First World War (1914 - 1918)

The period of 50 years preceding the First World War witnessed a bitter competition among the states to increase their respective military strength, to occupy new colonies in Asia and Africa and to redistribute territories already captured. The rich and industrialized countries were eager to earn more and more money and procure markets to sell their products. In order to meet their economic needs, they needed more and more colonies. France and Italy which were passing through a stage of balance between agriculture and industry wanted to establish their hold on Asia, Africa and east European countries to invest their excess wealth and to dump their products. This led to a scramble for colonies.

Destructive Impact of the War

The First World War lasted around 4 years and 65 million (6 crore 50 lakh) soldiers from 30 countries participated in this War. Both the victors and the vanquished had had to pay the price. The war was the bloodiest yet in human history, with about 10 million (one crore) dead- 1.8 million in Germany, 1.7 million in Russia, 1.4 million in France, 1.3 million in Austria-Hungary, 7,40,000 in Britain and 6,15,000 in Italy. France lost one in five males of fighting age, Germany one in eight. Over 23 million shells were fired during the five month battle of Verdun – two million men took part, half of them were killed. Yet neither side made any gains. One million died in the four month Battle of the Somme in 1916, with Britain losing 20.000 men on the first day.

About 1,95,36,000 people wounded during the war. The average deaths during the war period was 7,000 persons per day. There were 7,50,000 deaths through malnutrition only in Germany. On the whole various countries had had to suffer an economic loss to the tune of 40,000 million dollars. Loss of trade and commerce and property was enormous.

Second World War (1939-1945)

The Second World War was the direct outcome of the Nazi leader Adolf Hitler's ambitions to dominate the world to acquire bigger markets. The treaty of Varsailles was forced to sign on Germany after her defeat in the First World War and this was the most humiliating treaty in world history. The German people never forgave their government for signing this most disgraceful treaty. Hitler gave voice to German people to revolt against this treaty and take revenge on the very forces who imposed it on her. He denounced the Versailles Treaty as one-sided and partial. He stirred up the emotions of the Germans by condemning the treaty, heaped abuses on the victorious nations for imposing it and pledged that he would abrogate it if he came to power. Hitler built up a great war machine prior to the commencement of the war.

The crisis of nineteen thirties, known as-"the Great Slump" also led to tensions between states as well as between different classes. The government of each country sought to ease the economic pressure on themselves at the expense of their rivals abroad. They devalued their respective currencies in order to expand their exports of domestically produced goods which further enhanced tensions among states. In the east, Japan was another imperialist power which had already occupied Taiwan and Korea as colonies and controlled substantial concessions in northern China. Japan further occupied Chinese region of Manchuria in 1931 and began to cast her eye on the Western empires in south-east Asia. The Dutch East Indies, the British colonies in Malaya, Borneo and Singapore, the French colonies in Indo-China and the U.S. controlled Philippines.

In Europe, Mussolini's Italy sought to expand its colonial empire by grabbing Ethiopia to add to Somali land, Eritrea and Libya and cast an eye on an opportunity to grab Albania and the Adriatic coast of Yugoslavia. Actually, this all was once again an allout attempt by the imperialist powers of Europe and Japan to grab more and more territories at the expense of others. All these powers imposed heavy taxation on their respective people to build up an unprecedented war machine and to raise big armies to be able to wage another bloody war on the landscape of the world. Imperialist powers led by the U.S.A., Britain and France emerged victorious in this devastating war wherein the humanity tasted a shameful defeat.

Disastrous Impact of the War

There was enormous destruction of human lives, homes, industries and communication networks in Europe and Asia. Almost 40 million (4 crore) people were killed, another 21 million people were uprooted from their homes, some were taken to Germany to work as slave laborers and some were put in concentration camps. The number of stateless uprooted people in Europe was 40.5 million; about 13 million Germans were expelled from the parts of Germany annexed by Poland and the USSR, from Czechoslovakia and parts of south eastern Europe.

Large parts of Germany, especially her industrial areas and many major cities lay devastated. So was the case with Russia, France, Italy and Japan. The loss of productive capacities was also enormous. About 20% pre-war capital assets of the USSR, 13% of Germany, 8% of Italy, 7% of France and 3% of Britain were destroyed. The soviet Union which made the decisive contribution to routing Nazi Germany and its satellites, lost 20 million people in the fronts, in the enemy occupied territories, and in concentration camps. The war struck at every family, leaving behind millions of invalids, orphans and widows. It lost nearly one-third of its national wealth which had been created with the hands of many a generation. 31,850 industrial enterprises were destroyed during the war. Enormous damage was done to the country's fuel and energy industry. Over a thousand mines were destroyed in the Donetsk and Moscow coal fields. More than 3000 oil wells were damaged or ruined in the Grozny and Krasnodar oil fields. The German Army blew up 61 major and a great number of smaller electric power stations. The enemy did great damage to the railways and river-transport systems, destroying thousands of kilometers of railways, roads, railway stations and bridges. 1710 towns and cities and more than 70,000 villages and hamlets were burnt down and ruined. Great damage was done to the country's major cities, Leningrad, Kieve, Stalingrad, Minsk, Kharkov, Dnepropetrovsk, Smolensk and Kursk. 25 million people were rendered homeless.

The British casualties were, a total of 2,70,000 servicemen lost their lives in 6 year war, as well as over 60,000 civilians killed on the home front in German air raids. By 1945 German casualties on the Eastern Front totaled six million, and the total number of Russian dead reached 13 million soldiers and 7 million civilians. The war involved unbelievable brutality, and brutalized soldiers were prepared to tolerate if not join in, the mass murder of Russian and Jewish civilians, with excuse that they might provide support for resistance activities. The attempt to exterminate all of Europe's Jewish and Roma Gypsy population in secret.

Japan's loss of men and property was the heaviest. She lost her two big cities Hiroshima and Nagasaki, completely obliterated from the map of the world by the Atom Bombs dropped by the U.S.A. Neither any property nor life (human and others) could survive.

Cold War

With the end of the Second World War, the people and politicians of the world hoped that now a lasting peace would descend on the earth and the damages done owing to War could be replenished soon. The humanity would now move towards an economically prosperous and politically peaceful living. But these expectations did not come true. The post-War world was a divided world between the two super powers namely the U.S.A. and the U.S.S.R. They were representing contradictory ideologies with two entirely different social and economic systems. While the U.S.A. and its allies were following a capitalist liberal economic system with democratic polity, the U.S.S.R. and its allies were pursuing a socialist/communist regulated economic system with a dictatorial polity controlled by the communist parties of the individual countries. These divergent paths generated so much tension and animosity that a fierce war of charges and counter-charges with deep suspicion on each side continued for many years. This is known as 'Cold War'. They never indulged into a direct conflict with each other and maintained diplomatic relations, even then treated each other with hostility and tension. Both groups fought a proxy war through other countries and done a great damage to men and material in proxy war countries.

Military expenditure on both sides leapt to heights unprecedented in peace time, reaching about 20% of U.S. national output and up to 40% of Russia's smaller output. Russia built secret cities to develop an atom bomb to rival the U.S., while the U.S. developed the H-bomb-100 times more destructive than the atom bomb and maintained a fleet of armed nuclear bombers permanently in flight. It was not long before the combined arsenals of the two super powers were enough to destroy the world many times over. Yet generals on both sides played war games which assumed the use of these weapons.

The Korean War

The immediate aftermath of the 'Cold War' was the Korean War. North Korea under a communist leadership and South Korea under a capitalist leadership clashed in June 1950 and both the super powers came in support of the one and the other, the U.S. supported 'South' and the U.S.S.R. North Korea. The war lasted three years. The human cost was enormous. There were 5,00,000 Western casualties and 15,00,000 on the communist side. Two million (20 lakh) civilians were killed and half population of South Korea lost their homes and turned refugees. The general Korean people gained nothing at all. This animosity between North Korea and South Korea is still continuing and posing a great danger to world peace, even after the end of the 'Cold War'.

Vietnam War

Vietnam War was another aftermath of imperialism and then taken over by the 'Cold War'. The whole of Indo-China (Vietnam, Combodia and Laos) had been under the imperialist domination of France since the beginning of the twentieth century. Imperialist France fully exploited the people of Indo-China in every field. The nationalist revolution in China fostered the Vietnam national movement. Some native intellectuals went to France for study and came into the influence of the French liberal traditions alike Indian national leaders. These intellectuals began to take interest in the political philosophy of the eighteenth century French writers like Rousseau and Montesquieu. They began to organize national movements for the liberation of Indo-China.

After the end of the Second World War, national movement for the liberation of Indo-China gathered momentum under the leadership of Ho-Chi-Minh and became successful in constituting a free government which they named as 'Viet-Minh' in the northern part of Vietnam with Hanoi as its capital. Armed resistance to French occupation continued and Viet-Minh forces fought a guerilla warfare to overcome a powerful enemy. They got success in defeating French occupation army in the battle of Din-Bin-Fu in 1954 and compelled the French government to sign an agreement in Geneoa on April 23, 1954, according to which;

1- Vietnam was bifurcated into North & South;
2- All French troops had to be withdrawn from the Vietnamese territory;
3- It was agreed to hold a general election in 1956 to pave the way for the unification of the two parts; and
4- An international commission comprising India, Canada and Poland was set up to supervise the implementation of the terms of this agreement.

But this agreement could not get success due to non-observance of terms by the both sides and a fresh war erupted between North and South Vietnam. The U.S.S.R and China supported North Vietnam while South was supported by the U.S.A and her allies. American armed forces landed in South and its Air Force bombarded North with full force. This war continued for 15 years and millions of people killed on both sides. The world opinion began to demand cessation of this bloody and destructive war and finally an armistice was signed on January 27, 1973. As per the terms of the agreement, the U.S.A withdrew its forces from South Vietnam thereafter. But war did not stop there and ultimately forces of North Vietnam occupied Siogon, the capital city of South, thus unified the whole country. War in Laos and Cambodia continued for some more years.

India-Pakistan War (three times), India–China War, Iran-Iraq War, Iraq-Kuwait War and Israil-Arab War (three times) were other major wars in the world wherein millions of people had been killed and maimed and enormous valuable property destroyed. With the collapse of the Soviet Union, Cold War ended, but not the dangers of wars. The world is still not free from the dangers of large scale destructive wars.

Terrorism

This is a very different type of warfare used by the terrorist groups. The terrorists are invisible and they intermingle with the general public with an intention to kill and maim as many innocent people as they can. They even never hesitate to kill women and children. It is very difficult to fight them because of these factors. They are called terrorists, for they create terror in the minds of the common people who have nothing to do with them. Terrorists do there activities clandestinely and generally attack innocent civilians in crowded places. There aim remains to destroy maximum number of lives and property to harass their target governments or organizations by spreading terror into the minds of the people.

In our world, terrorism has done immense harm and inflicted sufferings through mass killings of innocent people. There are a number of terror outfits exist in many parts of the world, demanding separate state like the Basque in Spain, the IRA in northern Ireland, the Intifada in West Asia, the LeT in Jammu and Kashmir in India, the LTTE in Sri Lanka, Hamas in Jordan,

Hezbollah in Lebanon, the Abu Sayaf in Philippines and the most powerful Al Qaeda operating from several Islamic countries. It has masterminded several daring attacks on the pro-Israil western countries which include the U.S.A, the U.K., France etc. Its followers hijacked two American civilian aero planes and smashed them against the World Trade Centre at New York on September 11, 2011 and razed it to ground, killing around 4,000 people and causing a loss worth 90,000 million dollars. These twin towers were symbol of prestige and prosperity of the U.S.A.

In Sri Lanka, millions of people, both Tamils and Singhalese including army men and LTTE guerillas have been killed and wounded during the last 30 years of militancy. In India, LeT terrorists of Jammu & Kashmir have killed and wounded more than 3,000 civilians and many army personnels. Indian Army has killed more than 60,000 terrorists during the last 15 year-long militancy in that state. Terrorism is a sepsis of society and is born out of widespread disparities and regional differences, religious bigotry and intolerance. This emerges from the state of critical desperation among minority groups having no hope of justice from the ruling majority. **Abject poverty and massive unemployment give a fillip to it.**

Inferences Drawn

The purpose of looking back into history since the dawn of human civilization is to demonstrate that human societies have been clashing and conflicting with one another in order to secure maximum chunk of natural resources which were scarce and limited in comparison to the needs of the contemporary humans. They subjugated the weaker members of their own and exploited their labour to strengthen themselves further. These stronger sections gave birth to the institution of the state and state power and raised large armies to intimidate their neighbors and occupy their natural resources (land, cattle, forest, water bodies, slaves and women etc.). The ordinary and subjugated people were the majority soldiers to sacrifice their lives for the sake of their master's greed and whims. These masters turned into rich and propertied classes on account of plunder and exploitation. They built large empires on the basis of plundered and exploited money/wealth and labour and spent this easy wealth in building expensive forts, large magnificent palaces, tombs and mausoleums, magnificent temples and gothic churches, big mosques and other unproductive luxuries and whims. They spent large sums of money on the maintenance of large seraglios (*haram*) of the acquired enemy women and a large army of retinues to serve them. This situation continued till the end of the feudal society. The situation changed at the advent of capitalist society and Industrial Revolution, wherein emphasis shifted on investment in profitable enterprises to earn more profits, looking for markets all over the globe and building colonial empires. The feudal societies could not face famines and floods owing to their primitive knowhow and very limited means which culminated into demographic collapses.

Thus we observe that, though the human population from the dawn of its civilization to the feudal age was not large, can be termed as under populated and could easily be sustained with a rich supply of necessities of life, yet a peaceful, prosperous and scarcity-free secured life for commoners was as illusive as it is today.

The advent of Industrial Revolution along with advancement of science and technology produced a capitalist society wherein a commodity is produced on a mass scale to sell it in the market for profit. This society too could not procure a peaceful, prosperous, healthy and scarcity–free secure life to humans; instead capitalism gave a great fillip to a scramble for markets, intensified the exploitation of labour and extortion of peasantry, occurrence of two greatly devastating world wars and several other localized wars wherein hundreds of millions of people lost their lives, maimed and rendered homeless. Unemployment and underemployment rose to an unprecedented high level and left an environment full of pollution and dreadful diseases, rendering biodiversity endangered. It gave rise to imperialism and colonialism which intensified Third World extortion and exploitation which further gave birth to national liberation movements in all the Third World Countries. These national liberation movements culminated into getting freedom and independence to almost all the Third World Countries during the last half century. They began to pursue their own path of development and growth with an intention to providing their people a prosperous, peaceful & disease-free life; but we are sorry to note that none got success in this respect except China, where we do observe that her people are not free from fear and are not masters of their own will despite economic prosperity and general wellbeing.

On the other hand, the developed countries of the world too are not free from various economic problems and prevalence of a high rate of unemployment despite their prosperity. Another bewildering catastrophe emerged out of rat-race for 'physical' growth and development among all the countries of the world is the ecological damage, global warming and a great threat to biodiversity, looming large over the world. This all happened due to a blind and greedy exploitation of earth's natural resources, having no concern for ecological catastrophe and no consideration for the left-over for the future generations. Historian Chris Harman writes;

'The very economic dynamism that characterizes capitalism has vastly increased the speed at which negative ecological consequences make themselves felt. Nineteenth century accounts of what capitalism does to working class communities, from Dickens and Angels onwards, are also accounts of polluted atmosphere, endemic diseases, over crowding and adulterated food in slum life. But at a time when a maximum of ten million people worldwide were involved in industrial capitalist production, ecological devastation was a localized problem.' The author has endeavored to address these problems in this book and tried to locate the real problem behind all these distortions. The author feels that the excessive & uncontrolled increase of human population all over the globe (it has already crossed 7 billion in 2011), demanding every necessity and luxury enthusiastically, driving the capitalists and entrepreneurs to augment supplies of the same without taking into account its pros and cons, are the root causes for the imminent catastrophe pointed out by Chris Harman and several other environmentalists all over the world. Adherence to **optimum population** for every country as well as for the world as a whole is a **necessary** condition for maintaining a nice and prudent balance between the nature and the living species including humans. Further, use of a fruitful, eco-friendly technology and science in preventing damages to environment shall be a **sufficient** condition for a healthy and peaceful world. We shall be discussing the same in the subsequent chapters.

———◆———

Fig 05

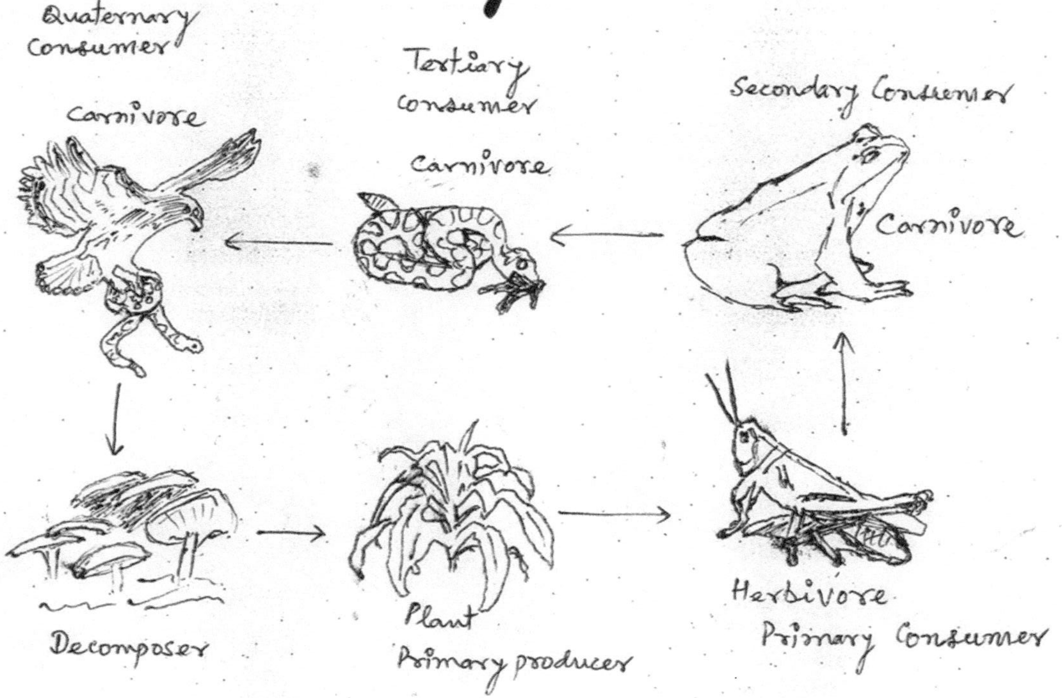

Tertiary
Consumer

Carnivore

Secondary Consumer

Carnivore

Herbivore
Primary Consumer

Quaternary
Consumer

Carnivore

Plant
Primary producer

Decomposer

THE FOOD CHAIN OF LIFE MATTER

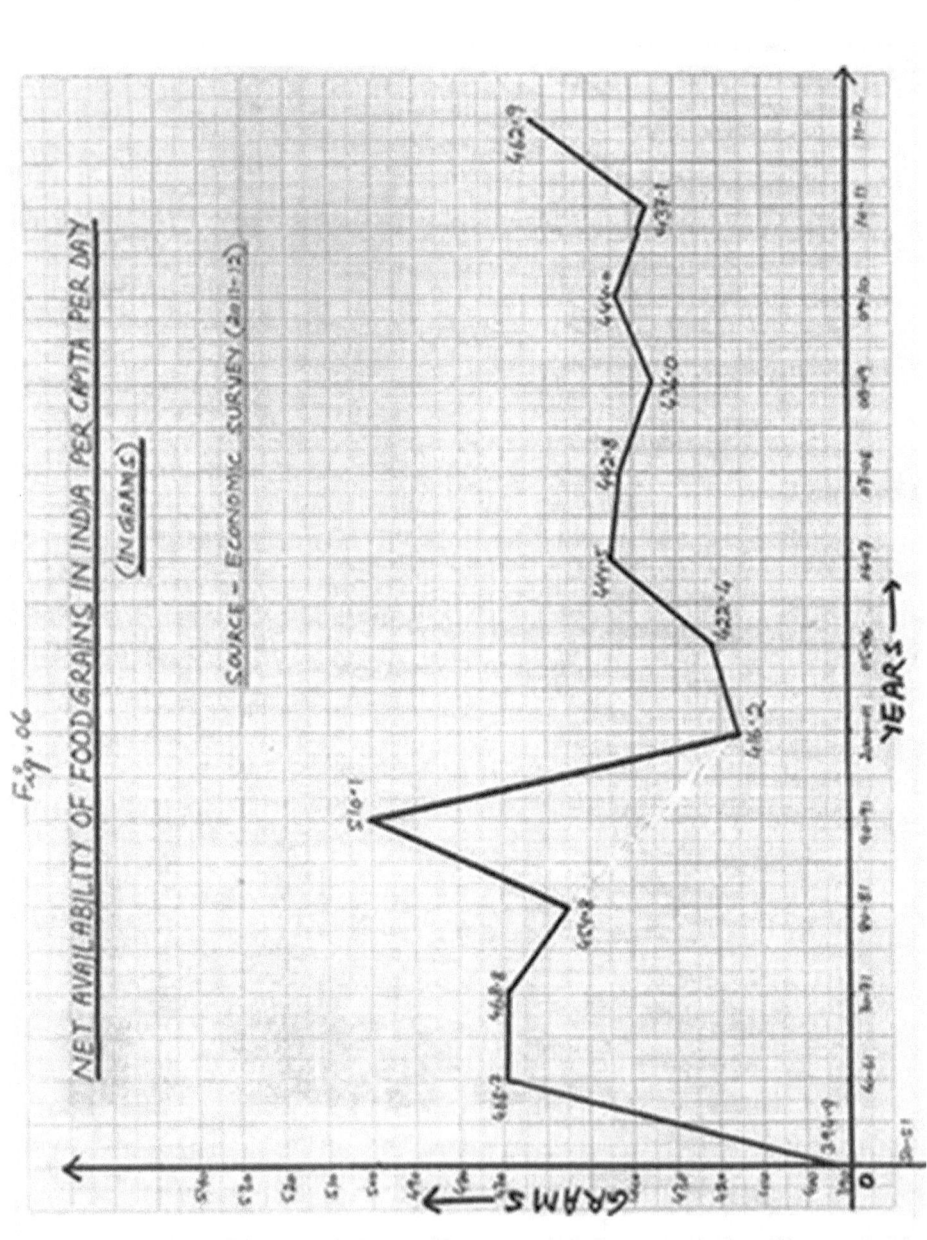

Fig. 06

NET AVAILABILITY OF FOODGRAINS IN INDIA PER CAPITA PER DAY

(IN GRAMS)

SOURCE – ECONOMIC SURVEY (2011-12)

Fig- 11

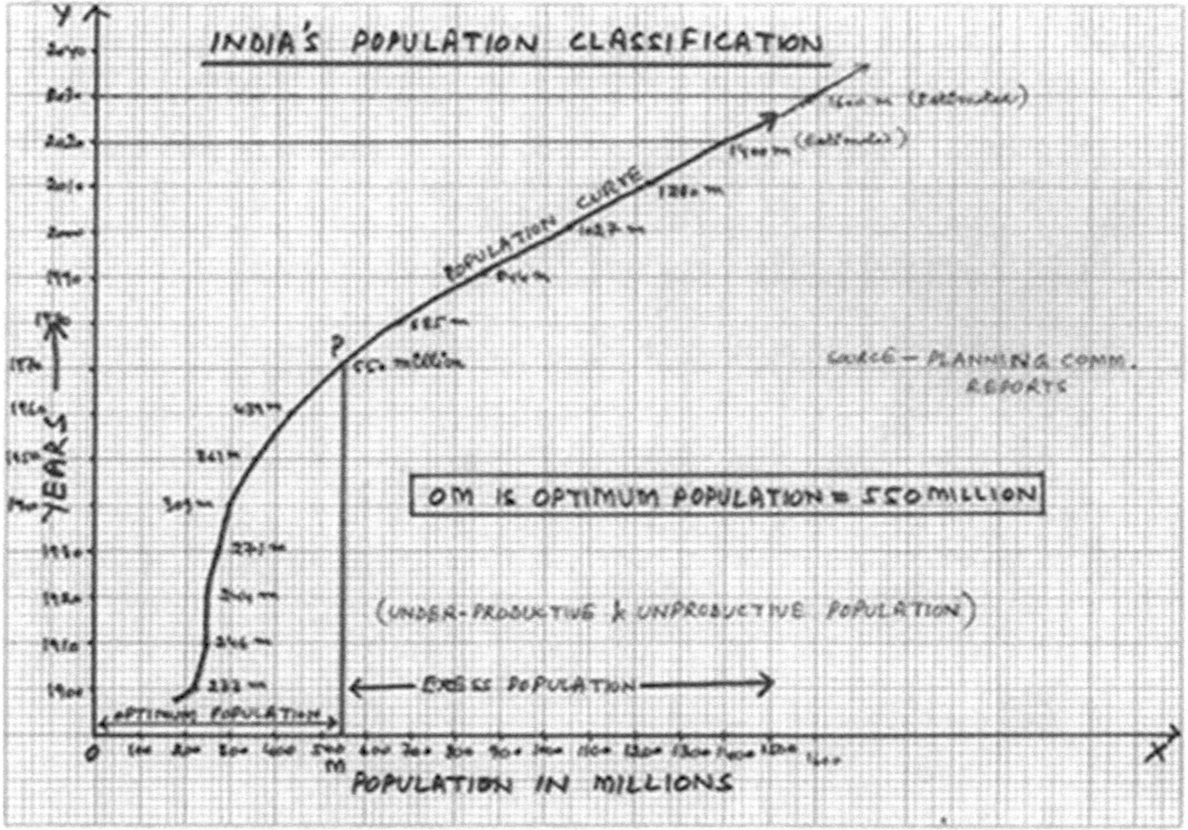
INDIA'S POPULATION CLASSIFICATION
POPULATION CURVE
550 million
OM IS OPTIMUM POPULATION = 550 MILLION
SOURCE - PLANNING COMM. REPORTS
(UNDER-PRODUCTIVE & UNPRODUCTIVE POPULATION)
EXCESS POPULATION
OPTIMUM POPULATION
YEARS
POPULATION IN MILLIONS
Y
X
O
M

POPULATION GROWTH OF INDIA

Fig. 4

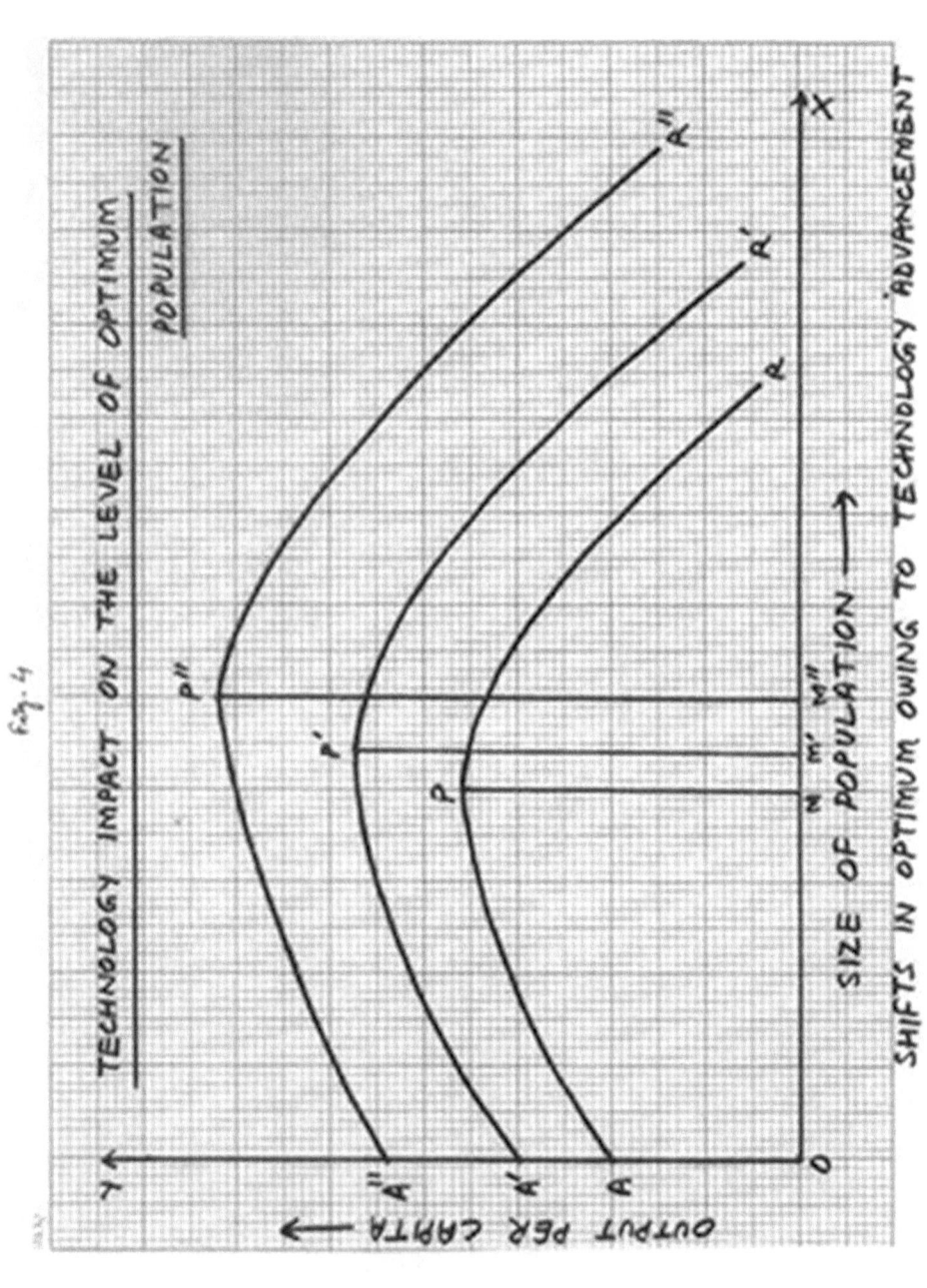

TECHNOLOGY IMPACT ON THE LEVEL OF OPTIMUM POPULATION

SIZE OF POPULATION →

OUTPUT PER CAPITA ←

SHIFTS IN OPTIMUM OWING TO TECHNOLOGY ADVANCEMENT

CHAPTER - 2

Various Theories of Popultion: An Evaluation

The subject of human population has never been viewed seriously in India since Independence, neither by the successive governments nor by the national economists. On the other hand, this issue was taken up during the Emergency days in 1975-76 by Smt. Indira Gandhi's government in such an erroneous fashion that it posted a negative and disdainful impact on the Indian people instead of making any useful positive good. People responded very disdainfully against this step of the government by giving a crushing defeat to the ruling Congress Party of Mrs. Indira Gandhi in the general elections of the Lok Sabha in 1977. The scheme of family planning was taken up by Mr. Sanjay Gandhi, the younger son of Mrs. Indira Gandhi who was a *de facto* head during those days. He implemented the scheme in a very arbitrary manner and resorted to the methods of highhandedness and intimidation to cow down the people to fall in line. The family planning programme became so hateful and anti-people that no other subsequent governments dared to even talk of the term family planning for years to come for fear of losing mass popularity. Once bitten twice shy. The result of this total apathy on the part of later governments is nothing but the jump of population in India to 1210 million as per 2011 Census. It is expected that population of India would cross the number of 1400 million by the end of 2020 or even earlier.

In fact, the imposition of Emergency in June 1975 was a desperate attempt on the part of the then Congress Party Govt. to suppress the growing disenchantment and unrest in the country on account of complete failure of the economic endeavors of Mrs. Gandhi's Government in the face of mounting mass unemployment, fast-rising prices, stagnant economy and widespread corruption, which, in turn was the outcome of the Indian polity's utter failure to control population explosion since Independence. Jawahar Lal Nehru, the first Prime Minister of Independent India and the main architect of India's economic planning had expressed his concern as back as in 1945 regarding population problem of India when he wrote in his 'The Discovery of India'; See page No.552.

These lines were written when the population of the 'united India' was only 400 million (40 crore) and post-partition India was having only around 300 million in August 1947. India's educated middle class and high class people, however by their own understanding and awareness, observed small family norms (i.e. 2 children norms), but majority of Indian people who constitutes lower middle class and poor people did not practice two children norm and generally having large families. These people are illiterate or semi-literate and are completely in the grip of ignorance. A rigid and torpor socio-religious super-structure which promotes large families, has overwhelmed them completely. Some religions like Islam is fundamentally opposed to family planning and its followers, with a few exceptions, do not adhere to small family norms and continue to increase their numbers. This creates a chain-reaction among the followers of other religions, for example, Christians, Hindus, Sikhs, Jains, Buddhists etc who are afraid of their diminishing numbers. Their religious leaders are making appeals to their followers not to adhere to small family norms and exhort them to increase their numbers. This unwise and negative exhortation on the part of religious leaders is pushing the population figures higher and higher without having any consideration for natural resources we have at our disposal in India. Further, there exists a very acute desire among the Indian families to have at least one male child to carry on the family traditions as well as to safeguard a place in 'the heaven' by the father- mother couple. This restricts them to hold on a small family size.

In next 15 years, India will emerge as the most populous country in the world, surpassing China. At 1.2 billion now, India's population will touch 1.4 billion in 2025 (here author predicts 1.4 billion by 2020 or earlier), surpass China in 2028 and reach 1.6 billion by 2050 before it starts declining by the 2100 at which point India will have 1.5 billion people, according to a study released on Thursday. The World Population Prospects __ The 2012 Revision __ released by the United Nations has projected the world population of 7.2

billion in 2013 to increase almost one billion people within the next 12 years, reaching 8.1 billion in 2025, and to further increase to 9.6 billion in 2050. by the turn of the century, the population will cross a whopping 10.9 billion.

Keeping the above scenario in view, we shall now take up population theories put forward by the economists hitherto;

Malthusian Theory of Population

Thomas Robert Malthus (1766-1834) was a British clergy man, who wrote his "Essays on Principle of Population" in the year 1798 and later modified the same of his conclusion in the next edition in 1803. At that time, the population of England was growing at a very fast rate and this perplexed him too much. He saw in it the disaster for England in the near future, and he considered it his solemn duty to warn his countrymen. His theory is very simple. He wrote, "By nature -human food increases in a slow arithmetical ratio; man himself increases in a quick geometrical ratio unless want and vice stop him. The increase in numbers is necessarily limited by the means of subsistence. Population invariably increases when the means of subsistence increase, unless prevented by powerful and obvious checks."

Every species, including humans has a prolific nature, but this prolificity has been subject to 'checks and balances' in the nature. The transfer of food energy from the producers, through a series of organisms (herbivores to carnivores to decomposers) with repeated eating and being eaten away, is known as a food chain which keeps a 'check and balance' among all the species in nature. The green plants occupy the first source of energy, and are called the 'primary producers' as plants utilize the radiant energy of the sun. This primary energy, in the shape of green plants and green grass, is then utilized by the plant eaters, known as 'herbivores', and are called the 'primary consumers'. Herbivores in turn are eaten away by carnivores and are called the 'secondary consumers'. Some carnivores are eaten away by some other carnivores and are called 'tertiary consumers'. Then comes 'quaternary consumers' who eat 'tertiary consumers'. Then comes 'decomposer' who provides nutritions to plants and grass. fig (5)

In any food-chain, energy flows from primary producers to primary consumers (herbivores), from primary consumers to secondary consumers (carnivores) and from secondary consumers to tertiary consumers (carnivores/

omnivores) and so on. This simple chain of eating and being eaten away is known as 'food-chain' or food-cycle.

Humans too belong to this 'food-chain' since the dawn of their existence, but they gradually became successful in pulling them out of this 'food-chain' by their wit and conceptualizing brain. They now participate into this food-chain from the 'eating part' and do not fall in the trap of 'being eaten away'. This pull out of humans from the 'food-chain' destroyed the natural phenomenon of checks and balances for them. They become part of food for primary producers (plants & grass) only when they die and their bodies decompose either by burning on the funeral pyre or through burial in the ground. They gradually learned to gather their food from the forests and hunting of animals through combined efforts and with the help of weapons and arms. The progress of man continued by developing the art of agriculture and living in groups in fortified dwellings. Discovery of fire further reduced their threat from the wild carnivorous animals and they were successful in multiplying their numbers very rapidly and soon became the master of the whole world. **Since the natural 'checks and balances' principle does not now apply on humans, it is now imperative for them to apply their own 'checks' on their population themselves to maintain a 'balance' with the nature and other species. But this did not happen.** Humans continued and still continue to multiply themselves irrespective of the availability of natural resources and this created conflicts and clashes among themselves. In due course of time, states, kings and their armies came into existence and powerful humans established first, master-slave relationship, then feudal-serf relationship, then landlord-peasant relationship and then capitalist-workers relationship. To subjugate large number of weak and poor people within the state and intimidate the neighboring states, kings raised large armies. This was possible only when a large number of people were available for recruitment in the armies. This competition to maintain huge armies by the states encouraged rapid population growth which necessitated a bitter scramble for land and other natural resources and turned human groups/societies as totally ignorant about the necessity of maintaining a balance between their numbers and relative availability of food and other necessaries of life for their survival.

What Malthus wanted to say is that, this very ignorance of humans has unwittingly encircled themselves in the trap of wars, famines, unrest, diseases etc.. Malthus asserted that the population of a country tends to double in every

25 years as it was actually happening in the American colonies and the U.K. at that time, but the supply of food and other necessities could not be increased with the same pace, as the power of land to produce grains, vegetables, fruits etc were limited. Since England was successful in shifting her population-burden on to her colonies where they sent large number of young men and women to man their large establishments and armies. They looted the natural resources of the enslaved colonies and benefited themselves, thus postponed her problem of over-population successfully. In this way, England was successful in keeping her population in good humor and satisfaction, thwarting the predictions of Malthus. The U.S.A. had had a large chunk of unutilized land in her western part which fulfilled the demand for food grains, fruits, animal meat etc, posed by the growing human population at that time.

As far as India is concerned, the theory of Malthus holds good perfectly as we have occupied all the land and other natural resources to the full and we are still growing our population. **Actually, Malthusian theory holds good for a country which has attained the level of optimum population (calculation of optimum population has been discussed in the next chapter).** If population keeps on growing beyond the level of the optimum mark, then Malthus' prophesy shall certainly turn into a reality. Malthus pointed out that there were two possible checks which limit the growth of human population;

1- Preventive Checks, and
2- Positive Checks

Preventive Checks

These are the checks which are to be applied by the man himself and they exercise their influence on the growth of population by bringing down the birth rate. They arise from Man's wisdom and foresight. We see the distress which frequently visits those who have large families. It is certain that with a large number of children the standard of living of the family will go down. Malthus thought that if he had to support a large family, he would have to face greater difficulties and work harder than otherwise would be the case. He would not be able to give adequate education to his children if there were many of them. Further, he might expose his children to poverty or charity by his inability to provide for them. These considerations force man to limit his family. Late marriages, self-restraint and other preventive measures fall under the category of 'preventive checks' to limit human numbers.

Positive Checks

Accounting to Malthus, positive checks exercise their influence on the growth of human population by increasing the death rate. They are applied by nature as preventive checks are exercised by the man himself. He recommended the use of preventive checks if mankind was to escape from the impending misery. If men fail to check their population in respect of resources they possess, then positive checks of nature will come into force and diseases, wars and famines would come into operation, cutting short the life of men by unnatural deaths. Has not the history of mankind proved this prophecy of Malthus correct from the dawn of human civilization? Is it not a fact that majority of wars and conflicts have taken place in human history because of revealed or concealed economic factors behind them? We may question the prophecy of Malthus regarding growth of population in geometric progression i.e. as 2, 4, 8, 16,.. so on and growth of food production in arithmetic progression i.e. as 1, 2, 3, 4, 5,... so on, yet his message is loud, clear and correct as far as Third World Countries are concerned and specially for India.

Food production in India has increased manifold since Independence, but its population growth too multiplied at the same speed, keeping her per capita availability of food grains at nearly constant level (fig 06), and the irony of food grains production-increase is that, this has been achieved at the cost of forest-covered land which has regularly been grabbed and cleared for cultivation. The result is there to be seen that only 12% of India's land surface is left as dense forests, threatening her biodiversity and increasing pollution level including global warming.

Here, author's view point is like this; when a country attains the level of 'optimum population', which India has achieved in 1971, when it crossed 550 million (55 crore) (fig-11), then Malthusian theory of population revealed its correctness. We have the highest birth rate and also the highest death rate in India compared with the others in the world. Abject poverty for 810 million people still haunts India when our Central Government passes a Food Security Bill-2013 in Parliament. Repeated occurrence of famines, epidemics, large number of farmer's suicides, communal and caste conflicts, prevalent malnutrition among women and children, widespread adulteration in food-items, very high level of unemployment and underemployment and steep rise in the prices of food grains and other essential goods for life clearly verify the correctness of the Malthusian Theory in India. Some intellectuals and economists have ridiculed the Malthus Theory on account of technological advancement in agriculture and on the basis of which they totally deny the possibility of food-shortage under any circumstances. This view is not correct as technology and agriculture growth both has their limitations. **As far as, the anxiety and warning for harmful consequences of over human population is concerned, Malthus stands tall and great as a sole torch-bearer among all the economists of the world. He may be called the father of demography whose significance in the modern world is more pronounced today than ever before.**

Modern Theory of Population

Modern economists have not only rejected the Malthusian theory of population, but ridiculed it too. They put forward a new theory of population which is known as the **Modern Theory of Optimum Population.** Cannan propounded this theory. This theory attempts to define an economically ideal size of population for a country. According to the theory, optimum population of a country is that number of people which at any given time, can secure the highest per capita income with the help of existing resources. This theory emphasizes on having a close relationship between the number of people a country possesses and it's resources. The optimum means the best and the most desirable size of a country's population. **It is the right number a country should have. When a country's population is neither too big nor small, but just that much which the country ought to have, then it is called the optimum population for that country. The optimum number can, therefore, be defined as the one at which per capita income is the highest with a given amount of resources, state of technology available and a certain stock of capital.**

As shown in fig-3, the size of population is measured on X-axis and the output per capita on Y-axis. It is evident from the figure that, in the beginning, as population increases, output per capita also increases and goes on increasing with every increase in population till OM level of population is reached. At

OM level of population, the output per capita MP is the highest. If population further increases beyond OM, the output per capita begins to fall. Therefore, OM is the optimum population. If it is less than OM, then country is under-populated and if it goes beyond OM, the country is said to be over-populated.

Variation in Optimum Population Level

However, the concept of optimum population of a country is conditioned by the availability of natural resources in a particular country and its level of technology used to exploit them. In other words, it may be said that the concept of optimum population is directly related to the available natural resources and level of technology in use, in a particular country. As shown in fig-4, with a certain given resources and technology, the per capita output curve is AR and the level of optimum population is OM, at which per capita income is MP, which is the maximum under the given circumstances. When the quantum of natural resources or the level of technology makes an advance, the output per capita curve shifts upward right, shown as A'R'. Here optimum population is OM', which is greater than the earlier OM. Now, in case, the resources further move upward or technology level improves ahead, the per capita output curve moves further upward-right to A"R". Here optimum population is OM", which is greater than the earlier OM and OM'. This theory of optimum population postulates variation in the level of population of a particular country according to its volume of natural resources and the level of technology used.

Evaluation of Population Theories

While Malthusian theory of population establishes a relationship between the movement of population growth and food supplies or natural resources in a particular country, the optimum theory of population portrays only a concept by which a level of optimum, under or over population is measured in terms of her per capita output conditioned by a given quantum of natural resources and level of technology. Both these theories fail to tell us as to what should be an actual optimum number or an ideal population level, beyond which a century's population must not go; or what means are to be taken into consideration to calculate the exact level of optimum population of a particular country, as the concept of per capita output is a vague one and can not be measured in real terms. It is not possible, in practice, to fix a point up to which the output per head goes on increasing and beyond which it starts declining.

Population experts have suggested different and conflicting numbers as the optimum. Thus, the concept has little practical utility.

No Concern for Ecology

Both these theories do not take into consideration the impact of population on a country's ecology and environment when output per capita keeps on increasing by over exploitation of natural resources in a short period which might damage that country's environment and biodiversity in the long run and might be beyond reparation. Over heating of the economy, high price-rise, hazardous diseases owing to pollution, global warming and climate change may occur by a wrong calculation of optimum population or no calculation either.

Since the birth of Industrial Revolution in England during the late eighteenth century to the present era of twenty first century, a great measure of industrial development has taken place in the whole world and every country, developed as well as under-developed has been pursuing a great deal of industrialization to maximize production of goods and services to outpace the others. They are blindly exploiting their respective natural resources with constantly advancing technology without taking into the slightest consideration the damage they are inflicting on earth's climate and environment and fast depleting the volume of non-renewable natural resources which are meant for future generations also. For example, fossil fuel like petroleum products, coal, natural gas etc. has limited deposits under the earth and cannot be renewed for re-use. Even then all countries of the world, developed and underdeveloped, blindly try to over- use them for their GDP growth. Even the renewable natural resources, for example ice/snow and rains are facing threats due to global warming and climate change which is a by-product of blatant release of harmful green house gases like carbon dioxide, ozone, nitrogen dioxide etc. into the atmosphere. Global warming is causing sea level to rise and pollution is causing several harmful diseases like cancer, T.B., asthma and several others.

All these negative aspects are also to be taken into account when economists want to determine the level of optimum population for a particular country and then for the whole world as usual, for the world pollution and climate is sum total of the pollution of all the countries of the world. The Malthusian theory and the Modern Theory of Population failed to address all these issues and simply view GDP growth in physical terms only. The author emphasizes and endeavours to arrive at a scientific and sustainable measurement of optimum population for any particular country, especially for India in subsequent chapter. He introduces a new concept of 'green growth' in place of self-defeating 'polluted growth'. 'Polluted growth' is that growth of economy which inflicts irreparable damages on our environment and ecology, threatening thereby, not only the mankind but the whole of biodiversity on the earth. 'Polluted growth' is an illusive growth which leads us to nowhere except to dreadful diseases, natural holocaust and extreme weather conditions, global warming and climate change. We urgently need a 'green growth' concept wherein these dangers of pollution and damages to environment are effectively checked and expelled and a healthy pollution –free climate is ensured not only for all the humans, but for the entire biological world along with the preservation/conservation of an enriched biodiversity, necessary for human existence.

How to switch over to 'green growth' from the present 'polluted growth' is discussed in the next chapter, wherein, a scientific method has been devised to calculate optimum population for India which encompasses 'green growth' in itself.

———◆◈◆———

LAND UTILISATION PATTERN IN INDIA 2009-10

NEEDED LAND UTILISATION PATTERN TO ABSORB AIR POLLUTION

TOTAL REPORTING AREA = 306 million Hectares = 100%

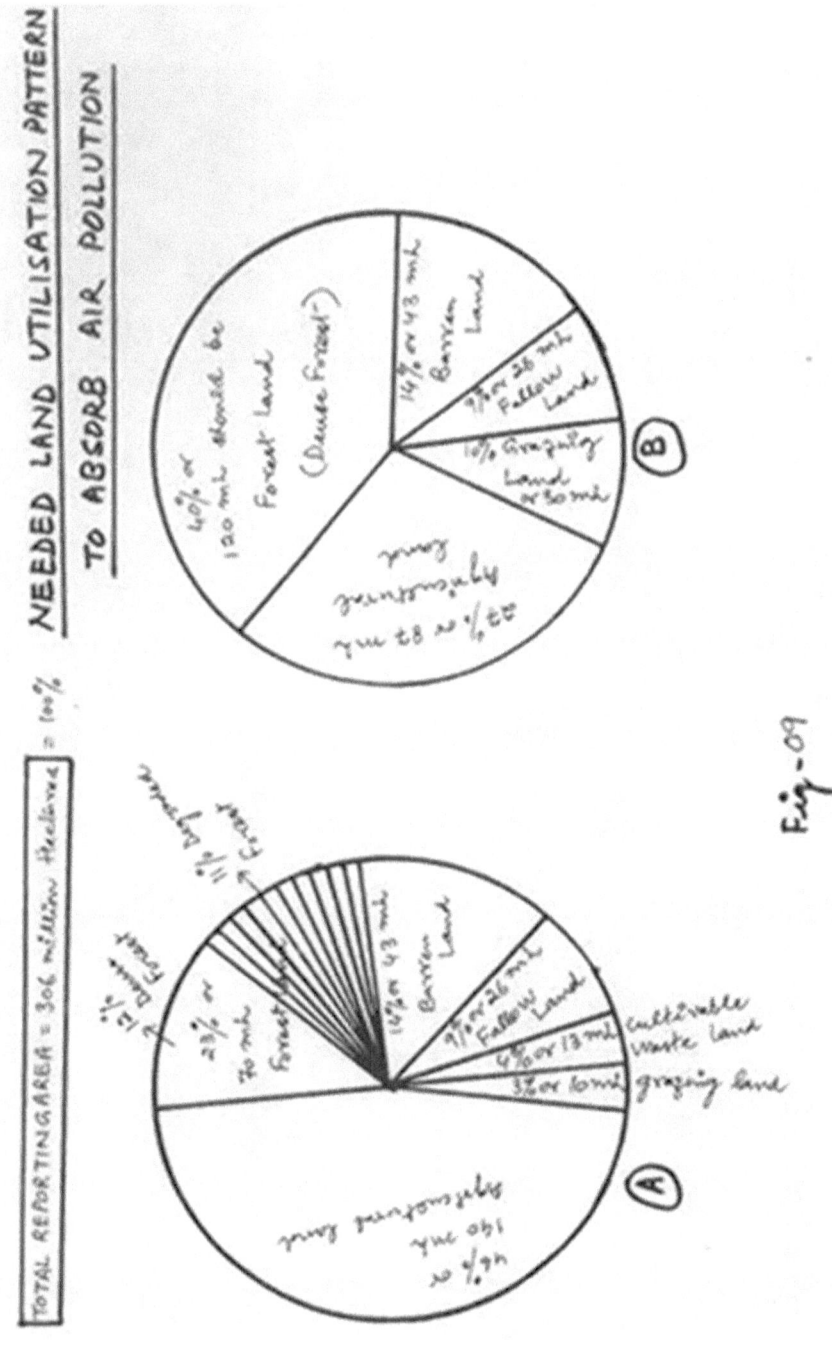

Fig - 09

Fig - 08

DISTRIBUTION OF LAND-SURFACE ON EARTH

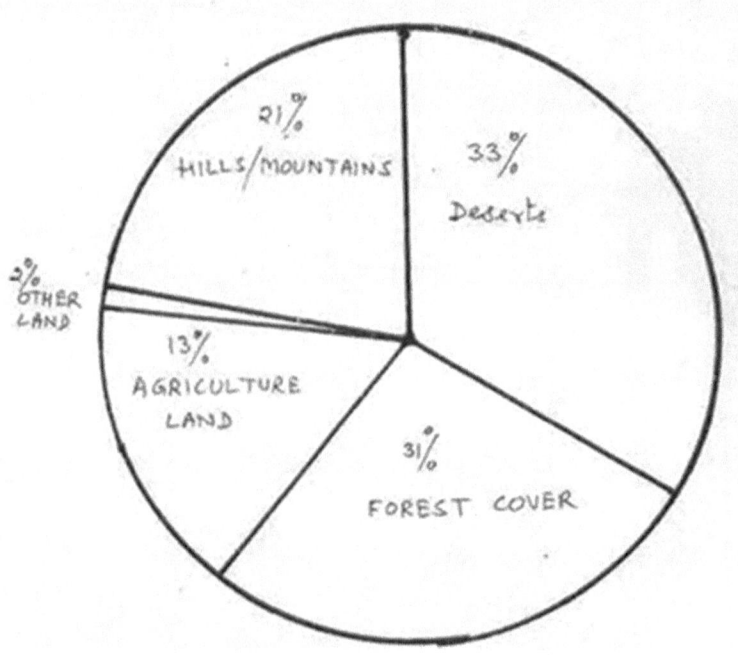

Fig - 07

AVAILABLE LAND SURFACE ON EARTH

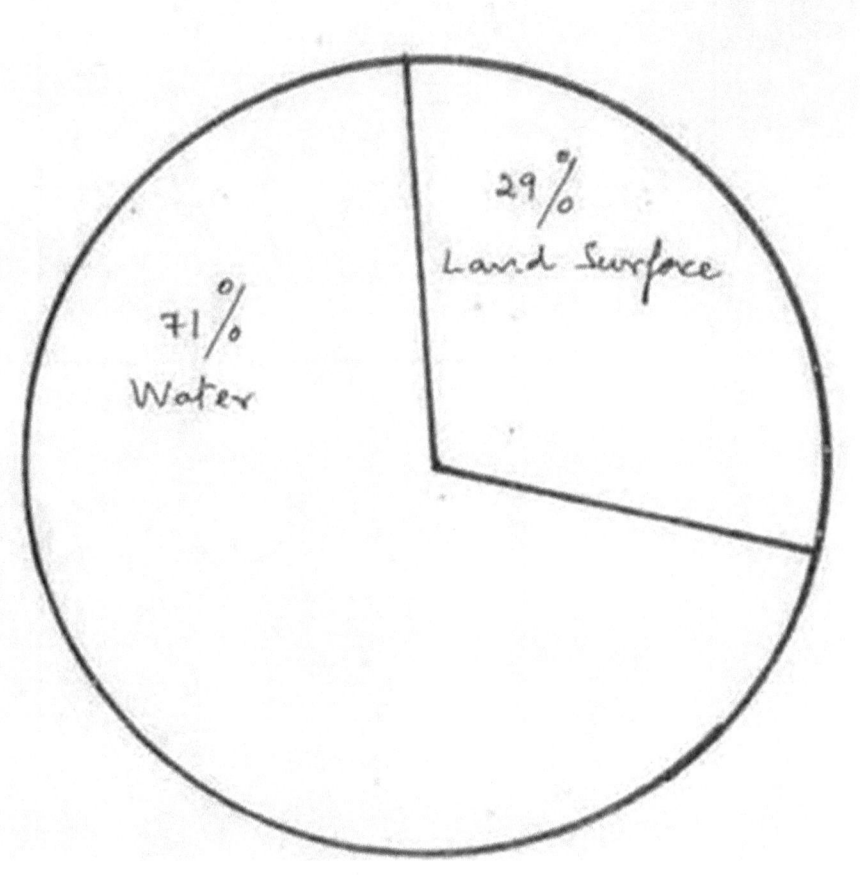

Fig. 12

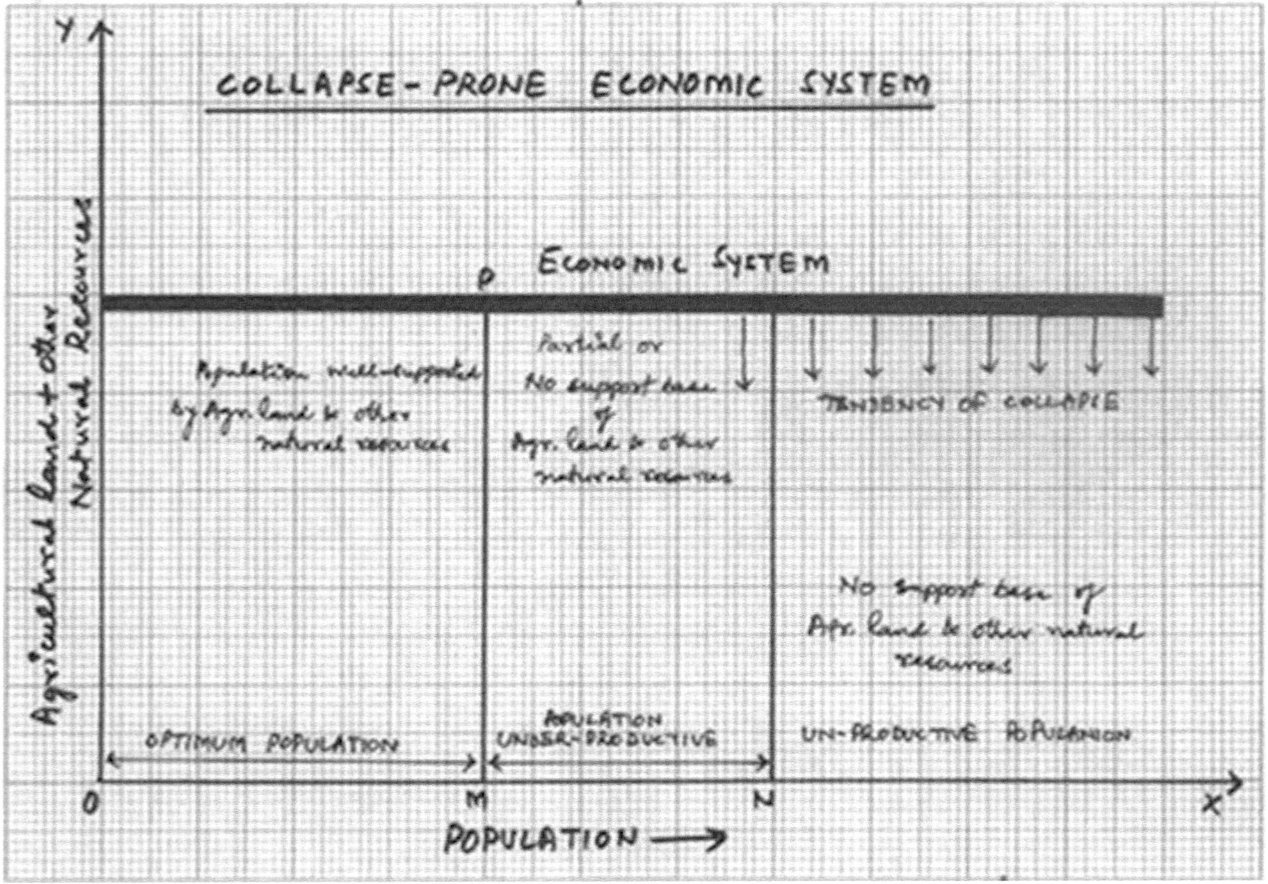

COLLAPSE - PRONE ECONOMIC SYSTEM

Economic System

TENDENCY OF COLLAPSE

No support than if Agr. Land & other natural resources

UN-PRODUCTIVE POPULATION

Partial or No support than if Agr. Land & other natural resources

POPULATION UNSATISFACTORY-PRODUCTIVE

Population well-supported by Agr. Land & other natural resources

OPTIMUM POPULATION

Agricultural Land & other Natural Resources

POPULATION →

0   M   2   X

Fig. 10

UNDER-PRODUCTIVE & UNPRODUCTIVE POPULATION CURVE

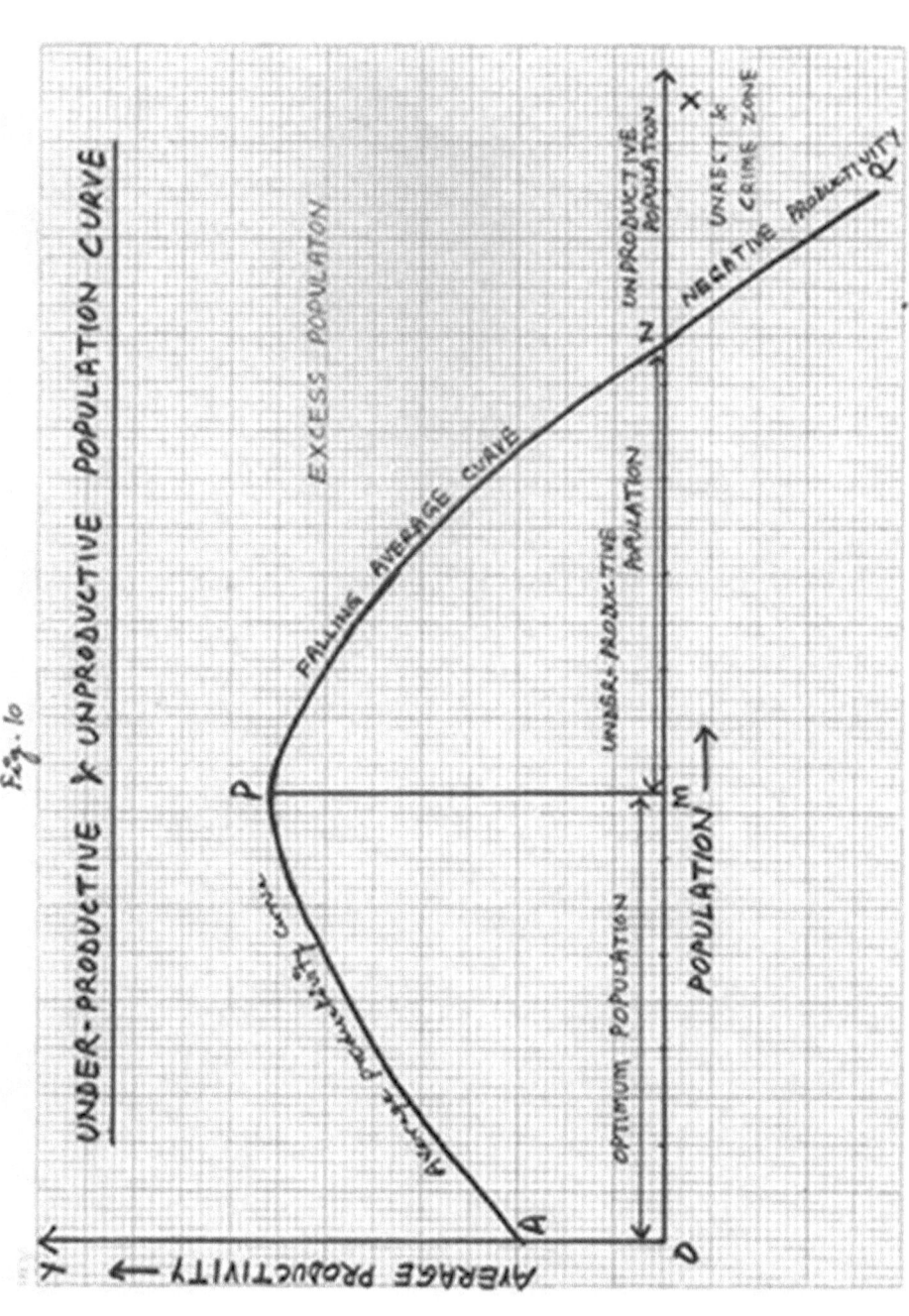

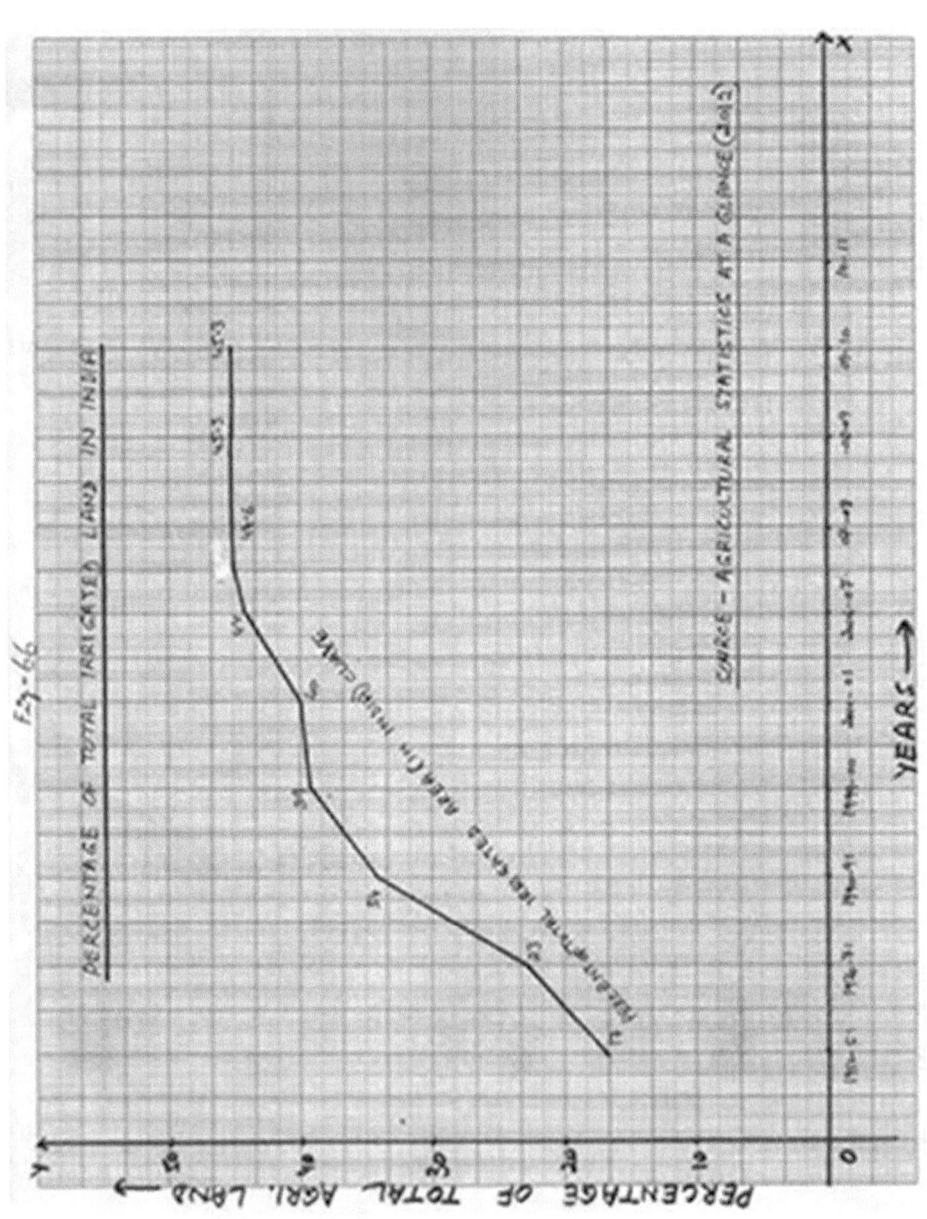

Fig - 66

VICIOUS CIRCLE OF OVER-POPULATION

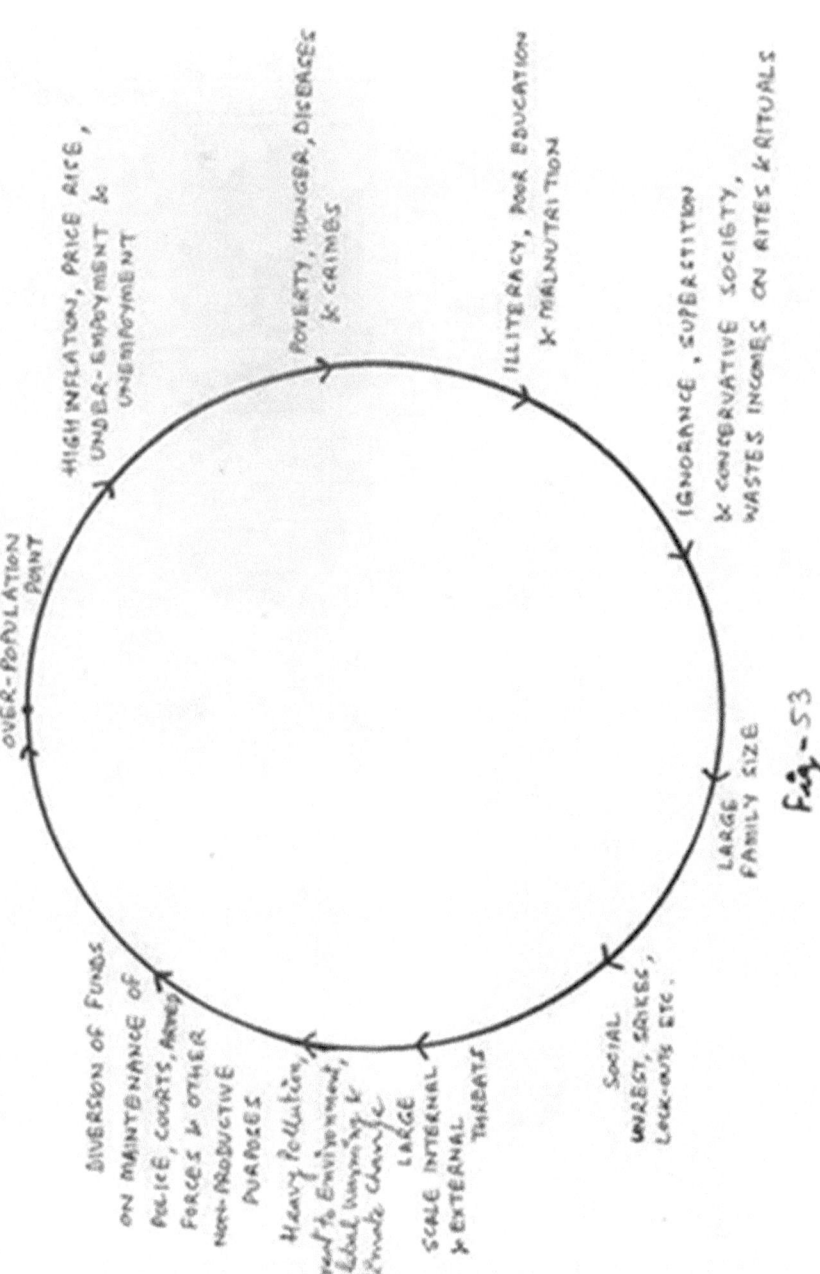

HIGH INFLATION, PRICE RISE, UNDER-EMPLOYMENT & UNEMPLOYMENT

POVERTY, HUNGER, DISEASES & CRIMES

ILLITERACY, POOR EDUCATION & MALNUTRITION

IGNORANCE, SUPERSTITION & CONSERVATIVE SOCIETY, WASTES INCOMES ON RITES & RITUALS

OVER-POPULATION POINT

DIVERSION OF FUNDS ON MAINTENANCE OF POLICE, COURTS, ARMED FORCES & OTHER NON-PRODUCTIVE PURPOSES

HEAVY POLLUTION, THREAT TO ENVIRONMENT, GLOBAL WARMING & CLIMATE CHANGE

LARGE SCALE INTERNAL & EXTERNAL THREATS

SOCIAL UNREST, STRIKES, LOCK-OUTS ETC.

LARGE FAMILY SIZE

Fig - 53

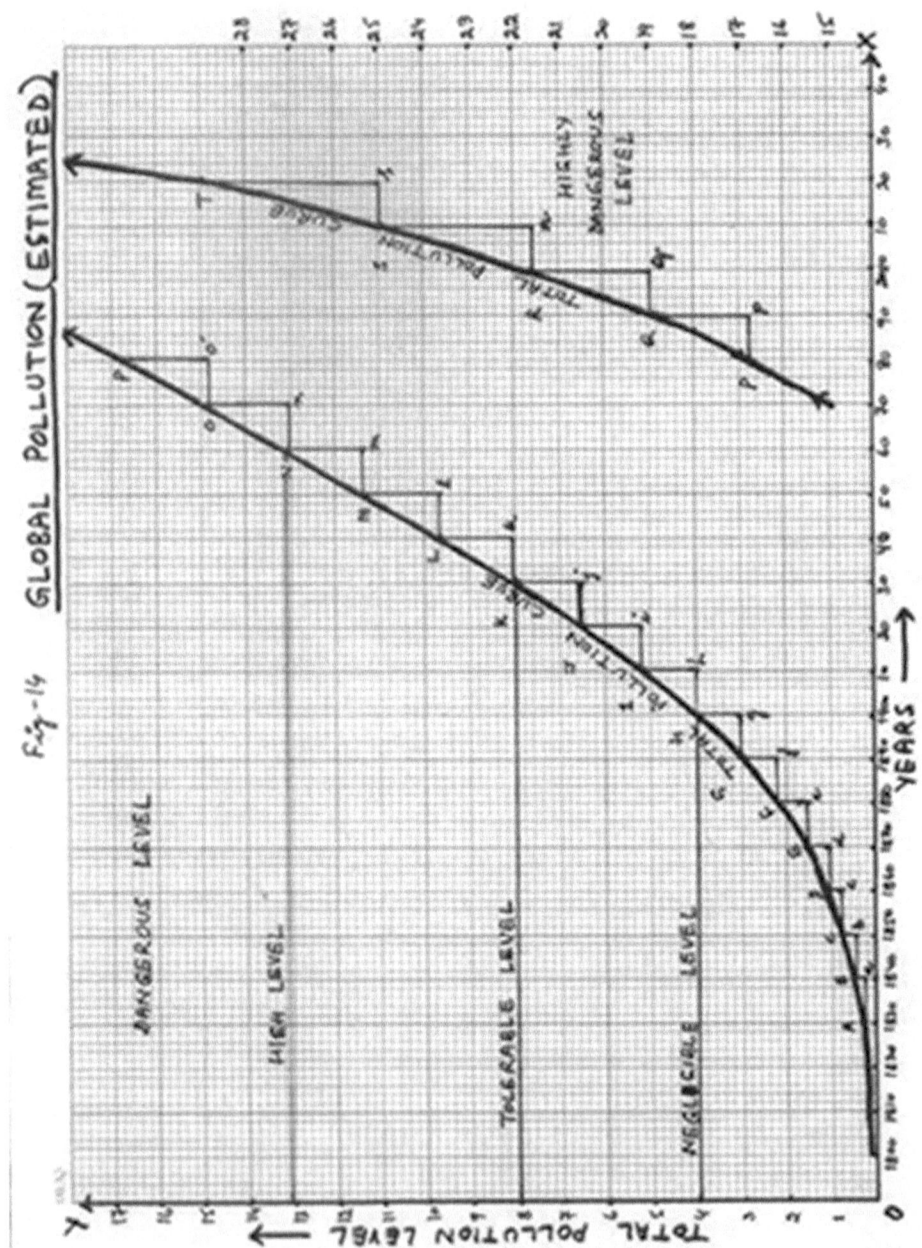

Fig-14 GLOBAL POLLUTION (ESTIMATED)

PRUDENTIAL DIVISION OF TOTAL AGRICULTURAL PRODUCE AND OTHER FOOD ITEMS
IN INDIA

33·35% To be consumed by the population engaged in manufacturing & Services Sectors

33·34% To be kept as reserves for exports & One year stocks To meet any contingency

33·33% To be consumed by the population engaged in Agriculture & allied activities

Fig - 13

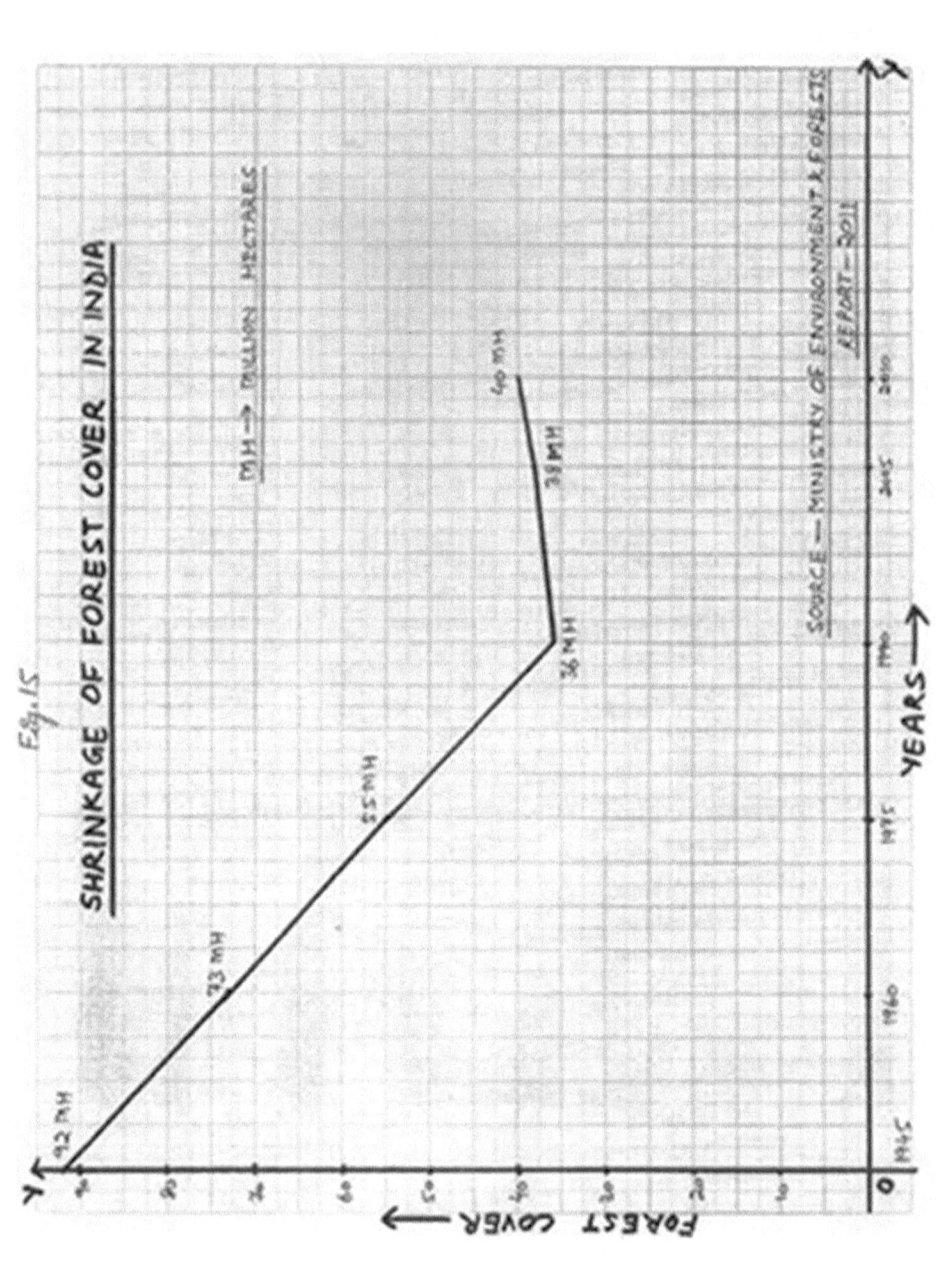

Fig. 15

SHRINKAGE OF FOREST COVER IN INDIA

MH → MILLION HECTARES

SOURCE — MINISTRY OF ENVIRONMENT & FORESTS
REPORT — 2011

CHAPTER – 3

Concept of Optimum Population & Green Growth

The concept of optimum population for any country is a desirable and healthy view to save the mankind from catastrophe, but as discussed in the previous chapter, the concept of maximization of per capita output/income is a vague one and cannot be calculated accurately. It has also not taken into account the damages it has been inflicting on the environment and biodiversity by ardently pursuing the monster of maximum output. Even then, the concept of optimum population is a positive step in the economy and must be adhered to in order to save the mankind from a certain catastrophe of anarchy and suicide. In this chapter, we shall be calculating to arrive at an optimum population for India in a scientific & realistic way.

As we observe from fig (07), the total surface area on the earth is fixed; around 29% is land area and 71% is covered with water (Oceans & Seas). Out of this global land area, we have 21% as mountains, hills and rocks, 31% as forests, rivers and other inland water bodies, 33% as deserts and only 13% as arable land. (Fig 08) When we look at India's topography, we find that only 46.24% of the total land area is agriculture land which comes out to nearly 141 million hectares and can be presumed as productive land. (Fig 9A) However, this productive land is regularly getting diminished every year due to its conversion into non-agricultural uses like, residential uses, setting up of small and large industrial estates, widening of roads and highways, establishing schools, colleges, universities, hospitals and other institutions, playgrounds and stadiums, commercial complexes etc. Latest data showed that as many as 20 states reported a drop in cultivable land of about 7, 90, 000 hectares in four years from 2007-08 to 2010-11. The decrease is attributed mainly to diversion of cultivable land for non-agricultural purposes including construction and industries.

For the purpose of our calculation of optimum population for India, we presume 140 million hectares as available agricultural land. Out of this 140 million hectares, only 40% is irrigated as of now (i.e. 56 million hectare) and the rest 60% (i.e.84 million hectares) is unirrigated or monsoon-fed, as per government of India reports. Now we shall calculate as to how many people can be profitably sustained on this productive land. According to the Agrarian Reforms Committee [1949] set up by the Government of India, a family of 5 members needs 4 hectares of irrigated land or 7.5 hectares of unirrigated / rainfed land for a profitable / respectful living.

1- For irrigated land

[i] Total number of families needed to sustain on 56 million hectares irrigated land = 56/4=14 million

[ii] Presuming one family consists of on average 5 persons, total persons needed = 14x5 = 70 million (maximum)

2- For unirrigated land

[i] Total number of families needed to sustain on 84 million hectares = 84/7.5 = 11.2 million;

[ii] Presuming 5 persons per family on average, total persons needed = 11.2x5=56 million (maximum)

[iii] some agricultural helpers / workers are also needed to perform some manual or other work on the field which we presume as needed in equal numbers, then total number of helpers / workers needed for agricultural operations = 70 + 56 = 126 million (maximum)

[iv] Thus total number of persons needed for agriculture and allied work operations =126 + 70 + 56 = 252 million or 25.2 crore (maximum)

[v] Now the question arises as to how many people are needed profitably in our services and manufacturing sectors? In other worlds, how many people can be sustained profitably in non-agriculture sectors with the help of agriculture sector? Because food grains and other edible commodities are supplied by the agriculture sector only. Here, the author has divided the total agricultural

produce into three equal parts. See fig (13) We must keep one third portion of the total food grain production as reserve stock for bad harvest days i.e. drought and floods. Another one third portion is needed for the consumption of people engaged in agriculture and allied sector only. The remaining one third portion is left for the consumption of people engaged in services and manufacturing sector or non-agricultural sectors. In this way, an equal number of people are required in services and manufacturing sectors as in agriculture sector. Thus according to our calculation, another 252 million people can be sustained in the secondary and tertiary sectors.

[vi] The total of primary, secondary and tertiary sector population is: 252+252=504 million. Since this is a mechanical calculation, practically some more people may be there in the country which we can not avoid. We add nearly 10% more to make it practical. **Thus around 550 million people are the optimum numbers for India. It should be noted that this is the maximum number. We can not sustain more than 550 million (55crore) humans under any circumstances.** Here, it would be appropriate to mention that 110 million working people (550/5) are gainfully and profitably employed under the optimum population level i.e. 550million people.

The population, over and above 550 million people may be termed as **excess population** and a burden on the labour and skill of 110 million gainfully working people. In the case of India, as of now, 700 million people (1250-550=700) are a big burden on the gainfully employed persons and come under the category of excess or over population. A major portion of taxes collected from this gainfully employed section's hard earned income is spent on this 'excess' population to prop up/sustain them. Practically, this excess population is contributing nothing or very little to out national income, for, all its working age groups are either underemployed or unemployed. Theoretically, some of them seem to be employed, but that is disguised unemployment, as we see in our agriculture sector. **As this 'excess population' keeps on growing, the burden on the economy would increase and inflation and price-rise would prevail, for, the simple fact that a large part of goods and services produced by the actually working optimum number is being consumed by the under-working or non-working excess population of the country.** In a democracy, no government can deny the benefits to excess population meant for the optimum population, for the simple reason of identification problem, as to who belongs to excess portion and who to optimum portion.

All the citizens of the country are bonafide members of Indian society and polity and have equal rights.

See fig 10. Here, growth of population is taken on X axis and average productivity measured in terms of average national income on Y axis. Intially, with the increase of population the average national income also keeps on increasing and attains the highest level at point P; thereafter average national income begins to decline with the increase of population beyond point M, which is the optimum level point. Here population OM is optimum. In countries like India, where population continues to increase, we have a falling average national income. Then at point N it becomes zero and further increase in population means emergence of negative productivity or income. MN is underproductive population which means that these people are not contributing their full capacity due to lack of natural resources and fall under the category of underemployment or semi-employment. Beyond point N, the increase in population means that these people will contribute nothing an they have no means of natural resources to support with and fall under the category of unemployment. This situation will create a phenomenon of very high price rise and inflation, widespread crimes, prevalence of diseases and malnutrition, social unrest and widespread discontentment. This type of situation compels the state/government to depend heavily on police and para-military forces to keep down the unrest and a large portion of national income is spent on these unproductive expenditures, which means that productive investment shall fall further. A vicious circle of overpopulation begins to operate wherein today's India has been badly entrapped. (See fig. 53)

The polity shall now head towards anarchy and economic collapse. The whole burden of producing and supplying goods and services falls on the actually fully employed persons and the symptoms of economic collapse begin to show in the polity. (See fig 12)

Sooner or later, the economic system is bound to collapse if corrective steps are not taken immediately. Interestingly in India, the area under agriculture is under extreme pressure of reduction and constantly being diverted towards non-agriculture uses. Nearly 50 million hectares of agriculture land is to be reverted to forest zone which was originally forest land. Further, fast growing population necessitates industrial expansion, increased residential accommodations, more hospitals, schools, colleges, universities / institutions, commercial complexes, widened roads/ highways, more canals, more rail lines and airports etc. etc. Naturally extra land is needed for all there purposes which shall gobble up agriculture land. The worst sufferer would be agriculture production which has been almost stagnant during the last decade. At the time of Independence in 1947, India had been facing a massive problem of achieving self-sufficiency in food grains. The famous "grow more food" programme initially aimed at increasing the total cultivable area in the country. As a result, till the beginning of the 1960s, the increase in agricultural production was more the result of expansion of cropped area. This was done by converting grazing lands and forest lands into crop lands; bringing cultivable waste lands under the plough, (See fig 15) and shifting the cropping pattern in such a manner as to divert land under fodder crops to food crops. According to the estimates of the National Commission on Agriculture, the net area sown up to 2001 was 145 million hectares. This net sown area is expected to shrink with the relentless growth of population and growing urbanization; cultivated and cultivable land is in fact disappearing under concrete buildings and metalled roads and good agricultural land is being destroyed to produce bricks for house construction.

CONCEPT OF GREEN GROWTH

Since the commencement of Industrial Revolution from the late eighteenth century in England, it set in motion an irreversible movement for world industrialization. Initially, West European countries followed the path of England by establishing industries and soon it spread to North America and other parts of Europe and Japan. It reached India through British domination during the middle of nineteenth century, but its progress was very slow, because British did not want to industrialize India for fear of losing British goods market in India. Even then, industrialization gradually took roots in India during the early twentieth century. All through these years, i.e. from the late eighteenth century to the early twentieth century, there was a great race for industrialization among the European countries, North America and Japan in Asia. This period witnessed a number of great inventions and discoveries in science and technology which boosted industrialization further. The First and Second World Wars saw the uses of war machinery on a big scale which had never been the case in earlier wars. Now the concept of powerful nation clearly shifted in favour of hightly industrialized country making a greater use of science and technology with the help of which a huge war and civil machinery could be built up. After the end of the Second World War in 1945, another great war has taken place, known as 'Cold War' which further gave a huge spurt to that phase of industrialization wherein large scale use of coal, fossil fuel and nuclear energy was freely done, thereby emitting very high volume of carbon di-oxide and carbon mono-oxide into the atmosphere. In the meantime, Third World countries, which hitherto were subjugated countries of several imperialist powers, became free and their national governments joined this race of rapid industrialization to achieve a higher growth rate to catch up with the West, as early as possible. This phase of industrialization began since the mid-twentieth century and turned sharper with every passing year. This extensive and intensive industrialization by all the countries of the world, developed and under-developed both, culminated into a massive volume of emission of harmful gases into the atmosphere collectively with a competitive zeal. Now they are not only discharging harmful gases into the atmosphere, they are polluting water bodies, soil, and noise too. Radioactive contamination is also posing a great danger to the existence of life on the earth. Serious sources of pollution include chemical plants, oil refineries, nuclear waste dumps, regular garbage dumps (many toxic substances are illegally dumped), incinerators, PVC factories, car factories, plastic factories and corporate animal farms creating huge amount of animal waste. Some sources of pollution, such as nuclear power plants or oil tankers, can release very severe pollution when accidents occur. Some more harmful pollutants are chlorinated hydrocarbons (CFH), heavy metals like lead, found in lead paints and gasoline, cadmium in rechargeable batteries, chromium, zinc, arsenic and benzene. All these pollutants are causing a variety of maladies, including cancer, lupus, immune diseases, allergies, T.B. and asthma. Mercury compounds cause Mina Mata disease.

Thus, in modern world, what we observe is that a rat-race for economic and industrial development is being competed among all the countries of the world. This large scale industrialization and bigger efforts to maximize production of goods & services including food grains (for which large amount of chemical fertilizers, pesticides and insecticides are used), mechanization of agriculture, increased use of automobiles and aero planes for transportation, nuclear powered ships into the seas and rockets into the space etc., created a combined effects of large scale damage to environment, causing global warming, rising sea level, birth of dreaded diseases and over-all, a greatest threat to bio-diversity. In this way, humans are pushing themselves towards a catastrophe and suicide. Here in fig (14), the author has endeavoured to demonstrate a graphical representation of the total pollution in the world since the birth of Industrial Revolution in England. The curve of world pollution slowly moves upward during the period of 1800 to 1850 which were the initial years of industrialization in England and was confined to England only. Then the curve moves more upward forming a 45° inclination, depicting the period from 1850 to 1900; another 50-year march towards industrialization wherein it spread it's wings in Western Europe and North America. During the 1800-1900 phase, the triangles shown are ABa, BCb, CDc, DEd, EFe, FGf, and GHg wherein perpendicular arms are slowly increasing and become equal to the base in triangle FGf (1890-1900 period). We consider this level of pollution as negligible for the world environment, for, it did not affect much as far as the world environment was concerned. We may call it the first phase of industrialization.

The second phase of industrialization began after 1900 and upto 1930. In these 30 years, industrialization spread to all over Europe and Japan in Asia, Canada, the U.S.A., Australia etc. Now England turned more industrialized. The mad race for rapid industrialization had already started among all these countries and the consequence of this was more rapid world pollution. Here, it should be noted that the First World War was already over which had done considerable damage to world's environment and preparations for the Second World War was in the offing. The triangles HIh, IHi, JKj depict the period 1900-1930; the vertical arms are gradually becoming longer in comparison to their respective bases. During this period (1900-1930), the pollution level all over the world turned 8 times higher to the level of 1800, but still it is within tolerable limits, because industrialization was confined to only one third part of the globe since all the Third World Countries were non-industrialized and Russia and Australia were semi-industrialized.

The third phase starts from 1930 to 1960. In this period, the Second World War was fought and ended in 1945, and this brought a process of decolonization and independence to Third World Countries. Cold War came into the picture and a renewed race for industrialization took roots in all the countries of the world, emitting ever larger volume of harmful gases into the atmosphere along with radio-active contents, thanks to the use of Atom Bombs in Hiroshima and Nagasaki in 1945. The tests for new Atom Bombs became a common feature in the U.S.A, the U.S.S.R, Britain and France. The world got divided into two great rival camps- the U.S.A, Britain, France, West Germany, Italy, Spain, Canada and Australia on the one side and the U.S.S.R, China, Rumania, Hungary, Mongolia, North Korea, Cuba on the other. Though the war never took place between the two camps, the extreme tension and cut-throat competition between them boosted the level of world industrialization to a very high point. Each camp wanted to outpace the other in the field of industrial growth. The newly independent countries too joined this race and turned it global.

Similarly, fourth and fifth phases came into existence when all the countries of the world began to participate in the mad-race for industrialization and nuclear proliferation. Now chemical weapons too came into existence and chemical fertilizers, pesticides and insecticides began to be used on a large scale to increase agriculture production to feed the ever growing population all over the world which has already crossed 700 crores (7 billion) in March 2011. Consumption of petroleum products, coal, natural gas and nuclear energy reached to a very high level all over the world, pushing the emissions of harmful gases and spread of radio-activity to an unprecedented level wherein air, water, soil, sound and light all became highly polluted which caused harmful hazardous diseases and unhealthy environment, endangering even the biodiversity. **This phase is highly dangerous and immediate corrective steps need to be taken by the U.N.**

Air pollution causes 29000 early deaths a year in the U.K. __more than twice as many per year as were caused by passive smoking before the ban. The World Health Organization has confirmed that air pollution causes cancer. Poor air quality also causes heart attacks and children living near busy roads in the U.K. have been shown to have underdeveloped lungs. EU said that nitrogen dioxide levels are excessive in many British cities.

Climate change may be world's most fearsome weapon of mass destruction and urgent global action is needed to combat it, says John Kerry, the U.S Secretary of States. In a speech to Indonesian students, civic leaders and Government officials in Jakarta, Kerry laid into climate change skeptics, accusing of using shoddy science and scientists to delay measures needed to reduce emissions of greenhouse gases at the risk of imperiling the planet. He also went after those who dispute who is responsible for such emissions, arguing that every one and every country must take responsibility and act immediately.

Mr. Edward Wong, correspondent of New York Times, reports from Beijing; On Thursday (16/01/2014), some residents of Beijing woke up with splitting headaches. A curtain of haze had fallen across the city of more that 20 million. It was the first "airpocalypse" of the year in the Chinese capital and nearby provinces, and it had come appropriately enough one year after a similar event had led to widespread anxiety. On Wednesday night (15/01/2014), the U.S embassy in Beijing began sending out online warnings that the air quality level had gone above 500, the upper limit of the measurement scale, and was now "beyond index". It stayed at that level until Thursday, when it dipped to "hazardous" from "beyond index". Hazardous means an air quality index above 300, at which point the concentration of fine particulate matter in the air is many times the exposure limit recommended by the WHO. American health officials say a hazardous rating means people should avoid venturing outdoors. Xinhua, the state news agency, reported that Chinese officials had ordered the closing of some highways, and visibility in some parts of Beijing was expected to drop to 500 meters.

Thousands of runners battled thick smog at the Beijing Marathon on 19/10/2014, with some athletes donning masks as air pollution soared to 16 times the maximum recommended level. Organizers rejected calls to postpone the race despite the soupy white haze over the Chinese capital, but said they had laid on extra medical staff to treat injuries among the more than 25,000 registered runners.

The level of small pollutant particles known as PM 2.5, which can embed themselves deep in the lungs, reached more than 400 micrograms per cubic meter in parts of Beijing as the racers lined up. The World Health Organization's recommended daily maximum average exposure is 25. The US embassy in Beijing described the air on Sunday as "hazardous". China has for years been hit by heavy air pollution, caused by enormous use of coal to generate electricity to power a booming economy, and by more cars on the roads. Public ire about the environment has grown leading the government to declare a "war on pollution".

Now it is a matter of satisfaction that some right-thinking people and environmental scientists have begun to express their concern towards the problem of growing pollution in the air through newspaper writings and seminars all over the world, telecaste by the T.V channels. This compelled many governments to pay attention to this problem. But they could do nothing more except spending more on health and medical facilities by establishing high-tech hospitals and clinics to palliate the sufferings of the affected people. This entailed a large amount of their annual national incomes. This expenditure on health, medicines and upkeep of hospitals on the one hand and negative effects on the working people's productive efficiency, if calculated in money terms, along with expenditures on floods damages and flood control measures, on drought control, soil conservation and on other environmental protection measures, shall constitute a large portion of a country's annual income on the other. **Here, it is to be pointed out that actually the 'real' annual national income would be much less if we deduct the above mentioned expenditures from the net national income.**

In other words,

'Real' Nation Income   = Net National Income – (Annual Expenditures on Health + Expenditure on pollution control measures + Expenditures on Floods, droughts etc)

In our projected fig (14), if we presume the annual net national income of a county as 100 in any year, then the 'real' national income for the year 1970 would be as below;

$$\text{'Real' National Income} = \frac{100 \times Oo}{Po} = \frac{100 \times 5}{10} = 50$$

Similarly, for the year 2010;

$$\text{'Real' National Income} = \frac{100 \times Rn}{Sn} = \frac{100 \times 5}{17} = 29.14$$

and for the year 2020;

$$\text{'Real' National Income} = \frac{100 \times Ss}{Ts} = \frac{100 \times 5}{20} = 25$$

Here, we see that as the industrialization goes on increasing to keep pace with the growing demand on account of population growth, the 'real' national income goes on declining. In other words, mere physical growth of national income is an illusionary concept and does not serve the purpose of 'real' or 'green' growth. **If the menacing growth of pollution is not checked, the people of the world would suffer immensely and what they earn by their hard labour shall be got snatched away by way of massive expenditures on the maintenance of heath and medicines, expenses on hospitals, flood and drought damage control measures, soil conservation and water purification efforts and above all incalculable damages to our biodiversity.** Here, we shall recall the tolerable level of pollution during 1930s. The governments of the world shall have to stick to that level for the sake of a healthy environment with a rich biodiversity and zero global warming. We shall have to investigate the ways and means to control pollution at tolerable level. This is possible only when we control human population to grow further which is the main factor for pollution and bring it to an optimum level for all the countries of the world as calculated above. Agriculture land and agriculture production is the base on which the human population thrives. This is the primary need without which humans can not survive. Simultaneously, at least 40% land surface in every country shall have to be reserved for forests and afforestation shall have to be completed soon on the entire 40% land surface to absorb the present and future pollution. According to data from the University of Maryland and Google, the world lost more than 500 million acres of forest between 2000 and 2012, a report in the blog said. That's the equivalent of losing 50 soccer fields' worth of forests every minute of everyday for the past 13 years. By contrast, only 0.8 million square km. have regrown, been planted, or restored during the same period.

Chemical fertilizers shall have to be replaced by organic fertilizers and alternatives be found to harmful pesticides and insecticides. Nuclear proliferation and chemical weapons will have to be abandoned in toto and wars and conflicts will have to be confined to history books only. This may be viewed by many as wishful thinking and a utopia, but for the survival and existence of life on the globe, this utopia shall have to be given a practical shape. **This is possible only when an optimum level of human population is targeted for every country of the world. The author's concept of 'green growth' encompasses all these things.**

The Indian Scenario

India had been under the British domination for about 200 years and got her Independence in 1947. During these 200 years, British did not allow Indians to go for industry owing to the fear of losing British goods market in Indian subcontinent. Even then, some Indian entrepreneurs like Jamshedji Tata, started industries on the Indian soil. It was in a nascent stage at that time and so the pollution was negligible. After Indendence, Govt. of India planned a massive industrialization programme for a rapid economic progress to catch up with the developed countries. India's Five-Year Plans on the model of the U.S.S.R. had been launched to bring about a rapid expansion in agriculture, industry, transport and other infrastructure, with a view to increasing production and employment, reducing poverty and inequalities in incomes and wealth in order to establishing an egalitarian society. Under successive Five Year Plans in India, additional land under cultivation has been brought with expanded irrigation facilities to increase agriculture production along with to enhance the employment opportunities in agriculture sector. Increased usage of chemical fertilizers, pesticides, insecticides and high yielding hybrid seeds have been encouraged ____ all collectively known as the New Agricultural Strategy. In order to achieve a rapid industrialization, new industries have been set up and the existing industries have been expanded and upgraded with modern technology as per international standards. Development of agriculture and industry have been accompanied by the development and expansion of infrastructure __ namely, power, transport, communication, banking and finance etc. At the time of partition, during 1946-47, a large number of refugees came to India from Pakistan (both East & West), leaving behind all their properties and wealth there. These homeless and penniless people were to be rehabilitated in India. A large number of them from West Pakistan had been allowed to settle in the Terai region of Himalayas, cutting down forests for agriculture. Further, growing population of India necessitated a high degree of mechanization, mindless and blatant exploitation of natural resources, cutting down of trees and clearance of forests for agriculture etc. degraded our natural environment. Natural environment includes the whole complex of climate, soil, water, and biotic factors whereupon we all subsist and whereupon our entire agricultural and industrial development depends. Rapid economic development to satisfy the colossal needs of our exploding population is actually converting India into a vast wasteland. In the table below, the position of soil erosion and land degradation has been shown:

		Million Hectares
1 -	Total geographical area	329
2 -	Area subject to water and wind erosion	130.16
3 -	Area degraded through special problems (ravines, salinity, water logging etc.)	43.65
4 -	Average area annually subject to damages through shifting cultivation	5.0
5 -	Annual average area affected by floods	8.0
6 -	Annual average cropped area affected by floods	4.0
7 -	Total drought prone area	40.0

Source – Water Commission of India Report - 2012

As shown in the above table, around 174 million hectares (total of 2&3) or 53% of the total land area of India is suffering from serious degradation. Soil erosion takes place when the surface soil is washed away through excessive rains and floods owing to indiscriminate felling of trees and conversion of forests into cultivated land, uncontrolled grazing of cattle and wrong methods of cultivation. The annual soil loss from erosion is tremendous with disastrous consequences, culminating into heavy siltation of the dams and reservoirs, tanks, streams and river beds, which reduces their capacity to hold water. This situation converts into disastrous floods with increasing frequency. According to some estimates of experts, the total annual loss due to soil erosion in India is around 6000-7000 million tonnes, which in terms of major nutrients, such as nitrogen, phosphorus and potassium alone is equal to an annual loss of 8.7 million tonnes, which if measured in money terms comes out to around Rs 60,000 crore.

Growing Urbanization

In order to accommodate our fast growing urban population, our cities' circumference is increasing year after year and trees and agriculture land are being sacrificed to meet the demand for land. A relentless population growth has put tremendous pressure on all natural resources, especially land. The scarcity of land resources has driven initiatives such as reclamation of land in coastal areas from the sea, even if they have detrimental effects on the environment and are accompanied by social ramifications. But unfortunately as the 'maximum city Mumbai' continues to develop in an unrestrained and unplanned manner, the reclamations provide the only solution. For instance, the total built-up area of the city in 1970s was 195.01 Sq. Km, as against the total area of 632.60 Sq. Km, it shot up to 338.38 Sq. Km in the 1990s, and 385.67 Sq. Km in 2011. This shows an alarming transition of natural land to a built-up area for urban use. As a result, more than 50 per cent of Mumbai's beaches, fresh lakes, creaks, inter tidal zones and mangroves got affected. It should be realised that the environment must not pay the cost of scarce resources. Instead of relying on an obvious and convenient choice of extracting more from nature, Government agencies should concentrate on measures that maintain the delicate balance between preserving the environment and accomodating the growth of mankind. The Lucknow Development Authority in its 151st board meeting approved construction of a new housing tower for IAS officers in the city, on 3.5 acres of CSI lawns, near CSI tower in Gomti Nagar. CSI tower is the only building for providing houses, exclusively to administrative officials. Since the area is a green belt, it would be converted into residential and LDA would be the construction agency. The board also gave their nod to land conversion of Chak Ganjaria farmlands on Sultanpur Road. The 850 acres of farmlands have to be developed into facilities like IT city, IIIT, UP Administrative Services Academy, modern milk processing unit, world class cancer hospital, super specialty hospital, and various types of residential/commercial projects. The layout plan of about 133 acre land near IIM on Sitapur-Hardoi Bypass Road proposed by Eldeco City under Integrated Township policy has been approved. Similarly OMAXE has got green signal for acquiring land in Saraswan village to be developed into an integrated township. Ansal Properties and Infrastructure limited's proposal for swapping of land use in partial areas of Sushant Golf City's D P R is also being considered. The U.P. state government is all set to give Jhansi City a new master plan that would almost double the development area of the historic city. The state housing department headed by Mulayam's son and U.P. Chief Minister Akhilesh Yadav, has issued a notification, under which more than 62 villages will be acquired by the Jhansi Development Authority for the expansion of the city. The previous development area of the city had

39 villages in its orbit to make around 32000 hectare of land. But with the new notification another around 38487 hectares of land in 62 villages will be incorporated in the new master plan. Top housing department official said that the Jhansi Development Authority board has already given it's nod for the acquisition of the land.

Around 7000 trees across 32 acres (think 1.5 times the size of Oval maiden in south Mumbai) of forest land have been cut down in an eco- sensitive zone of the Western Ghats between December 2013 and January 2014 to make way for a toll plaza on N H- 17. If built, it will involve flattening of hills on either side of a road. The issue is currently in appeal in the Bombay High Court.

Days before the Lok Sabha poll dates are to be announced, the government is likely to notify the revised regional plan for NCR-2021 (National Capital Region) which allows tourism activities in ecologically sensitive zones and permits constructions in these areas beyond the current 0.5% cap-moves that environmentalists claim will be disastrous for green belts such as the Aravalis. Top sources said urban development minister Kamal Nath, who chairs the NCR Planning Board, has approved the minutes of the last board meeting in which it was decided to allow tourism activities in nature conservation zones and construction beyond current limit.

Depleting Forest Cover

In India, since Independence, the forests have been subjected to large scale destruction for the purposes of agriculture and other uses for the last 65 years. According to FAO report, around 3.4 million hectares of forest land has been cleared and diverted towards agriculture (2.4 million hectare) and another 1.0 million hectares towards the development of river valley projects, industries, roads and communications. This process of cutting down and clearance of forests had continued till today at the rate of 1.3 to 1.5 million hectares annually. The dense forests in the Tarai regions of Uttar Pradesh were cut down and cleared during the 1950s to convert into agriculture land to be allotted to the refugees from West Pakistan during partition. It is now estimated that the rate of depletion of forests in Himalayan range from Kashmir to Assam which constitutes 25% of India's forest cover is so great that this mighty mountain range is fast converting into barren land by the year 2030. Now the position in the Himalayan ranges below the height of 2000 meters is 'no-forest cover left'. **The National Committee on Environmental Planning states that only 12% or 36.72 million hectares of country's land surface is under adequate tree cover and can be termed as dense forests despite the official claim of 22% or 68 million hectares.**

As we have shown in fig (15), the actual forest cover in India has been depleting regularly since Independence. The progressive depletion of India's forest cover is virtually pushing the country towards an environmental collapse. Apart from destroying India's bio-diversity, it is increasing floods and droughts, soil erosion, heavy siltation of dams, constructed at enormous costs, and air-pollution. Floods and droughts are becoming too frequent and causing a very heavy loss of life and property over the years. There is acute shortage of fuel-wood in the whole country and has turned into a fuel-famine like situation in certain parts of the country.

Why did this happen? Actually, apart from corruption, the exploding population of India has created a huge demand for food grains and other agriculture products owing to which demand for agriculture land increased progressively. Further, demand for land for residential purposes, schools, collages, universities/institutions, widening of old roads and construction of new ones, industrial base establishment, construction of airports, hospitals and commercial buildings etc. is also on the rise and forest land and agriculture land both are being occupied to satisfy the insatiable needs of the growing humans.

The devastation caused to the Indian economy by continued and excessive deforestation is indeed enormous. It has caused increased suffering to the landless laborers, marginal and small farmers, who have steadly lost their traditional sources of fuel-wood and fodder for their cattle. Loss of fuel wood, in turn, has led to the use of cow dung as fuel, resulting in loss of precious organic manure. Continuing deforestation, therefore, has brought us face to face with a major ecological and socio-economic crisis.

According to the forest policy of the Govt. of India, it was decided to re-acquire steadily the lost area under forest and raise it to 100 million hectares or 33% for the country as a whole, which means that the present agricultural land shall have to be brought under forest cover, thereby reducing the existing agricultural land area and decline of food grain production in addition to displacement of a large number of farmers from their fields and livelihood. **This is not possible under the present circumstances until pressure of**

population on agriculture land is drastically reduced. This is possible only by adhering to the limiting of human population strictly around optimum level (i.e. 550 million) as suggested above. **But now we are too late to achieve this in the near future, even if we adopt 'two-child' norm immediately.** If we adopt 'two-child' norm with immediate effect, even then its effects will be felt in the coming 20 or 25 years. What shall happen till then? The household size data released by Census authorities on 13/06/2014 shows that the country's average family size is 4.8 people per household. Uttar Pradesh has the most crowded households with an average of 6 people per household. Tamil Nadu, with 3.9 members per household is now the lowest in the nation.

Further, **increased life expectancy in India** is another factor which is ballooning the volume of population.

Data released by the Union ministry of Health shows that life expectancy in India has gone up by 5 years, from 62.3 years for males and 63.9 for females in 2001-2005 to 67.3 years and 69.6 years respectively in 2011-2015. Experts attribute this jump __ higher than in the previous decade __ to the better immunization and diet, along with prevention and treatment of infectious diseases. Average life expectancy which used to be around 42 in 1960, climbed to 48 in 1980, 58.5 in 1990 and around 62 in 2000. The World Health Organisation defines life expectancy as "the average number of years a person is expected to live on the basis of the current mortality rates and prevalence of distribution of health states in a population.

Increased life expectancy is not only ballooning the volume of human population in India, but raising the number of 'dependent people' in the total also who survive on the toil and labour of the working people in the age group of 21-60. **One should not swear at the long-life expectancy, as it is a healthy sign of human health of a country; at the same time we must apply a brake on the fast running train of child birth to keep the human population under optimum level.**

Factually, in India, we need at least 40% land surface under dense forest cover which comes out to 120 million hectares. This much forest cover is necessary to neutralize the negative effects of industrialization, present and future. As we have shown in fig (9) the distribution of land area as we have in 2009-10 (9A) and what should have been (9B) from the view-point of having a healthy environment and rich biodiversity. If we set apart 40% of our total land area for dense forests, then, only 27% land is left for agriculture production as 10% is left for meadows while the rest 23% land area in India is fallow and unproductive. We should utilize our fallow and unproductive land area for industrialization and other non-agricultural uses, but this has not been the case in India. As of now, we unhesitatingly occupy agriculture and productive land for non-agricultural purposes without considering its negative impact on the production of food grains and other edible goods. The outer boundaries of all the major cities in India are regularly expanding to accommodate growing homeless families by erecting concrete buildings and houses on a large scale. For example, a 300 hectare township at Greater Noida and another 218 Sq Km industrial region at Dadri-Noida – Ghaziabad location near New Delhi are being developed which will reduce agriculture land. Similarly, all the cites of India, big or small, are witnessing the same expansion in their perimeter, gulping the agriculture land as well as forests into their orbits.

Now, the position of our economic development has reached to such a level where environment and development are clashing with one another. If we move ahead for industrial development, our environment is in acute danger, and if we do not develop this sector then country shall be stagnant. 'The easing of excise duties for the automobile sector announced in the recent Budget (2014-15) is an example that has the potential to increase the emission levels and fuel consumption. Close on the heels of this, the National Capital Region Planning Board gave it's nod to the State Government to allow more construction activities in notified 'green zones' such as the Aravalis. The NCRPB has empowered the State Governments that are armed with a tourism policy to commercially develop these green zones in the guise of tourism projects. Priority towards infrastructure development is scoring over environment. In November 2013, the Union Government, keen to boost power output in an electricity-starved country, is prepared to bypass environmental hurdles in order to clear ultra mega power project. In addition to power, road construction too has now been allowed to exemption for environment clearance. The Ministry of Road Transport and Highways has proposed to the Environment Ministry to have "no green" nod for roads up to 200 Km. and expansion of existing stretch by another 60 meters. Relaxation of environmental norms in order to speed up development is a disturbing initiative that should at best be a one off and not be a practice. The norms are a product of intense debate and deliberation by experts and well-wishers of the environment and, therefore cannot be brushed aside in the name of economic progress.

Had we had a 40% forest cover together with an optimum population level of 55 crore people in India, this conflict between development and environment might have been avoided/resolved.

———◆◈◆———

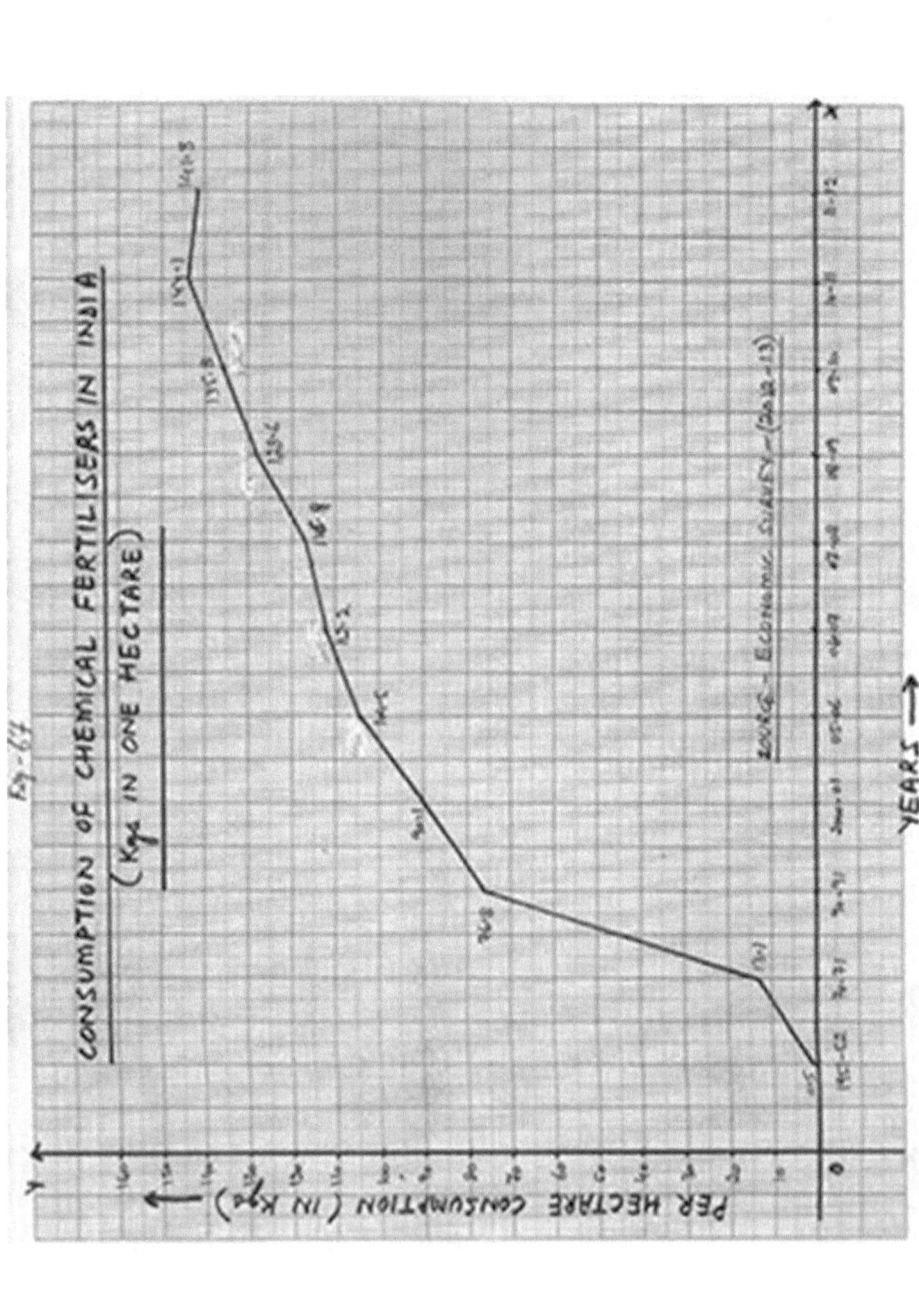

Fig-6.4

CONSUMPTION OF CHEMICAL FERTILISERS IN INDIA

(Kg. IN ONE HECTARE)

SOURCE— ECONOMIC SURVEY—(2012-13)

YEARS ⟶

PER HECTARE CONSUMPTION (IN Kg.) ⟵

CHAPTER – 4

Consequences of Over Population

Over population of India as well as of the whole world has been posing a great threat and incalculable harm to the human existence as well as to the entire existence of life on the earth. Apart from various nations' endeavour to satisfy the high demand for various types of luxury and necessary goods and services of their respective growing populations, their capitalist systems of production and market oriented approaches have induced them to a ruthless and unmindful expoitation of every available natural resource whether it is renewable natural resource or non-renewable, set to get exhausted in the near future. They are also unmindful and oblivious of the damages which they are inflicting on the environment and ecology, whereupon not only the existence of humans depends but also every form of life on this earth. In our endeavour to produce more and more goods and services, we humans have been billowing and belching forth carbon dioxide, carbon mono oxide and other harmful gases from the chimenies of factories unhindered since the Industrial Revolution from mid-eighteenth century to the present day. In order to augment agricultural production further, people have been using chemical fertilizers, pesticides, insecticides etc on a large scale which have polluted our soil, water, air etc and posed a great danger to our biodiversity on the one hand and inducing global warming, thereby smelting of ice and rising of sea level on the other.

In the following Chapters, we shall be taking up the harmful effects of over-population on our environment, biodiversity, health and education of masses, existence of mass poverty etc, and its consequences as threat to the world peace, spurt in crime and corruption, on woman's upliftment & empowerment, child-labour problem, democracy, capitalism and last but not the least, global warming and rising sea level in detail.

Environment And Over-Population

As we have discussed above, humans are creations of 'Nature' as well as a part of it and they act on Nature to influence it and also get influenced by Nature. They have been participants in Nature, subject to its rule of checks and balances. But humans, by their conceptual brain, immunized themselves from the rules of natural checks and balances. By living in groups in fortified dwellings with the invented arms and weapons to defend themselves from wild and rapacious animals bestowed them with comparatively a long and danger-free life. Further, discovery of fire illuminated their nights thereby lessened the threats of wild animals on the one hand and vagaries of extreme cold on the other, to a great extent. In this way, early humans were successful in defending themselves from the life-threatening factors, thus escaped from an early death. This resulted in facilitating the growth of their numbers frequently. They successfully subjugated domestic animals for their food and other needs and killed or driven away the wild animals to far off places. This process further accentuated when humans developed the art of agriculture. Gradually they were successful in converting large land surface into agriculture land by cutting down the forests.

But, till the medieval times, prior to the advent of Industrial Revolution, human activities, their expansion and development did no harm or negligible damage to the world's environment, as their population was still below the optimum level and forest cover on the earth was sufficient enough to absorb the harmful effects of human activities, if any. Organic fertilizers were in use to manure the agriculture and no chemicals, pesticides and insecticides were known to humans. Air, water and soil were not polluted to any extent.

Thereafter, as the humans progressed on the path of science & technology, they invented new machines and discovered new medicines which made their life more comfortable and long. Soon Industrial Revolution took place in England which was to change the face of the earth completely. The Industrial Revolution gave birth to capitalism which soon converted itself into imperialism and colonialism. The whole world soon became slave of major industrial powers of the world, namely, England, France, Spain, Germany, the U.S.A, Japan, Italy etc. These industrial powers began to exploit the natural resources of the subject countries as well as their subject population for the benefit of capitalists turned imperialists and soon they began to fight with one another to scramble for the empires of others. This process continued till the culmination of the Second World War. Then began Cold War. Slave countries became independent and they too embarked upon an ambitious industrialization programme to develop themselves on a big scale as they were hitherto prevented by the imperialist countries to establish their indigenous industries. The cumulative effect of all these industrial expansion all over the world was very damaging for world environment and ecology. Now all the countries of the world, developed, underdeveloped and backward, were in the mad-race for rapid industrialization and began to exploit their natural resources indiscriminately, just to increase their GDP. In this process of mad-racing for industrialization and boosting production of goods & services, all were and still are contributing their respective share of pollution in a big way, when taken together as a whole. The level of total world pollution has now reached to a highly dangerous level, encompassing every thing, i.e., air, water, soil, noise, etc. and proliferation of radioactivity. (see fig.14) In the last 30 years, a third of the natural world has been obliterated. 40 to 50 per cent of earth's ice-free land surface has been heavily transformed or degraded by human activities, 66 per cent of marine fisheries are either over-exploited or at their limit, and atmospheric carbon dioxide has increased more than 30 per cent since the advent of industrialization. The current pattern of resource consumption shows a gradual erosion of the natural capital of the planet. Instead the survival of mankind should be linked to the income generated by this capital. This will help prevent the erosion of nature's resilience. **The emerging challenge today is to reverse the collision course between humans and nature.**

Air Pollution

Air pollution is a broad term applied to all physical, chemical and biological agents that modify the natural characteristics of the atmosphere. Air pollutants are classified as either primary or secondary. A primary air pollutant is one that is emitted directly into the air from a given source. Carbon mono oxide is an example of a primary air pollutant because it is produced as a byproduct of combustion. A secondary air pollutant is formed in the atmosphere through chemical reactions involving primary air pollutants. The formation of ozone in photo-chemical smog is an example of a secondary air pollutant.

Our atmosphere is a complex, dynamic and fragile system. The combined effect of air pollutant emissions globally is causing a great concern among the environmentalists all over the world. These emissions are the main villains in creating global warming, climate change and stratospheric ozone depletion. The World Health Organization (WHO) has rated air pollution as a class 1 carcinogen and estimates that one fifth of the global burden of disease is attributable to environmental health problems. **The 'Global Burden of Disease' report 2013, categorized air pollution as the fifth largest killer in India.** Left unchecked, air pollution combined with toxic chemicals and wastes have the potential of fuelling a global epidemic.

A study entitled 'Pollution in Lucknow City and its health implication on the exposed venders, drivers and traffic policemen' was conducted by the Indian Institute of Toxicology Research (IITR), Lucknow. Those surveyed complained of various eye related problems. About 62% of drivers, 57 % of vendors and 68% of traffic policemen complained of eye problems. Majority of the subjects were suffering from burning sensation in the eyes. Category-wise, 93% of drivers, 74% of vendors and 77% of traffic policemen complained of eye burning sensation. Eye watering problem was reported in 51% of drivers, 44% of vendors and 72% of traffic policemen. Constant irritation and redness in eyes was reported in 33% of drivers, 21% of vendors and 26% of traffic policemen. Impaired eye vision, too, was reported in 25% of drivers, 20% of vendors and 13.5% of traffic policemen.

For each city, the exact causes of pollution may be different which depend upon the geographical location, temperature, wind and weather factors. Sometimes, pollution is dispersed into the atmosphere and becomes diluted. Sometimes this does not happen and builds up to dangerous levels. A temperature inversion occurs when air close to the earth surface is cooler than the air above it, and pollution cannot rise in the air. Cities surrounded by mountains also experience trapping of pollution. Inversion can happen in any season. Winter inversions are likely to cause particulate and carbon mono oxide pollution. Summer inversions are more likely to create smog.

Another consequence of air pollution is acid rain. When pollutant, such as sulphuric acid combines with droplets of water in the air, the water or snow becomes acidified and acid rains occur. It damages plants by destroying their leaves, poisons the soil, and changes the chemistry of lakes and streams. It kills trees and harms animals, humans, fish and other wildlife. The Greenhouse Effect, also referred to as global warming, is generally believed to occur from the build up of carbon dioxide gas in the atmosphere. Carbon dioxide is produced when fuels are burned. Plants convert carbon dioxide back to oxygen, but the release of carbon dioxide from human activities is much higher than the world's plants can process and absorb. The situation is made worse since many of the earth's forests are being removed by concrete constructions, large industries and agriculture land. Thus the amount of carbon dioxide in the air is continuing to increase without any treatment. This accumulation of carbon dioxide into the atmosphere is acting like a blanket and traps heat close to the surface of the earth. This causes global warming and a change of few degrees in temperature will affect us thoroughly. There is the possibility that the polar ice caps may melt and its consequences would be a rise in global sea level, resulting in widespread coastal flooding. **Large scale destruction of forests and trees cause soil erosion which goes into the seas by way of rivers and deposits upon the surface of the seas. For thousands of years, this silting of soil on the surface of the seas has been going on and causing sea level rise too, apart from ice-smelting.**

Ozone depletion is another result of air pollution. Chemicals released by human activities affect the stratosphere, one of the atmospheric layers surrounding the earth. The ozone layer in the stratosphere protects the earth from harmful ultraviolet radiation from the sun. Release of chlorofluorocarbons (CFCs) from aerosol cans, cooling systems and refrigerator equipment removes some of the ozone, causing "holes" in the ozone layer; this causes open up of the layer and allowing the radiation to reach surface. Ultraviolet radiation is known to cause skin cancer and has damaging effects on plant and wildlife. Every year, 10 lakh (1 million) Indians are diagnosed with cancer and another 6 to 7 lakh die of it. And it's feared that, by 2035, these numbers may almost double to 17 lakh new patients and 12 lakh deaths per year. These projections are part of a special research paper on Indian cancer published in Lancet Oncology journal. Stating that cancer has "devastating economic and human costs" in India, over 40 experts from across the globe have asked Indian politicians, who are busy with electioneering at the moment, to concentrate on family health programmes for cancer. More cancer specialists, more hospitals and more money for research for India-specific affordable treatment are needed to change the cancer graph of India, said the paper, written mainly by researchers at King's College in London and Tata Memorial Hospital in Parel, Mumbai.

There is sufficient evidence that exposer to outdoor air pollution causes lung cancer with a positive association with an increased risk of bladder cancer. Particulate matter, a major component of outdoor air pollution, was evaluated separately and was also classified as carcinogenic to humans (Group 1), said an IARC (International Agency for Research on Cancer) statement. IARC Monograph Section head Kurt Straif said the air we breathe has become polluted with a mixture of cancer – causing substances. "We know how that outdoor air pollution is not only a major risk to health in general, but also a leading environmental cause of cancer deaths." Studies indicate exposure levels have increased significantly in some parts of the world, particularly in rapidly industrializing countries with large populations in recent years. **The most recent data indicates 2.23 lakh deaths of lung cancer worldwide resulted from air pollution in 2010.** In the past, the programme evaluated many individual chemicals and specific mixtures that occur in air pollution. These include diesel engine exhaust, solvents, metals and dust. But this is the first time that experts have classified outdoor air pollution as a cause of cancer. The predominant sources of air pollution are transportation, stationary power generation, individual heating and cooking. This report should send a strong signal to the international community to take action without further delay.

Shanghai authorities ordered children indoors and halted all construction on 06/12/2013 as China's financial hub suffered one, its worst bouts of air pollution, bringing visibility down to a few dozen metres, delaying flights and obscuring the city's skyline. The financial district was shrouded in a yellow haze, and noticeably fewer people walked the city's streets. Shanghai's concentration of tiny, harmful PM (particulate matter) 2.5 particles reached 602.5 micrograms per cubic meter on Friday afternoon, an extremely hazardous level that was the highest since the city began recording such data last December. That compares with the World Health Organization's safety guidelines of 25 micrograms. The dirty air that gripped Shanghai and it's neighboring provinces for days is attributed to coal burning, car exhaust, factory pollution and weather patterns, and is a stark reminder that pollution is a serious challenge in China. Beijing has seen extremely heavy smog several times over the past year.

Air pollution causes 29000 early deaths a year in the U.K. The WHO last said air pollution has emerged as the world's single largest environmental health risk, having caused seven million deaths in 2012 __ 80% of which were from heart attacks and stroke. The European Commission has already dragged Britain to court for failing to deal with air pollution. The Commission has launched legal proceedings against the U.K. for its failure to cut excessive levels of toxic nitrogen dioxide.

Delhi's major chunk of pollution comes from vehicular emissions. There are 7.5 million vehicles plying in Delhi today. Around 1400 vehicles are added to this number every day. In this, inter-state vehicles, which are mostly diesel based, are the major contributors. The environment department has very little to do as vehicles, the key polluters, are out of their jurisdiction. After vehicular emissions, small scale industries and thermal power plants are the next major air pollutants emitting poisonous sulphur dioxide and nitrogen oxide gases. Construction activities and open burning and harvest haze are also major reasons. In winters we have a lot of smog accumulated in Delhi's air. This is because neighbouring states like Punjab and Hariyana burn their dead crops leading to major rise in air pollution. It also includes a specific strategy for two-wheelers as the state pollution data claim that 54 per cent of the total pollution levels in Delhi are due to two-wheeler.

Now we shall take up the major pollutants of the air and their harmful effects on humans and other biological world;

1- Ozone

This gas is found in two places in the atmosphere. First is near the ground in the trotosphere where it constitutes major part of smog. The second is higher in the air in the stratosphere where it blocks radiation from the sun. Ozone is formed when nitrogen oxides and volatile organic compounds mix in sunlight. Ozone near the ground can cause more frequent asthma attacks in people who have asthma and can cause sore throats, coughs, and breathing difficulty. It may lead to pre-mature deaths and can do harm to plants and crops.

2- Carbon Mono Oxide

This is also a gas formed by burning of fossil fuels, mostly in cars. This gas is released when engines burn fossil fuels. Untuned engines of automobiles cause higher emissions. Furnaces and heaters in our homes emit high concentration of carbon mono oxide if they are not properly maintained. Exposure to carbon mono oxide makes people feel dizzy and tired and gives them headaches. It prohibits oxygen intake and make body parts hard to run correctly. It is more harmful to elderly people with heart diseases when exposed to higher amounts of this gas.

3- Nitrogen Dioxide

It is a reddish-brown gas which comes from power plants and cars or automobiles. Nitrogen dioxide formed when nitrogen in the air reacts with oxygen at very high temperatures. High levels of nitrogen dioxide exposure can cause coughs and breathing problems in humans. This gas is responsible for acid rains which harms plants and animals.

4- Sulphur Dioxide

This gas is produced by the burning of coal or oil in power plants and from factories that make chemicals, paper or fuel. Exposure to sulphur dioxide harms people who have asthma and create breathing problems. It causes acid rains and irritates people's eyes, noses and throats. It damages crops, trees, buildings and make it harder for people to see at long distances.

5- Lead

Lead is a metal having blue-gray colour and very toxic in nature. The cars which are not run on unleaded petrol, emit lead in the atmosphere which causes lower IQs and kidney problems among small children. For adults, its exposure can increase the chances of heart attacks or strokes. Lead can also come from lead paints, power plants and other industrial sources.

6- Particulate Matter

These are very small particles, solid or liquid, found suspended in the air. These particles are as small as 0.00005 mm. These are of two types; coarse particles and fine particles. Coarse particles are formed from sources like road dust, sea spray and construction. Fine particles are formed by burning the fossil fuels in automobiles and power plants. These particles, when enter in lungs, can cause health problems, like more frequent asthma attacks, respirating problems and premature deaths. Further, large number of chemicals is also found in the air which includes arsenic, asbestos, benzene and dioxin. These chemicals are responsible for causing cancer, skin and eye irritation and breathing problems.

7- CFCs

Chlorofluorocarbons (CFCs) are very harmful chemicals used in air conditioners and refrigerators as coolants. They can also be found in aerosol cans and fire extinguishers. These CFCs are responsible for depletion of Ozone layer in the stratospheric zone of the earth. If the ozone layer in the stratospheric zone is destroyed, the ultraviolet rays from the sun can not be prevented and its exposure on humans and animals can cause skin cancer and eye problems. Plants may also get harmed by its exposure.

8- Greenhouse Gases

The gases that stay in the air for a long time, like carbon dioxide, methane and nitrous oxide, warm up the planet by trapping sunlight. This is called 'green house effect' because these gases act like the glass in a green house. Carbon dioxide is the most important green house gas. It is released by burning the fossil fuels in auto-mobiles, thermal power plants, houses and in industries. Methane is released during the processing of fossil fuels, and also from natural sources like cows and rice paddies. Nitrous oxide comes from industries and decaying plants. These gases can bring about climate change of the earth by temperature rise, which causes melting of ice at the poles and rise of sea level. Sea level rise damages the land near the coast and floods the coastal areas where humans reside. Global warming is causing climate change and extreme whether conditions seen recently. It has been a strange winter in the Kumaon hills in Uttarakhand following a strange monsoon earlier. Heavier snowfall than any in recent history, and unusually bitter cold stretching into March, have chilled bones and disturbed the pattern of plant life after floods, one of the worst in history, had killed hundreds and swept away habitations, and prolonged downpours had caused landslides and eroded vast stretches of roads. People here are attributing havoc to climate change, which is altering weather patterns the world over. It is not just a matter of coping with floods, snow storms, and the loss of lives but of reckoning with a changing environment. Global temperatures are going up, glaciers are melting and the sea level is gradually rising.

In what appears to be another grim outcome of climate change, a study has found that forests in easterm Himalayas are gradually 'browning', with trees withering and foliage declining even during productive seasons. Similar changes were noted in tropical mountain forests across the world. The study used satellite images from 1982 to 2006, which revealed a common trend; mild greening till the mid 1990s and then a sudden and steady reversal which is making these forests appear drier and brown. The study has been accepted for publishing in the Global Change Biology journal. A study has found a worrying increase in 'browning' in forests in the eastem Himalayas. This may mean that the trees in these forests are not able to transpire at the optimum level and their photosynthesis activities has reduced due to temperature rise. Among the 47 protected areas across five biodiversity hotspots selected for the study, were Kangchendzonga national park in Sikkim and Namdapha national park in Arunanchal Pradesh.

Acid Rains

Acid rain was first reported in Manchester, England, which was an important city during the Industrial Revolution days. In the year 1852, Mr. Robert Angus Smith, a scientist, first of all found a relationship between acid rain and atmospheric pollution. He used this 'acid rain' term in 1872 and observed that acid rain could lead to natural destruction. The problem of acid rain is therefore not a new one, but now it has taken an international problem from being a local problem for industrial towns and cities in England and Europe.

Acid rain is a term used to describe all forms of acid precipitation i.e. rain, snow, hail, fog etc. Harmful gases pollutants in the atmosphere, particularly oxides of sulfer and nitrogen, can cause precipitation to become more acidic when converted to sulphuric and nitric acids, called acid rains. The increasing demand for electricity and the rise in the number of motor vehicles in recent decades all over the world has made the emissions of acidifying pollutants on a much larger scale, particularly since 1950s. Emissions of such pollutants are heavily concentrated in the northern hemisphere, especially in Europe and North America and during 1970s and 1980s, Scandinavian countries began to notice the effects of acid deposition on trees and fresh waters.

The fast growing human population beyond the optimum level and its byproduct – industrial growth has increased the problem of acid rain as a world wide phenomenon. Trees and plants are harmed by acid rain in many ways. The way surface of leaves is broken down and nutrients are lost, making trees more susceptible to frost, fungi and insects. Root growth slows down and as a result less nutrients are taken up. Toxic ions are mobilised in the soil, and valuable minerals are leached away. These toxic ions released due to acid rain form the greatest threat to humans. Diarrhea in young children is caused by mobilized copper and Alzheimer's disease is caused by water supplies contaminated with aluminum.

Water Pollution

Water occupies over 70% of the Earth's surface and a most precious natural resource that exists on our planet. Water is a compound of oxygen and hydrogen and existence of life is impossible without it. Although, the inevitability of water is recognized by humans, its pollution on large scale is also due to human activity. With the advent of industrial revolution and thereafter two great wars coupled with a huge increase of human population all over the world brought about a large scale water pollution every where, in rivers, lakes, oceans and even in ground water. The result of this large scale water pollution is death of organisms at a very alarming rate. According to recent estimates of the Central Pollution Control Board (CPCB), faucal coliform levels in the river Ganga mainstream, a stretch of about 2500 km. from Gangotri to Diamond Harbour, remain above the acceptable level. According to the CPCB, 138 drains flow directly into the Ganga river catchment, of which nearly 76% of the population load is being contributed by Uttar Pradesh alone. As cities and industries thrive at the cost of rivers of our country, the collateral damage is borne by the common man, as these polluted water bodies are unfortunately the only water resources for many but also the hotbed for numerous diseases. This is not a local issue but a global challenge. It is estimated that 764 grossly polluting industries discharge waste water into the Ganga. Accounting to a study, the river Thames, in the United Kingdom, will fail to meet pollution standards in 2015 unless farmers use 20% less fertilizers and water companies reduce phosphorus discharges from sewage treatment. Similarly, a United States Geological Survey study shows the threat of nitrate pollution in the Mississippi river.

The CPCB has identified 150 polluted river stretches in the country with Maharashtra and Gujrat topping the list of having maximum of them. The CPCB has identified 150 polluted stretches along various rivers in the country based on Bio-Chemical demand (BOD), Environment Minister Jayanti Natrajan told Rajya Sabha. While 28 such stretches have been identified in Maharashtra, 19 polluted stretches have been found in Gujrat. Uttar Pradesh too has 12 such polluted stretches.

Many causes of water pollution include sewage and fertilizers which contain nutrients such as nitrates and phosphates. These nitrates and phosphates, when reach excess levels, stimulate the growth of aquatic plants and algae. Excessive growth of plants and algae clogs waterways, use up dissolved oxygen as they decompose and block light to deeper waters. This phenomenon proves very harmful to aquatic organisms as it affects the respirational ability of fish and other invertebrates in water. Another source of water pollution is silt and other suspended solids carry by rain water such as soil, wash off ploughed fields, construction and logging sites in urban areas and eroded river banks. When these sediments enter various water bodies, fish respiration becomes impaired, plant productivity and water depth get reduced, aquatic organisms and their environments get suffocated, many types of fish and bottom-dwelling aquatic life cannot survive when levels of dissolved oxygen drop below a certain level, thus kills aquatic life in large numbers which leads to disruption in food-chain. By the end of 21st century, billions are likely to be gripped by water crisis. So say hydrologists who forecast that on present trends, fresh water faces a double crunch __ from a population explosion, which will drive up demand for food and energy, and the impact of climate change. Already today, around

768 million people do not have access to a safe, reliable source of water and 2.5 billion do not have decent sanitation. Jump forward in your imagination to mid-century when the world's population of about 7.2 billion is expected to swell to around 9.6 billion. By then, global demand for water is likely to increase by a 55%, according to the U.N World Water Development Report.

Sea water pollution is another alarming zone where immediate attention has to be paid if we have to save our environment and biodiversity. The main pollutants of sea water are petroleum, plastic items, radio-active substances and heat. Petroleum often pollutes water bodies in the form of oil, resulting from oil spills. Large scale accidental discharges of petroleum are the main cause of pollution along shore lines. Apart from the supertankers, off-shore drilling operations contribute a large share of sea pollution. According to one estimate, one ton of oil is spilled for every million tons of oil transported. The 11000 km Indian coastline, with 202 ports, 27 thermal power plants and hundreds of fishing harbours, has a further 76 ports and 59 thermal power plants planned for future. Given this scenario, the future poses a grim challenge for Indian coastal ecological stability. Chemical industries along the coast aggravate an already delicate situation, with the chemicals seeping into the sea water. This affects the quality of ground water as well. The West coast of India suffers yet another environmentally detrimental industrial activity of ship-breaking. Most of the ship-breaking activity is concentrated in Alang and Sosiya ship-yards in Gujarat. The State has 171 ship-breaking yards which produce 4.6 million tones of scrap metal a year and provides enormous employment to locals. But the industry has severely polluted the coastal region. Over the years, the fish catch along Alang has reduced by 60% due to the presence of heavy metals like lead, cadmium and mercury in the sea water. The National Institute of Oceanography, in its 2011 report, had stated that the coastal waters of Goa are unsafe for bathing or fishing.

Radio-active substances are produced in the form of waste from nuclear power plants, and from the industrial, medical and scientific uses of radio-active materials. Specific forms of nuclear waste are uranium and thorium mining and refining. Accidents in nuclear power plants like Japan's Fukushima disaster, pose a big danger not only to sea life but humans also. A new leak of 100 tonnes of highly radio-active water has been discovered at Fukushima, the plants operator said on 20/02/2014, after it revealed only one of nine thermometers in a crippled reactor was still working. The toxic water is no longer escaping from a storage tank on the site, said a spokesman for Tokyo Electric Power, adding it was likely contained, but the news is a further blow to the company's already battered reputation for safety.

Accidents in nuclear plants can be highly disastrous not only to humans but to all living species. But the fact is, nuclear plants can be most fragile and such incidents can have disastrous consequences. Any case of a nuclear meltdown would cause leakage of radiation, which not only can lead to an unimaginable high death toll and permanent physical and mental disorders, but in the long run, can also make the vicinity uninhabitable for tens of decades. If nuclear leakages can happen in developed nations like Japan, which have a focus of zero defects, then given India's level of work ethics in general take it as good an assurance that in India a nuclear disaster will happen for certain.

Plastic proliferation is relatively a new phenomenon. Use of plastic bags and other plastic items have increased very rapidly and almost every article of use is being made of plastic, since it is handy, unbreakable and never decayable. In India, according to the Central Pollution Control Board, 56 lack tonnes of plastic waste occurs annually. At best, about 40% of this is recycled. The rest is largely uncollected and remains littered, finding it in landfills, dumped conveniently away from urban sight in remote villages, forests, rivers or seas. Most of the plastic is generated, of course from urban centres. The impact of plastic waste on marine life is well documented. **Simply put, the ocean is the world's garbage dump. A conservative estimate indicates that the oceans contain 157.5 million tons of plastic, 80% of which is dumped from land, and the rest off ships, rigs etc.** Plastic usually breaks down into smaller pieces, and mimics the prey of several marine species, causing them to ingest it till it blocks their digestion, causing slow death by starvation. Sea creatures get entangled in plastic and may get choked or suffocated. According, to the United Nations Environment Programme, over one million seabirds and 1,00,000 marine mammals and turtles are killed annually as a result of plastic ingestion or entanglement.

Humans have polluted earth's vast oceans by their activities pertaining to excessive commercial exploitation of sea creatures and negligent dumping of plastic and other waste into the sea. A French undersea explorer and a visionary Jacques Cousteau had made a television series in 1968 named 'The Undersea World of Jacques Cousteau' wherein he demonstrated the pollution level of our oceans carried out by the humans all over the world. Cousteau himself had begun to realize and saw first hand how human activity was in fact rapidly destroying the oceans. There was probably once a time not too far back when the ocean did seem endless and limitless in the bounty it held, but that bubble has burst much sooner than what many have expected. The ocean did have a breaking point and today we have shattered this mega-earth system and cracked the very foundation of life on our planet. According to one estimate, nearly 1.5 billion (150 crore) people lack safe drinking water and that at least 5 million (50 lakh) deaths occur per year on account of water borne diseases. With over 70 per cent of the planet covered by oceans, people have long acted as if these water bodies could serve as a limitless dumping ground for wastes. Dumping of raw sewage, garbage and oil spills in large quantities has prevented the diluting capacities of the oceans, and most of the coastal waters are now polluted. The rapid growth of the urban population all over the world and especially in Latin America, Asia and Africa, has outpaced the ability of governments to expand sewage and water infrastructure. While water borne diseases have been eliminated in the developed world, outbreaks of Cholera and other similar diseases still occur with alarming frequency in the developing countries. The increased prevalence of pollutants in the air and pesticides in food is believed to further lower the immunity of people who are genetically prone to allergies. According to the World Allergy Organization (WAO), almost 30-40% of the globe's population suffers from some kind of allergy. The number of people reporting allergies keeps increasing every year, says Ruby Pawankar, president of WAO, who also serves as the president of Indian Academy of Allergy. She points out that in India, allergies are often dismissed as a non-serious condition. But given the number of people who now react badly to an array of substances __ some allergies can even be fatal __ that perception is changing.

Even ground water is not free from pollution. Chemical composition of ground water in some areas has revealed a high concentration of nitrates, potassium and even phosphates. In areas of intensive industrial activities, there is high concentration of heavy/toxic metals in different proportions in ground water in India. This is the result of contamination of surface and ground water due to discharge of untreated/partially treated water from industry, domestic sewage and fertilizer/pesticide run-off from agricultural fields. Since World War II and the birth of 'Chemical Age', water quality has been heavily impacted worldwide by industrial and agricultural chemicals. Eutrophications of surface waters from human and agricultural wastes and nitrification of groundwater from agricultural practices has greatly affected large parts of the world. Acidification of surface waters by air pollution is a recent phenomenon and threatens aquatic life in many areas of the world.

President of India, Mr. Pranab Mukherjee said while inaugurating the 37th Indian Social Science Congress at Kennedy auditorium of Aligarh Muslim University on 27/12/2013 as, despite having water on three fourth of its surface, Earth had only one per cent drinking water, a large quality of which was polluted. He said rivers were drying and there was over exploitation of ground water. Where there is water, there is life and where there is no water, there is on life. So we need to conserve as well as replenish our water resources. ... India is one of the mega-biodiverse countries in the world and with global biodiversity hotspots, it ranked among the top ten species rich nations. ... Human beings are product of evolutionary and historical process. So far, the desire to be master of nature has guided most human activities. This desire needs to be replaced now by a philosophy of cooperation with nature and urge to evolve new paradigms of ecologically sustainable development.

In the same Congress, President of the Indian Academy of Social Sciences, Prof. P. S. Ramakrishnan said that continuous destruction of ecology through deforestation, mining, chemicalisation of agriculture and industries, nuclearisation etc. had endangered the very existence of human beings.

The major environmental problems in the West are those arising out of waste disposal, that is problems of air and waste pollution and of disposal of highly toxic, industrial and nuclear wastes. In India as well as in all the Third World Countries with progressive rate of industrialization, the waste disposal problems are getting worse day by day. Newly industrialized countries such as China, India, Thailand, Brazil and Mexico are now facing all these problems simultaneously.

Soil Pollution

Soil pollution is defined as the build up of persistent toxic components, chemicals, salts, radioactive materials or disease causing agents in soils, which have adverse effects on plant growth and animal health. Modern wars that hit the earth surface and air are the immediate causes of soil pollution. After World War II, the population of all the countries, especially in the Third

World Countries increased rapidly and they suffered from the problem of food shortage. To cope with the problem of food shortage, almost all the countries of the world introduced the use of chemical fertilizers and other chemicals to boost up the agricultural production. The KNP fertilizers (Potassium, Nitrogen, Phosphates) found its uses on a large scale which degraded the soil and its elements immensely. (fig. 67)

Use of pesticides like DDT was widely done to prevent yellow fever and malaria. It was later also used to control and eradicate disease carrying and crop eating insects. It was later on discovered that destruction of insects led to the endangerment of birds who survive on these insects, thus destroying an important food-chain. DDT is also harmful for bird's egg formation and a threat to human health too. Dioxin is another chemical used by the American army in Vietnam War as a defoliant to make dense forest denuded of leaves which made enemy visible from the sky to bombard. After the war, it was found that the after effects of Dioxin were congenial deformalities and mental defects to the children born to the American soldiers and in the area over which Dioxin was applied.

It was also discovered later that even the smallest amount of Dioxin had the ability to cause cancer, chloracne, miscarriage and fatal abnormalities. Arsenic is used in Glass industries to eliminate a green colour caused by impurities of iron compounds, which is a violent poison and its compounds, namely, lead arsenate, calcium arsenate and paris green are very harmful compounds for humans as well as for other species.

Noise Pollution

Noise pollution is another monster generated out of the Industrial Revolution. As science and technology progressed, new inventions took place which regularly enhanced the level of noise in the atmosphere. Apart from industrial noise, cars, trains, motor-cycles, aero planes, helicopters, tractors, trucks and buses, oil-engines, flour and oil mills, high decibel crackers etc, all contribute their respective noises which become intolerable in cities. High level noise harms the body and mind. It creates deafness in humans. Increased human population has made noise pollution more acute and serious. Every type of machines have increased manifold with the increase of human population. **More than 20 million (2 crore) new motor vehicles annually are being** introduced in India alone. One can imagine what would be the worldwide figure if all the countries are taken together. Similarly, the number of running trains (goods and passenger both), aeroplanes, helicopters, trucks, buses and other commercial vehicles, ships etc are on the increase and polluting the air, water and increasing the decibel level.

In India especially, in addition to the above, religious and social functions also contribute a lot in polluting the noise when people use loudspeakers freely in day and night; even one can not sleep the whole night when high noise music is played. Noise pollution is harmful for animals too. Very high levels of noise pollution may interfere with the natural cycles of animals and they may change their migration paths to avoid the sound. The most extreme damage is done by the noise pollution when it kills the marine mammals by rupturing their various tissues and organs.

Green House Effect And Global Warming

Green house effect was first discovered by Joseph Fourier in 1824 and is a process by which an atmosphere warms the planet. This is of two types ___ natural and manmade. Natural green house effect is a process through which earth's atmosphere balances the incoming solar radiation by reflecting an equal amount of radiation from the earth. Instantly reflected radiation accounts for 30% of the earth's total radiation, of which 6% of the incoming solar radiation is reflected by the earth's atmosphere itself, 20% is reflected by clouds, and 4% is reflected by the surface. The remaining 70% of the incoming solar radiation is absorbed by the earth surface, of which 16% is absorbed by the atmosphere, 3% by clouds and 51% by the land and oceans. This absorbed energy heats up the atmosphere, oceans and land. This converted thermal energy is again radiated back into the atmosphere through which it is lost into the space. In this way, the natural green house effect balances the temperature of the earth's surface and its atmosphere.

Man-made Green House Effect

As described above, the 'natural Green House Effect' refers to the temperature regulating effect that such atmospheric gases have on the earth. The temperature regulating gases are called 'green house gases', which form a blanket around the earth, keeping some heat from the sun, within the earth's atmospheric orbit and thus keeping the planet warm and habitable. Six types of gases have been identified as 'Green House Gases';

1- Carbon dioxide (CO_2)
2- Methane (CH_4)
3- Nitrous Oxide (N_2O)
4- Hydrofluorcarbons (HFCs)
5- Perfluorocarbons (PFCs)
6- Sulfur hexafluoride (SF_6)

Though, these green house gases make up only 1% of the atmosphere, but they act like a blanket around the earth. But human activities make the blanket 'thick', as the natural level of these gases are being regularly increased by the emissions of carbon dioxide from the burning coal, oil, and natural gas; by adding more methane and nitrous oxide produced by farming activities and changes of land use; and by several long lived industrial gases that do not occur naturally. Large scale destruction of forests for industrial, house construction and agricultural uses have further added the green house effect to an intolerable level, for the carbon absorbing factor reduced considerably. In urban areas, pollution has increased to dangerous levels and breathing fresh air has become a luxury.

Amid the frenetic pace of 'development' and busy life styles, urban communities are unable to keep a check on the cost at which the growth is taking place. Cities are becoming exceedingly inhospitable due to newer environmental challenges paired by an ever-increasing threat to human health. Recently, Delhi shot environmental notoriety by overtaking Beijing for excessive levels of air pollution. Smog in cities across India is beginning to extract a heavy price on the collective health of the population, in the form of chronic respiratory symptoms, asthma, chronic obstructive lung diseases and severe coronary disorders, especially in the elderly. Toxicants such as lead, mercury and chromium cause mental retardation, cancers, neurological damage, gastro-intestinal and auto-immune disorders. In extreme cases, such exposures result in death.

According to the Human Development Report 2007-08, high-income OECD [Organization for Economic Cooperation and Development] countries' total emissions of carbon dioxide were 10055.4 million tonnes in 1990 and rose to 12137.5 million tonnes in 2004. The United States of America alone emitted 4818.3 million tonnes in 1990 which rose to 6045.8 million tonnes in 2004. As of now, the U.S. having only 4.6 per cent of world population and emitting 22 per cent of world's pollution, whereas India having 17.4 per cent of world population emitting hardly 4 per cent of co_2. **This large scale emission of co_2 into the atmosphere causing global warming which is man's creation. Since Industrial Revolution in England, this man- created emission is regularly on the increase and now has touched a dangerous level.** (see fig.14) A leaked report of a U.N. panel has predicted severe impact of global warming on food grain production, fresh water resources and human settlements across the globe with Asia facing the brunt of it. The document, second in series of the Intergovernmental Panel on Climate Change's [IPCC] fifth assessment report which is to be made public in Tokyo on March 31, 2014, also carries details of how the global warming will create a civil-war kind of situation in many parts of the world due to huge pressure on available resources.

Asia is facing the brunt of climate change and will see severe stress on water resources and food grain production in the future, increasing the risk of armed conflict among India, Pakistan Bangladesh and China, the latest report of a U.N. panel has warned. U.N.'s Intergovernmental Panel on Climate Change (IPCC), in its report assessing impacts of climate change on human health, settlements and natural resources released on March 31, 2014, carried a dire warning. "The worst is yet to come", it said, if no measures are taken to curb the ill-effects of global warming. India, like other developing economies, may lose up to 1.7% of its gross domestic product (GDP) if the annual mean temperature rises by 1 degree celisus compared to pre-industrialization level, hitting the poor most. The report also predicts an increase in extreme weather events such as last year's flash floods in Uttara- Khand and cyclone Phailin in Odissa, if steps are not taken to control the rise in temperature.

Climate change is also another important threat hanging like a demoniacal sword over Indian agriculture. Climate change is expecting to increase dry lands by 11%. Due to global warming, the average temperature has increased. In has affected the yield of major crops. A 1°c increase in the temperature will reduce the duration of wheat and rice in north and western India by a week. This will result in reduction of rice yield by 4 to 5 quintals per hectare. In Northern parts of country in December, the day temperature has risen from 14°C to 20°C and night temperature has increased from 4°C to 7°C, has reduced the wheat yields in Northern parts of the county, especially in Hariyana from 4106 kg per hectare in 2000-01 to 3937 kg per hectare in 2003-04. Climate change would also result in the emergence of new insect pests besides reducing the milk yield in cattle and affecting fruit crops such as Apples in Himanchal Pradesh and Jammu & Kashmir. **A survey by National Sample Survey Organization (2005) reveals that 41% of farmers want to leave agriculture if any other option was available.**

Rising Sea Level

This man-created global warming manifested into a general rise of temperature on the surface of the earth. According to one estimate, the temperature of the earth's surface has risen 0.60 Celsius since late 1800s and is expected to increase by another 2.0° Celsius. The impact of the general rise of global temperature is melting of the glaciers into the sea and rise of sea level. According to one estimate, average sea level has increased by 10 to 20 centimeters hitherto and is expected to rise further by another 40 centimeters by 2100, which will contaminate the underground sources of water all over the world. Global warming is also creating conditions for global climate change and we are witnessing extreme weather conditions, sudden floods, hurricanes, droughts etc. Millions of people around the world are likely to be pushed back into poverty as climate change is undermining economic development in poor countries, warned the World Bank. In its report "Turn down the heat ____ Climate Extremes, Regional Impacts, and the Case for Resilience" has predicted major droughts, floods, heat waves, sea level rises and fiercer storms in the days to come. In South Asia, shifting rain patterns will leave some areas under water and others without enough water for power generation, irrigation or drinking. The report projects India's two largest coastal cities, Kolkata and Mumbai, as "potential impact hotspots" threatened by "extreme river floods, more intense tropical cyclones, rising sea levels and very high temperatures." President of the World Bank, Mr. Jim Yong Kim has warned that climate change should not be seen as a future problem that could be put off: "The scientists tell us that if the world warms by 2°C ____ warming which may be reached in 20 to 30 years__ that will cause widespread food storages, unprecedented heat waves and more intense cyclones. With South Asia close to the equator, sub-continent would see much higher rises in sea levels than higher latitudes, with the Maldives conforming biggest increase between 100 to 115 cm. Pakistan would suffer the most extreme increase in heat.

'Vast glaciers in West Antarctica seem to be locked in an irreversible thaw linked to global warming that may push up sea levels for centuries. Six glaciers, eaten away from below by a warming of sea waters around the frozen continent, were flowing fast into the Amundsen Sea, according to the report which was based partly on satellite radar measurements from 1992 to 2011. Evidence shows a large sector of the West Antarctic ice sheet has gone into a state of irreversible retreat. The coastal ends of the glaciers rest on bedrock below sea level, holding back a vast weight of ice and making them vulnerable to melt. Scientists likened the process to uncorking a full bottle of wine while it was lying on its side.

The devastating effect of storms, tsunamis, floods and other natural catastrophes across the world is mostly a consequence of rising sea levels____ a direct impact of global warming. The last few years have seen the consequences of global warming like perhaps never before. More than 110 people were killed in the U.S. alone by Hurricane Sandy, apart from 67 casualties in the Caribbean and two in Canada. In the Philippines, the deadly typhoon Bopha killed at least 540 people, injuring another 1100. Topping the misery chart in recent times is Japan's tsunami, which claimed, a jaw dropping 15700 lives. All these calamities, are posing an impending danger to human lives. This year (i.e. 2013) itself has begun with a scary chill across the world (also in 2014) with temperatures falling to new lows and pollution smogs hitting new highs. Delhi is a good example where the shivers of winter were felt like never before.

In today's world, many weather-related disasters are not merely chance occurrences. Extreme weather and related disasters are becoming more common. In an analysis published in 2012, Munich Re, global insurance giant, reported that disasters tied to extreme weather events have more than doubled worldwide since 1980. So far in 2013, many examples stand out __ record high temperatures in Australia and the United States (including the highest June temperature __ 54°c __in Earth's recorded history at Death Valley California), heavy rainfall and catastrophic floods in northern India, the U.S., Canada, Central Europe and Argentina. Parts of the Central U.S. also experienced record snowfall as late as May. Simultaneously, other parts of the U.S., such as southern Texas, are in the midst of record drought. According to the U.S. National Oceanic and Atmospheric Administration [NOAA], the city of Lincoln in the State of Nebraska registered a record low of 0.5°c on May 12, rising to a record high of 37.7°c within two days. As scientist Kevin Trenberth remarked, "all weather events are affected by climate change, because the environment in which they occur is warmer and moister than it used to be. There is now clear, overwhelming, scientific consensus among 97 per cent of climate scientists that current warming is largely man-made, fuelled by emissions of greenhouse gases such as carbon dioxide (CO_2) from fossil fuels and human activities.

In India, during the period from 1990 to 2004, carbon dioxide emissions have approximately doubled, thanks to our efforts to 'improve' the standard of living of our people and poverty removal efforts. Factually, India, China and Brazil owing to their large populations and developing nature of economies, are causing enormous emissions into the atmosphere although they are still far behind from the U.S. and other European countries in this respect. But the overall effect of the total emissions of harmful gases into the atmosphere has reached to a highly dangerous level and this emission is to be checked without any 'ifs & buts' or blaming one another. **Since global emission is a global problem, its solution shall have to be sought jointly and unitedly.** It is true that today's developed countries of the world had started industrialization in their respective countries very early and deliberately prevented the third world countries to industrialize themselves, as they were colonized by the developed nations, better known as 'imperialist powers.' These colonial nations started industrialization in their countries only after gaining their respective independence from their imperialist masters and this happened mostly after the end of the Second World War. These third world backward countries were new entrants in the field of industrialization and till then, the developed world had already emitted large volume of greenhouse gases into the atmosphere. As soon as, these newly independent third world nations joined the race of industrialization enthusiastically, the level of greenhouse gas emission got boosted up further. Since then, the rate of total emission is regularly increasing owing to their zeal for rapid development in shortest time to satisfy their people's desires for necessaries and luxuries alike. Since their population levels are very high and constantly on the increase, their volume of emissions is also increasing year after year. **Thus, the total volume of emissions from all the nations of the world taken together has now reached to such a high level**

that it is causing global warming and climate change. As the atmosphere of the world will not discriminate against as to who is developed and who is developing nation and shall affect all equally, therefore, the time has come to think and act unitedly by all the nations of the world to contain and reduce the level of greenhouse gas emissions forthwith. This, *ipso-facto*, entails the reduction of population size on the part of over-populated nations and bringing to the level of optimum number respectively. This will pave the way for an optimum number of humans required on the globe vis-à-vis it's natural resources and environmental conservation taken into account.

Fig – 16

PERCENTAGE SIZE DISTRIBUTION OF HOLDINGS
IN INDIA

SOURCE – MINISTRY OF AGRICULTURE
ANNUAL REPORTS

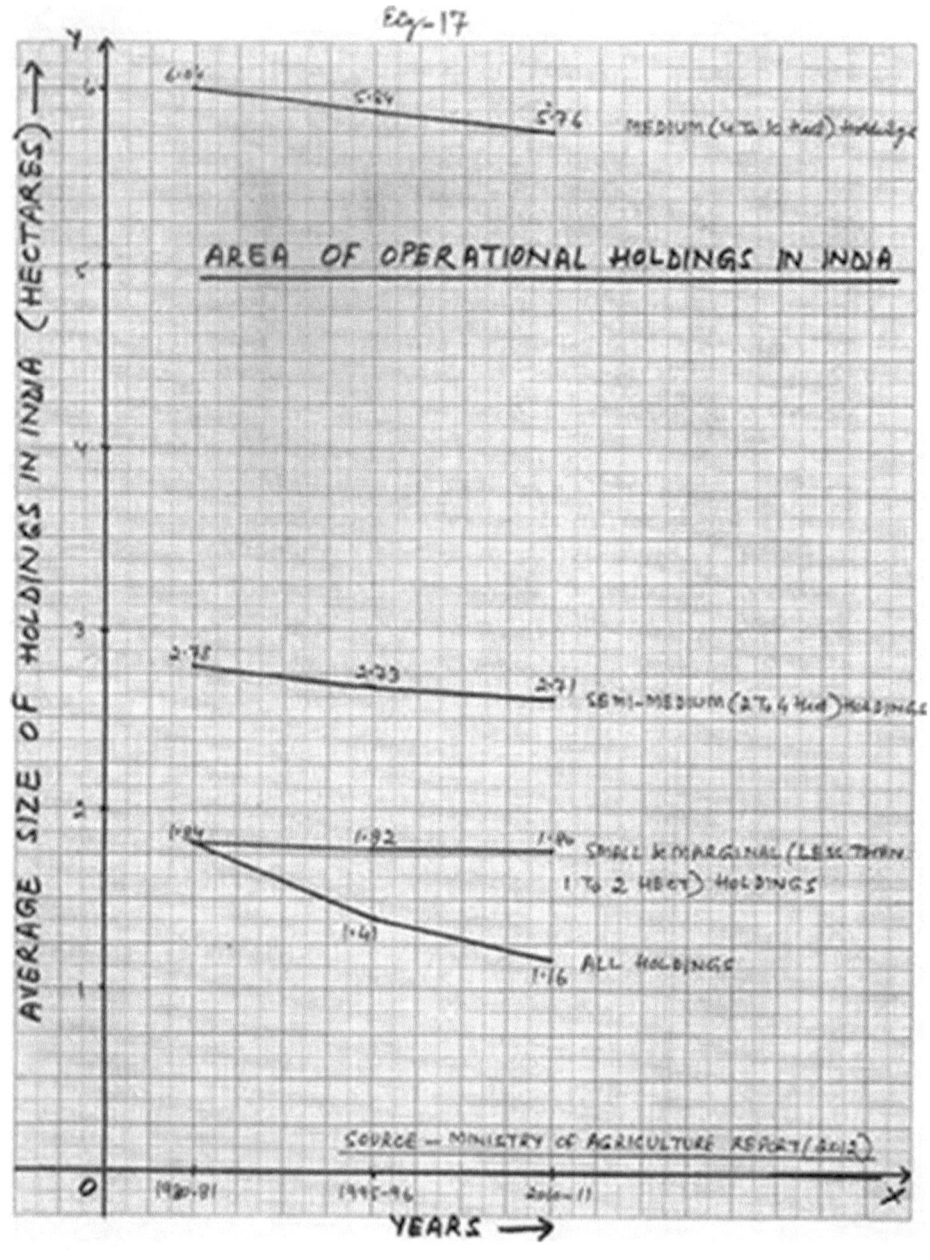

Fig- 17

AREA OF OPERATIONAL HOLDINGS IN INDIA

SOURCE — MINISTRY OF AGRICULTURE REPORT/2012

Fig - 60

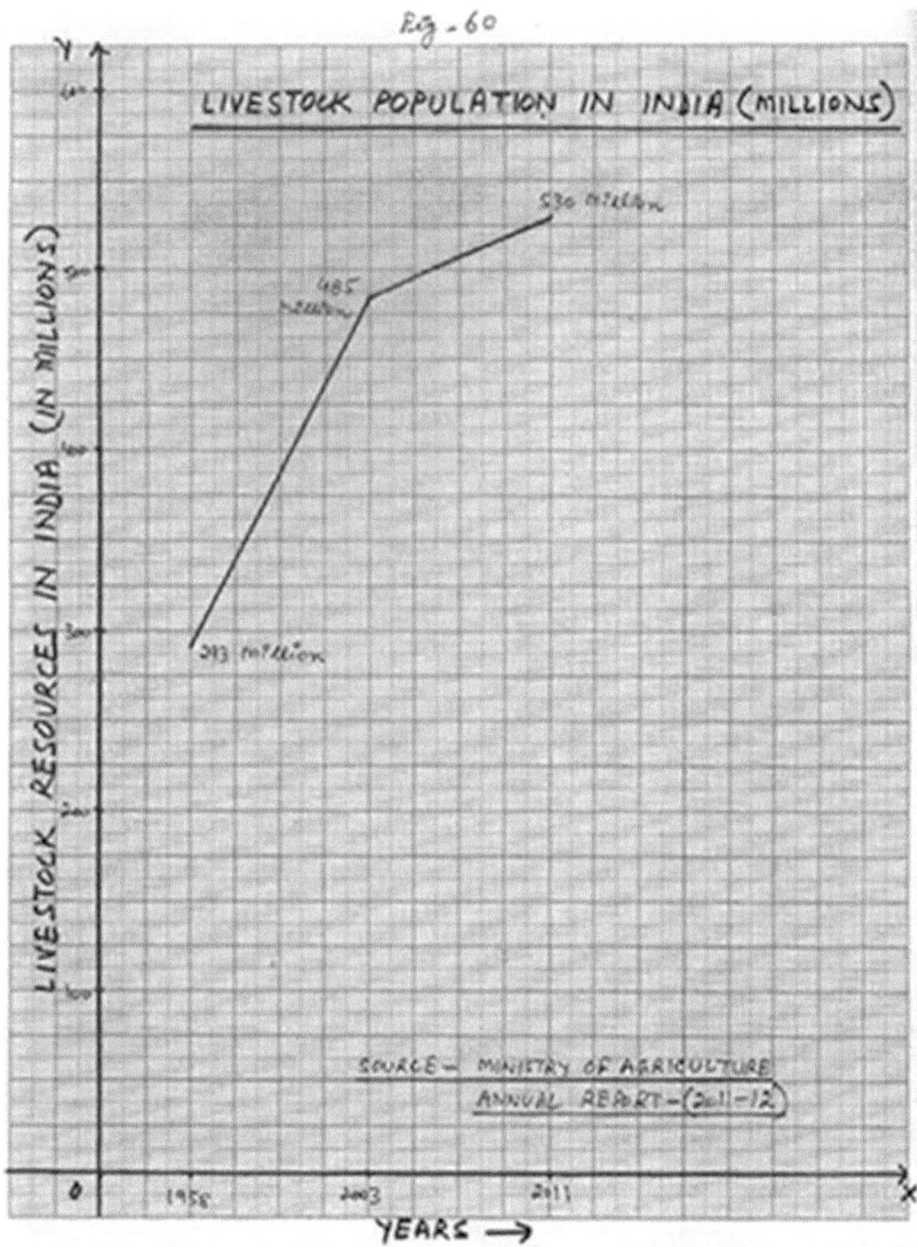

LIVESTOCK POPULATION IN INDIA (MILLIONS)

530 million

485 million

293 million

SOURCE — MINISTRY OF AGRICULTURE
ANNUAL REPORT - (2011-12)

LIVESTOCK RESOURCES IN INDIA (IN MILLIONS)

YEARS →

1958   2003   2011

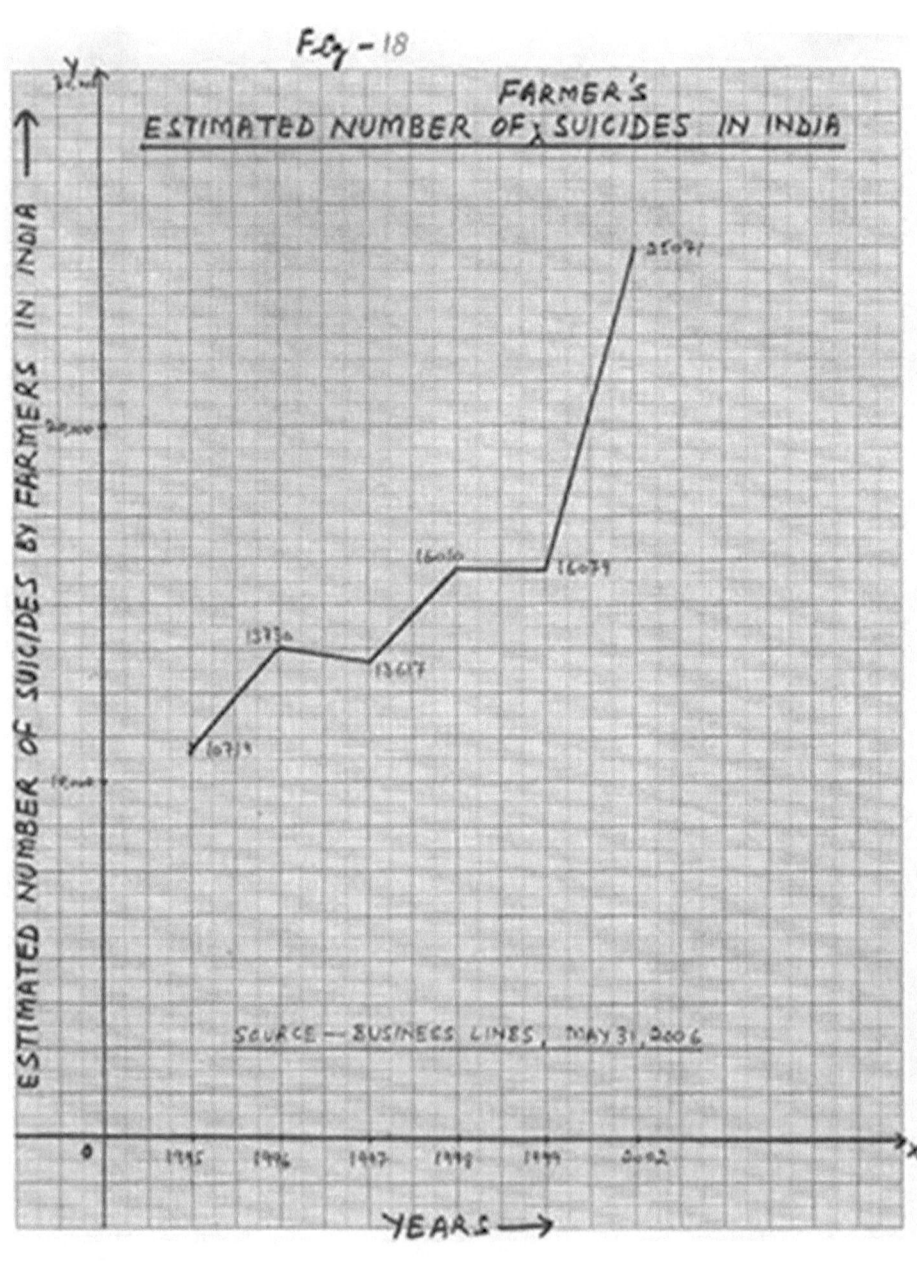

Fig - 18

FARMER'S
ESTIMATED NUMBER OF SUICIDES IN INDIA

SOURCE — BUSINESS LINES, MAY 31, 2006

YEARS →

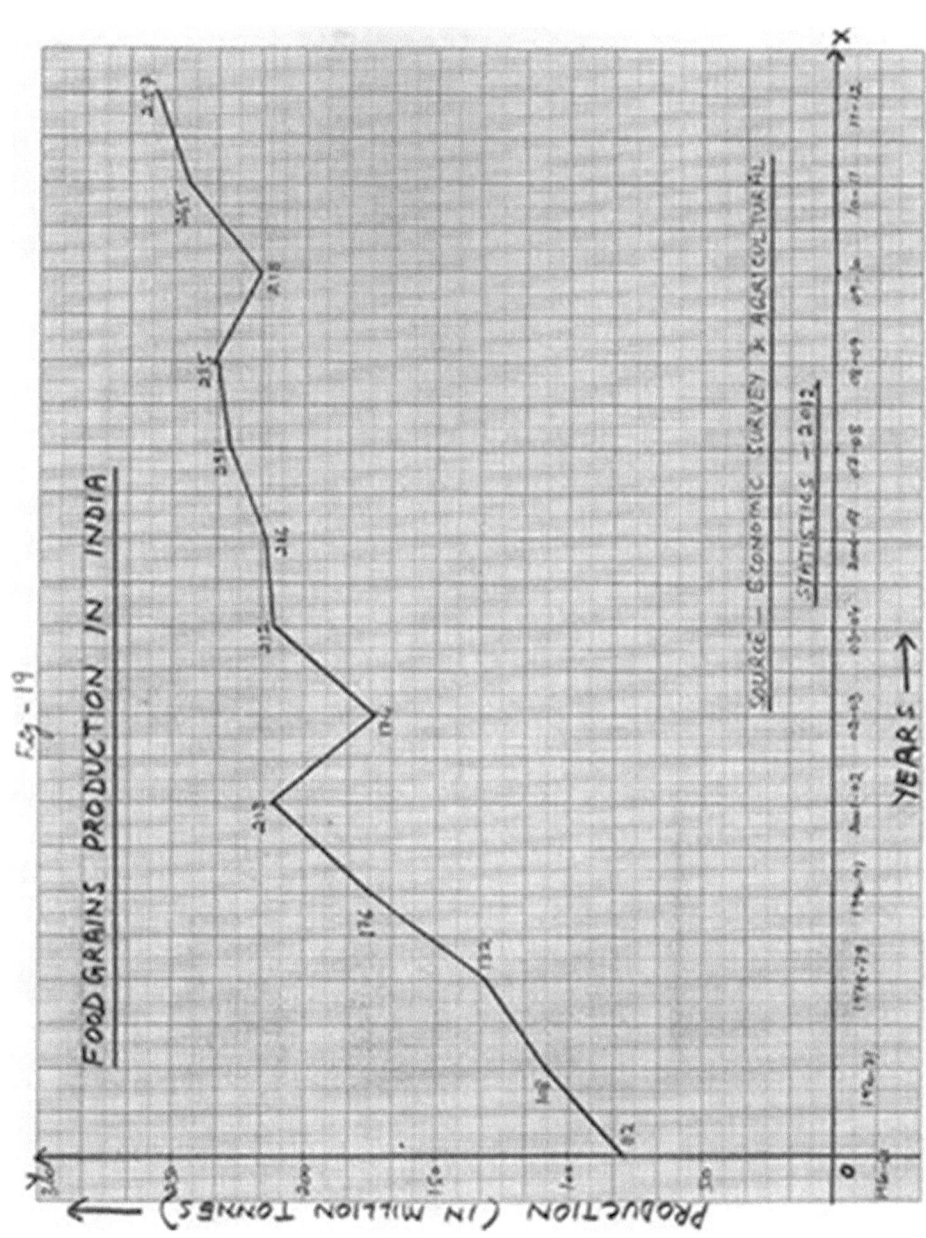

Fig - 19

FOOD GRAINS PRODUCTION IN INDIA

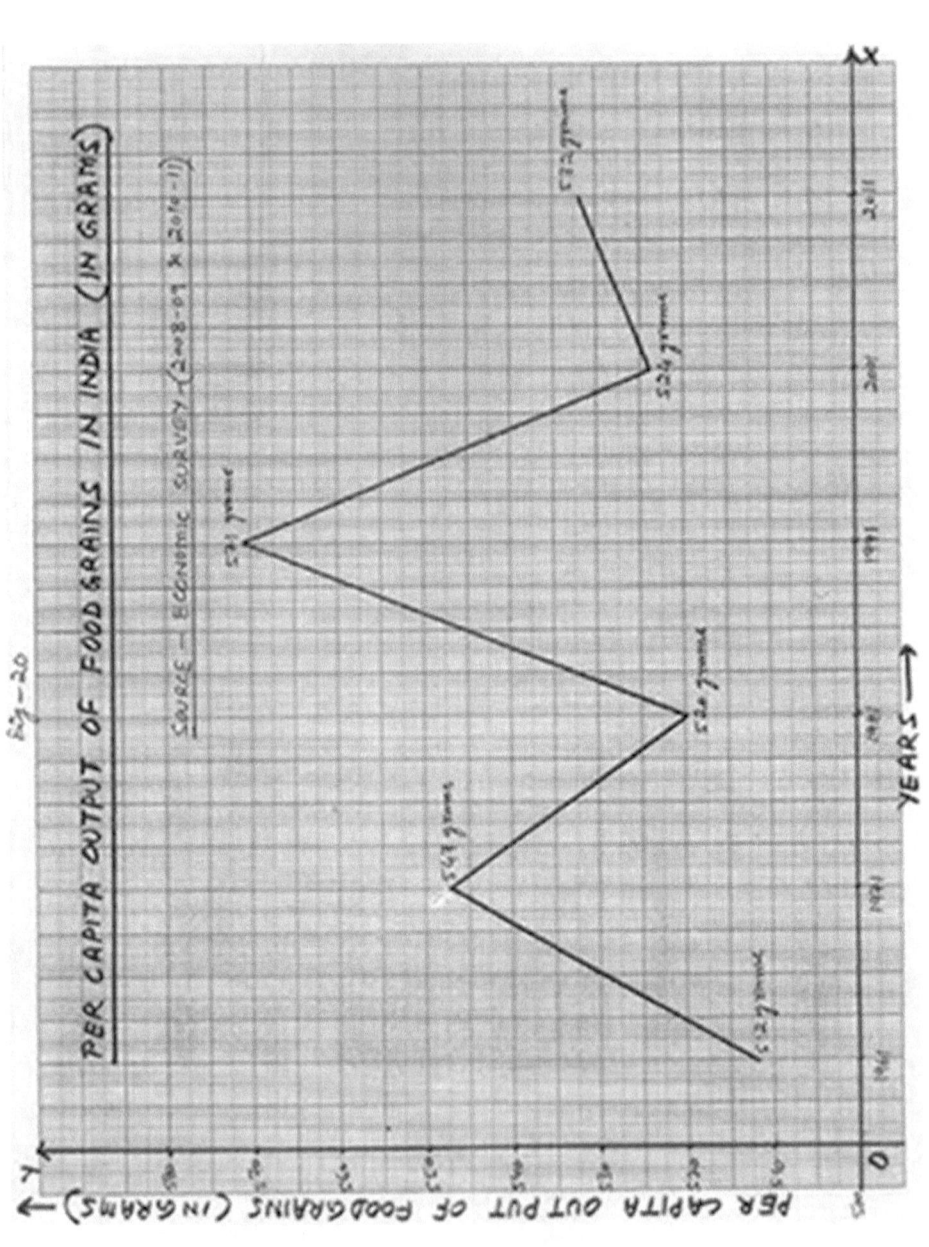

Fig – 20

PER CAPITA OUTPUT OF FOOD GRAINS IN INDIA (IN GRAMS)

SOURCE – ECONOMIC SURVEY (2008-09 & 2010-11)

CHAPTER – 5

Agriculture Sector & Over Population

The worst sufferers by the impact of over-population are agriculture sector all over the world in general and India in particular, because agriculture sector is the only sector where surplus population can get absorbed in the form of under employment or semi employment. Here, this surplus population can atleast survive with the barest of minimum. India's 60% population is dependent on agriculture and allied activities which comes out to around 750 million (75 crore) people, taking the total population of India in Dec. 2013 as 1250 million (125 crore). Comparison can be made between the positions of agriculture in India with that in the other countries as regards the share of agriculture in employment. In the United Kingdom and the United States, only 2 to 3 per cent of the working population is engaged in agriculture, in France, the population is about 7 per cent; and in Australia, this is around 6 per cent. It is only in backward and less-developed countries that the working population engaged in agriculture in quite high. For instance, it is 35 per cent in Egypt, 59 per cent in Bangladesh, 50 per cent in Indoneshia and 68 per cent in China.

As on March 2003, 90.4% of total farmers in India were small & marginal formers and agriculture labours. In the year 2011, this figure was 85%, which indicates migration of agriculture labour to the cities for job search. On the other hand, semi-medium and medium farmers, having holdings above 5 acres and below 10 acres were 9% of the total farmers in March 2003. (See fig-16) It went up to 14.4% in 2011, which indicates the fragmentation of agriculture land on account of population growth; while the percentage of big farmers having 25 acres and above land remained almost the same i.e.

0.6% in 2003 and 0.8% in 2011. Average land holdings have also gone down since Independence. In 1981, average land holdings (See fig -17) for small & marginal farmers was 1.84 hectares, went down to 1.80 hectares in 2011 and semi-medium and medium average holdings went down from 8.82 to 8.47 hectares during the same period. Total average land holdings in India went down from 1.84 hectares to 1.16 hectares during the same period.

The small size of holdings is thus explained by division and sub-division of ancestral property due to the growth of population, breakdown of joint family system, the attachment of landed property, the decline of cottage industries, the laws of inheritance, the consequent pressure on land etc. On the other hand, fragmentation of holdings is due to the sub-division of property among joint owners, each of whom wants a share in each plot of the ancestral land. Such a process of sub-division and fragmentation of agricultural land may continue to such an extent that every plot may become extremely tiny. According to a study in a Maharashtra village, fields measuring less than half an acre were found to be sub-divided into more than 20 separately owned plots. In Ratnagiri district of Maharashtra, plots were often as small as .006 acre, so that it was not possible even to turn a pair of bullocks on the tiny bits of land.

Rapid rural population growth has compounded the problem by causing great pressure to be exerted on existing resources. Where fertile land is scarce, especially throughout South and Southeast Asia, but also in many parts of Latin America and Africa, rapid population growth has led to an increase in the number of people living on each unit of land. Given the same farming technology and the use of traditional non-labour inputs (e.g. simple tools, animal power, traditional seeds), we know from the principle of diminishing returns that as more and more people are forced to work on a given piece of land, their marginal (and average) productivity will decline. The net result is a continuous deterioration in real living standards for rural peasants.

Please see Nehru's observation, written by him around 82 years ago on December 01, 1932; 'Glimpses of world History', pages 487& 488.

No other vivid description of village life of India can be had than this. Nehru portrayed the actual scenario of villages in India. But the situation did not improve after Independence, rather deteriorated further owing to unabated growth of human population over the years. The size of land-holdings turned smaller and smaller over the passage of time and even after 67 years of Independence, the position of rural India became deplorable. Large scale suicides by the farmers have been committed during the last ten years despite Government's efforts to ameliorate the lot of the farmer's community. They were not in a position to repay the loans of the Banks/ Financial Institutions and more than 15000 farmers have committed suicides during the last 3 years in different parts of India. More than 1500 farmers have committed suicides in Bandelkhand area alone in U.P. during the last 3 years. According to one estimate, more than 2,70,000 farmers have commited suicides due to unbearable debt burden following crop failures. What would be the situation of those farmers who are totally dependent on monsoon, in the event of its failure in any year, one can only imagine as 60% agriculture land in India is still rain-fed. What Nehru wrote some 80 years ago (in 1934) is still true for the Indian farmers; see page 318, 'An Autobiography' by J.L.Nehru.

Existence of very small and fragmented land holdings in Indian agriculture sector is the root cause of farmers' abject poverty and suicides, for they can not generate sufficient income out of these tiny bit of land holdings to sustain their families' expenditure and always remain hand to mouth round the year. Even cheap bank loans can not increase their earnings to that level where they can be able to create a reasonable surplus to repay the loans. Since the loans of sub-marginal and marginal farmers were at very high rates of interest from non-institutional lenders, they increased the burden of debt. These poor farmers with very low capacity found it impossible to repay them and thus, borrowed more for the payment of interest as well. Consequently, the vicious circle of indebtness and poor repayment capacity pushed quite a large number to commit suicides. A very large number of suicides were committed by farmers in Punjab, Andhra Pradesh, Karnataka, Maharashtra and Kerala. In most cases, the suicide victims were small and marginal farmers. Tata Institute of Social Sciences (TISS) in its study of 644 suicides in Vidarbha (Maharashtra) reported 83% of suicides were committed by small and medium land holders (see fig-18). The causes of suicides were common; repeated crop failures, inability to meet the rising cost of cultivation and indebtedness. The TISS report states: The other important points were the mismatch between the cost of production and the low minimum support price or the market price leading to huge losses; debt from a low of Rs10,000 to Rs3,00,000 and the inevitability of half the amount borrowed from private lenders who charge an usurious 5 per cent per month.

Given the poll season (electioneering for 16th Lok Sabha), every Partys' heart is beating for the farmers. While AAP's Arvind Kejariwal has brought out figures of farmer suicides in Gujrat, Narendra Modi has repeatedly lamented about such deaths under the UPA regime. However, a look on data on farmer suicides since 1995 till 2012 shows that no party or politician has done any thing for the farmer. In fact, BJP fares poorer than Congress. During the NDA regime at the Centre (1999-2003), a total of 84235 farmers committed suicide. This was a 31% increase compared to the previous five years (1994-1999). (This figure comes out around 64302). Under UPA's next five years (2004-2008), the figure marginally increased by 2% to reach 85960 and in the next five years decreased by13%. Data on farmer suicides were computed by the Nation Crime Record Bureau since 1995 and are available till 2012. Even among top four states, no Party heading the state governments seems to have any successful plan for decreasing farmers' suicides. In Maharashtra, during the 1995-1999 BJP-Shiv Sena regime, around 10,000 farmers committed suicide with an increasing year-on-year trend. From 1083 suicides in 1995, the regime witnessed 2409 farmers' suicides in 1998. The following Congress regime was worse. Between 1999 and 2003, over 16000 farmers committed suicides in the state. In the next nine years of Congress-NCP rule, a whopping 33702 farmers ended their lives. In MP, the situation has been no better. During the Congress regime of 1998-2003, over 13000 farmers committed suicide. Since then over 22000 have committed suicide in MP under the BJP regime.

More than 3,00,000 farmers have committed suicides from 1994 to 2013, in 20 years. **This shows the fact that the problem of abject poverty among the farmers is independent of the Party in power. Now, no Party has got any worthwhile solution to offer to stop such things in future and our Indian polity is on the brink of drowning in the turbulent waters of over population. (See fig.50)**

As we have calculated in chapter 3, around 252 million (25.2 crore) people can be profitably engaged in agriculture sector in India. (This is the maximum number). In India, we have only 140 million hectare agriculture land (decreasing every year) of which only 56 million hectare is irrigated and the rest 84 million hectare is rain-fed or un-irrigated. Even this 140 million hectare landmass is facing a constant shrinkage on account of conversion for other needs; for example, residential needs, industrial needs, for establishment of hospitals, schools/colleges/universities/other institutions, for widening of roads etc. Even, if we implement our new forest policy, we shall have to re-occupy at least 36 million hectares of agriculture land to cover 33% of India's total land surface under forests. Under such a scenario, agriculture land shall go further down to only around 100 million hectares. It means the number of people profitably engaged in agriculture will have to be brought down to only 200 million (20 crore) or even less. This will render 550 million (750-200) people surplus in agriculture sector. Where shall these people go?

According to NSSO Survey Report 2011, the agriculture sector still provides employment to around 55 per cent of India's total work force and is the single largest private sector unorganised occupation. It is mentioned in the report that percentage of agriculture labour has increased from 20 in 1951 to 25 in 2010 on the one hand and the number of total cultivators registered a decline from 50 per cent in 1951 to 29.7 per cent in 2010. This clearly shows the growing pauperisation of the peasantry. **One cannot deny a close relationship between the prosperity of the peasantry and the prosperity of industry and services sector. Likewise, bad crops and pauperisation of peasantry lead to depression in industry, business and other services. Agriculture is the backbone of India's economy and its strength and firmness consolidates the health of its industry and services.** Conversely, since Independence, agriculture sector in general and peasantry in particular is regularly on the path of decline and neglect in India. Food grain production has increased due to Green Revolution, but simultaneous growth of population resulted in wiping out its surpluses and imports have often been resorted to in the past. A country of 1250 million people can not be dependent on imports for basic items like food grains and edible oils. (Please see figs 12, 19 & 20.)

The food grain production from 1960-61 to 2011-12 increased by 313.41% or slightly above three times and population grew by 284.59% or slightly below three times during the same period. It means our growth in food grains production vis-à-vis population growth remained almost the same which indicates that per capita availability of food grains in India remained almost the same (see fig 20). As per Govt. of India's Food Security Bill-2013, 810 million (81 crore) people of India do not have even the basic security of food as on December 31, 2013. If this is the situation after 67 years of Independence, this indicates that we are as backward today as we had been during the British Raj, for our 67% population still does not have even the basic need of food security. How shameful it is, when our rulers boast to have converted India into a growing super power? It is all humbug and deception.

The green revolution has boosted agricultural output substantially, increasing it 2.85 times to 235 million tones, helping feed the county's population from 440 million to 1200 million. The mid '90s marked a shift in which agricultural production slowed down causing stagnation or even decline in farmer's income and agrarian distress turned serious with passing time. Agriculture is no more productive for small or marginal farmers, many of whom have committed suicide because of bebt burden. Reason is not far to seek. In spite of the success of green revolution, contribution of agriculture and allied sector to the gross domestic product (GDP) has fallen from 61% to 19% in the last five decades. Presently, India sustains 16.8% of world's population on 4.2% of world's water resources and 2.3% of global land. Per capita availability of resources is four to six times less compared to the world average which will decrease further with increasing demographic pressure and consequent diversion of the land for non-agricultural uses. While sparing virtually negligible land from agricultural use, around 51% of India's geographical area is already under cultivation compared to 11% of the world average. Rain-fed dry land constitutes 65% of the total net sown area. India's population will grow to 1.3 billion by 2017 which means fresh demand for food grains in terms of quantity, quality and affordability, so current agricultural output needs to be doubled against odds like changing climate conditions, declining ratio of arable land to population and water getting scarcer. Presently excess exploitation of groundwater has caused sharp depletion of water table in central Punjab, Hariyana, and west Uttar Pradesh, Rajasthan, Tamil Nadu and West Bengal. In U.P., over 260 out of total 800 blocks are already declared 'dark zones'. Production capacity of the ecosystem is constantly wearing away due to reckless use of chemicals and poor management of natural resources.

It is now clear that owing to green revolution, we have somehow maintained the level of food grains production with that of the growing population and averted famines and acute food shortage/scarcities, yet we have not been able to provide food 'needed for an active and healthy life' to our large population. In other words, the goal of a balanced and healthy diet, consisting of needed cereals, necessary quantity of pulses, vegetables, milk, meat, fish, fruits etc. is still a distant dream. Excessive use of chemical fertilizers, pesticides and insecticides resulted into deterioration of soil quality and its fertility. 'Food grains production in Uttar Pradesh has stagnated over the last two years, with soil health deteriorating in nearly 70 out of the 75 districts of the state dependent primarily on agriculture. This has put a brake on growth in production of food grains in the state. In 2006-07, food grains production was around 418 lack metric tonne (MT), which rose to 472 lakh MT in 2010-11 and in 2011-12 it reached 520 lakh MT. By this year, it should have been 659 lakh MT but since 2011-12 it is stagnant around 520 lakh MT. It is an emergent situation where both state and central governments should intervene urgently to improve soil health which is turning sterile. The sick soil is surviving on maximum pouring of chemical fertilizers and pesticides, said soil scientist CP Srivastava. The soil survey department's report states the organic materials and micro nutrients like zink, iron and copper have almost depleted and if the green manure programme for improvement is not implemented, the day is not far when U.P poses a threat to the nations food security mission.

An immediate implementation of 'two-children' norm per couple is extremely necessary to halt the further growth of population and then bringing it down slowly to optimum level (around 550 million) is the only way as a necessary condition to achieve the above goal. This shall take at least 100 years or more to achieve this, if we take-up 'two-children' norm immediately. Shrinkage of agricultural land with the increase of population is another cause of concern among agro-economists. At the time of Independence in 1947, India had the massive problem of achieving self-sufficiency in food. Various "grow more food" programmes initially aimed at increasing the total cultivable area in the country. As a result, till the beginning of the 1960s, increase in agriculture production was more the result of the expansion of cropped area. Grazing lands, forest land and waste land have been brought under cultivation. As the National Commission on Agriculture (1976) estimated, the net area sown could increase only marginally up to 145 million hectares by the year 2001. With the relentless increase in population, the net sown area could be expected to decline after every passing year. The cultivable land, in fact, is fast disappearing under concrete buildings and metalled roads and good agriculture land is being destroyed to produce bricks for house construction.

Odissa Chief Ministre Naveen Patnaik's first meeting with the Prime Minister (Narendre Modi), Patnaik raised the issue of granting special category status to Odissa and scrapping of the controversial Polavaram Project situated on the border between Andhra Pradesh and Telangana. Odissa fears the project would submerge 130 odd villages in the malkagiri district and lacks of hectares of land.

Agriculture land is in danger of losing its status every where in India.

———◆———

SECTORAL DIVISION OF WORKING FORCE IN INDIA

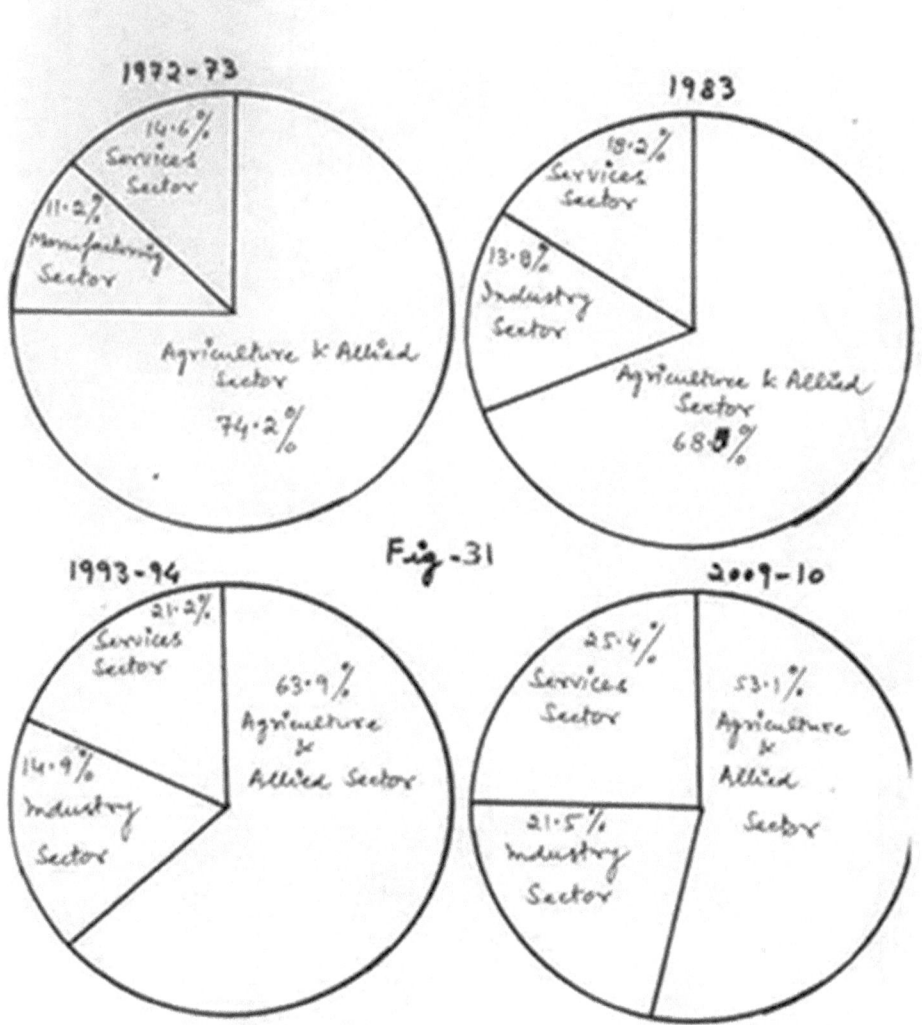

1972-73

14.6% Services Sector

11.2% Manufacturing Sector

Agriculture & Allied Sector 74.2%

1983

18.2% Services Sector

13.8% Industry Sector

Agriculture & Allied Sector 68.5%

1993-94

21.2% Services Sector

63.9% Agriculture & Allied Sector

14.9% Industry Sector

2009-10

25.4% Services Sector

53.1% Agriculture & Allied Sector

21.5% Industry Sector

Fig.-31

SECTORAL CONTRIBUTION OF GDP IN INDIA

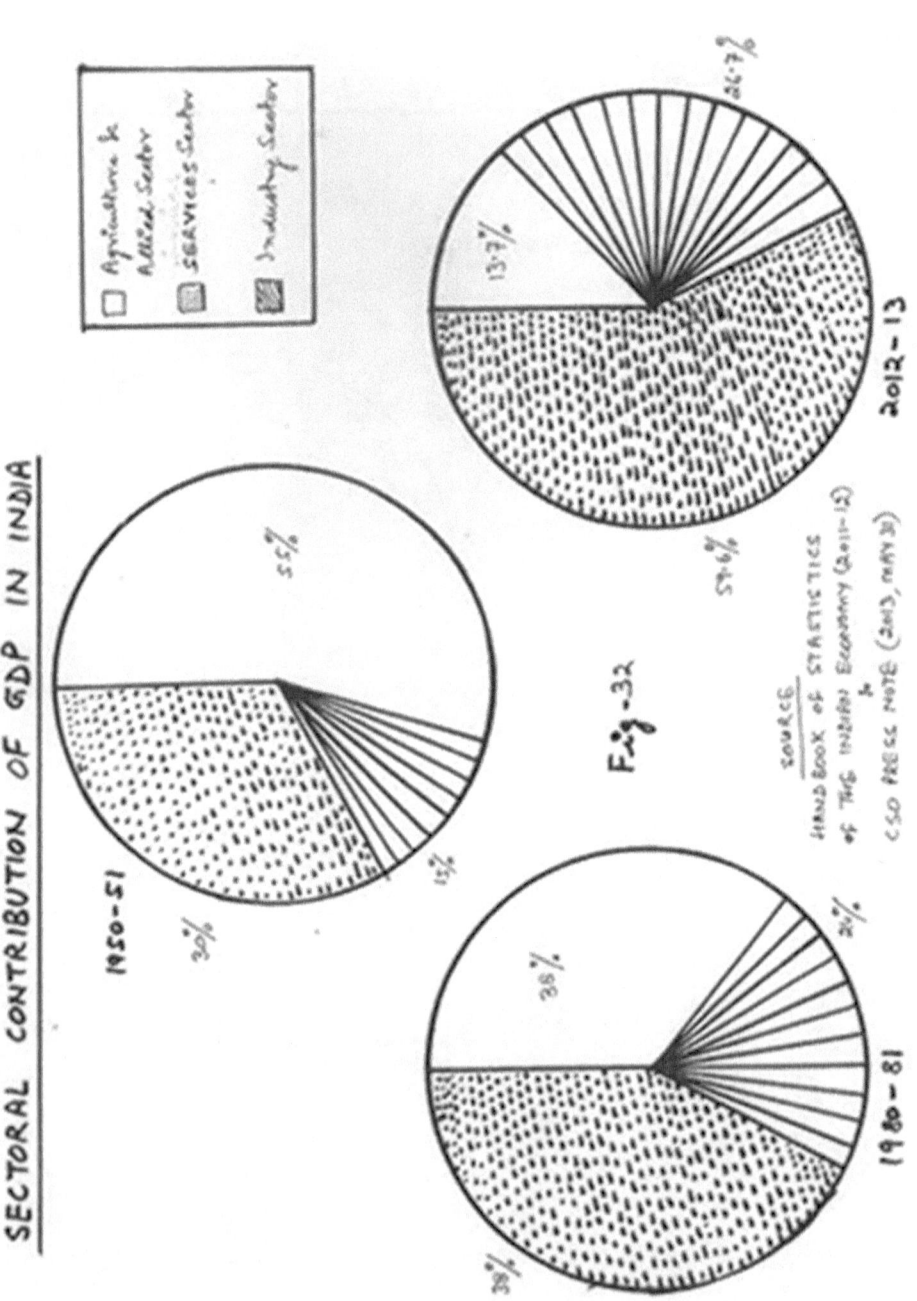

Legend:
- ☐ Agriculture & Allied Sector
- ☒ SERVICES Sector
- ☒ Industry Sector

1950-51
- 55%
- 30%
- 15%

1980-81
- 38%
- 38%
- 24%

2012-13
- 13.7%
- 26.7%
- 59.6%

Fig.-32

SOURCE
HANDBOOK OF STATISTICS
OF THE INDIAN ECONOMY (2011-12)
&
CSO PRESS NOTE (2013, MAY 31)

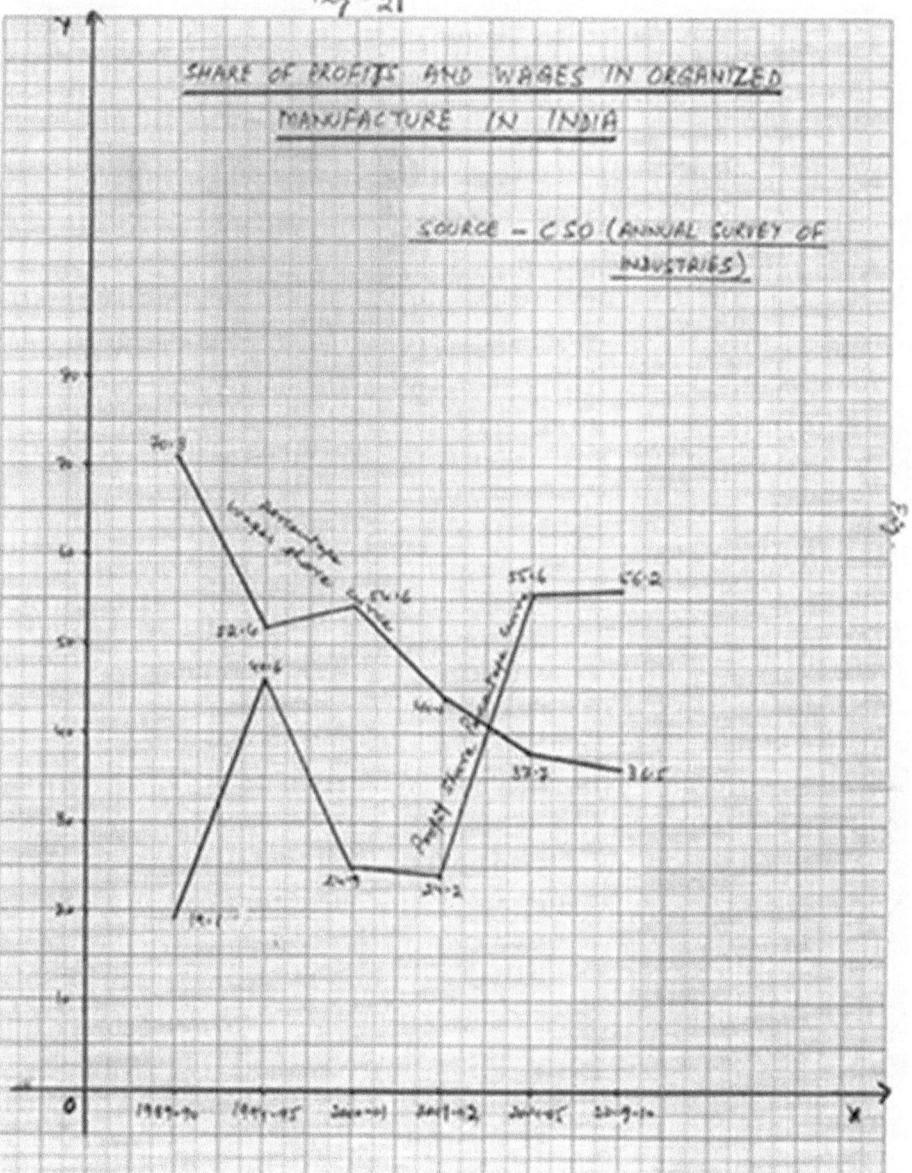

Fig - 21

SHARE OF PROFITS AND WAGES IN ORGANIZED MANUFACTURE IN INDIA

SOURCE - CSO (ANNUAL SURVEY OF INDUSTRIES)

Unemployment and Over-Population

India's massive unemployment and underemployment problem is quite different from the industrially developed countries of the West as it is a developing economy started from a position of social and industrial backwardness. Since India had been under subjugation of the British for almost 200 years, this imperialist power prevented Indians to industrial opening on the Indian soil to protect its own economic interests. India's long history of foreign subjugation also kept it socially backward. At the time of Independence in 1947, Indian polity was backward both socially and industrially. At the time of Independence, nearly 80% population of India was engaged in agriculture and allied activities and having a literacy rate of 18% only. This clearly depicts the backwardness of its economy and society.

After Independence, our governments of free India planned to develop India industrially and socially, and 'Five-Year-Plans' were organized to achieve targeted goals. But after completion of several plans, the problem of massive unemployment and underemployment still persists; rather became more pronounced than at the time of Independence. Though, in 1947, the population of India was around 330 million (33 crore), much below the optimum level of 550 million (55 crore), even then there was unemployment and underemployment on a large scale. This was due to the fact that our technological know-how was at the very low level and extremely limited. We could not exploit our land and other natural resources profitably. Our economy developed during plans (now we are under twelveth plan 2012-17) and an alround progress has been done in industry, agriculture, infrastructure development, social and services sector etc. Our GDP increased manifold since Independence and so the per capita income.

In 1950-51: GDP was Rs 2,23,899 crore and per capita NNP was Rs 5708

In 2011-12: GDP was Rs 83,62,495 crore and per capita NNP was Rs 38037 (At 1999-2000 prices)

Even then, our unemployment and underemployment problem turned more severe and acute and its number grew with every plan. According to a Planning Commission report, total number of unemployment in India in March 2000 was 106 million (10.6 crore). The Eleventh Plan (2007-12) was having a backlog of 37 million unemployed and according to the Planning Commission, 45 million more have been added as new entrants during the Plan period. Thus total job seekers in the Eleventh Plan were 82 million. **In other words, the development plans in India failed to absorb even the normal increase in labour force during the period, not to speak of reducing or vanishing the backlog of unemployment and underemployment.** More than 20% of Indians in the 15-24 age group were jobless and seeking work, according to startling data in Census 2011 released on July 01,2014. In absolute terms, this army of unemployed youth is staggeringly huge __ around 4.7 crore of which 2.6 crore were men and 2.1 crore women. These definitive figures for 2011 reveal the deep and pervasive unemployment that has gripped India in the past decade even as economic growth was over 8% per annum for most of this period. Overall, the unemployment rate in the 15-59 working age population group was a worrisome 14.5% including marginal workers seeking work. The figures include the entirely unemployed and marginal workers who get work only for up to six month in a year. Among dalits, unemployment rate in the working age population of 15-59 years was a shocking 18%, much higher than the general population. Among adivasis, the unemployment rate was even higher at over 19%. These are the two most marginalized sections of Indian society, and clearly they are struggling with widespread unemployment.

Over 11.3 crore persons are "seeking or are available for work", that is, they were unemployed, according to Census 2011 data released on 23/09/2014. This huge number made up around 15% of the working age population of about 74.8 crore in the 15 to 60 years age group. These unemployed persons were distributed over nearly 7 crore families or households. That's about 28% of all households in the county. This appears to be an all-time high for Census years. In 2001, about 23% of households had members that were unemployed. Within a decade, this has risen to 28%. In the past three years, on particular spurt in employment growth or policies that would catalyse job creation have emerged and the situation continues to be dire. Over 20% of youth between 15 to 24 years of age were jobless and seeking work according to Census 2011 data released earlier. In absolute terms, this army of unemployed youth is about 47 million. The number of unemployed persons is actually more than 113 million because the Census office has released data in terms of how many persons per household are seeking or available for work, and the highest number in that is "more than 4". For the purpose of the present computation, this has been taken as four persons only.

Poverty and unemployment and underemployment have a close relationship and they are two sides of the same coin. When unemployment and underemployment persist largely in any economy, it is but natural that poverty and abject poverty will also be there. India with a population of 1210 million in March 2011, and with its per capita income of U.S $ 1410 is among the poorest of the economies of the world. It has had a share of 17.5 per cent in world population, but accounts for only 2.6% of world's Gross National Income (GNI) on exchange rate basis. Whereas China's share of world population is 19.3% and her per capita income is U.S. $ 4940 and accounts for 10.5% of world GNI on exchange rate basis.

The question arises; why we could not deal with the problem of unemployment and underemployment despite a remarkable alround growth in the economy? **The answer lies in the fact that our population growth raced much ahead of our development and more and more people joined the work-force than the absorption of the same into the growing economy.** In 1970 itself, we crossed our level of optimum population which was 550 million or 55 crore, as per author's calculation. Since then, the problem of unemployment and underemployment turned more acute and serious for the simple reasons that the base of agriculture land and other natural resources have completely exhausted and there remained no solid base for the exceeding population beyond 550 million to depend upon. (see Figs 11 & 12) **Hence every increase in population beyond the level of 550 million optimum shall render a mass of unemployed and underemployed people, for the capacity of the economy to generate gainful employment would diminish.** As shown in Fig 12, OM is the optimum population level whereat the entire workforce can be employed profitably and gainfully and per capita income and 'green output' will be the highest. When population crosses that level, the underemployment begins to grow because, now there are no agricultural land and other natural resources to give support to these portions of population. As the population reaches ON level (Fig 10 & 12), capacity of the economy to absorb the entire workforce diminishes and full and gainful employment can not be provided to this MN portion of population, consequently, underemployment, semi employment and small volume of unemployment emerge in the economy. Even the optimum population OM also gets affected and its incomes fall due to heavy taxation and inflation (inflation is also a form of disguised taxation) which is levied on the fully employed workforce to lend a support to underemployed, semi employed and unemployed in the form of provisions for subsidized goods and services and other unproductive purposes.

Data from the department of industrial policy and promotion shows that between August 1991 and March 2014, the government received about 94,000 investment proposals. Put together, these proposed investment of more than Rs. 102 lakh crore and were supposed to create to 2.3 crore jobs. The data on actual implementation of these proposal shows that only Rs. 5.1 lakh crore was actually invested and just 20.1 lakh jobs created. That's less than 5% of the proposed investments and 8.9% of the proposed jobs. So, what is the investment to job creation ratio? Overall, the Rs. 5 lakh crore actually invested created a little over 20 lakh jobs, which amounts to four jobs per crore of investment.

For example, the ruling Congress Party in its 'Election Manifesto' for the 16th Lok Sabha has promised 100 million (10 crore) jobs during the next five years, which was a total deception. Even hoping to increase 10 million jobs in the organized sector as against the total of 8.24 million jobs at present implies a 121% addition to the existing job creating potential is highly ludicrous. The estimates are thus highly over-optimistic and uttarly unrealistic. In unorganized sector, 95% jobs are having the characteristic of underemployment as their incomes are not sufficient to lead a dignified life. Now, Indian economy has reached to that level of development where 'real' job creation is impossible, since it has crossed the level of 550 million population (optimum level) as back as in 1970. Now it is more than twice of that level. **At this level, whatever jobs are created, they will be of 'nominal' nature, as they would not generate any real national income without raising inflation in the economy due to the fact that all our natural resources including agriculture land (natural resources of a country include its productive land, water resources, fisheries, mineral resources, forests, marine resources, climate, rainfall, and topography) are fully exploited.** It is not surprising that despite all efforts of the government to boost GDP growth through liberal economic policies failed and it is less than 5% per annum only with around 10% inflation. Even this nominal GDP growth does not have higher employment generation potential. The authorities are now realising their folly because the country is faced with the phenomenon of demographic dividend for the next 30 years and the rate of increase of labour force is likely to remain above 2.5% per annum. As shown in figs. 31&32, agriculture and allied sector of India's economy is contributing only 13.7% of the GDP in the year 2012-13 and engaging 53% of the total work force of India. This clearly demonstrates the heaviest pressure of population in this sector and here more than half workforce is surplus. While in industrial sector, its contribution in our GDP is 26.7% in 2012-13, wherein the total workforce engaged is around 22% which seems adequate. On the other hand, the services sector contributes around 60% of the total GDP in 2012-13, while the workforce engagement is only around 25%, which shows that this sector is under-engaging the workforce. This is perhaps due to the alround deployment of computer technology which replaces man-power. **If productivity has to be improved and to be brought to the level of developed countries, then it is imperative to computerise the services sector and introduce large scale automation in the Industrial sector.** Farm mechanization with better quality high yielding seeds is the need of the hour for agriculture sector, not only to feed our growing population, but also to export as well as to stock for bad days.

Incidence of unemployment and underemployment in developed countries of the world is different from the developing countries like India. Developed countries are generally not over populated, however, immigration from the third world countries is enormous, which creates unemployment problems in these countries. These developed countries, generally, face the problem of unemployment / underemployment on account of economic depression and deficiency of effective demand. **It would be worthwhile to emphasise here that the massive problem of unemployment / underemployment in developing economies like India is not due to deficiency of effective demand in the Keynesian sense, but a consequence of shortage of capital, land and other natural resources vis-à-vis large supply of work-force on account of relentless growth of human population.**

According to a Eurostat report, the EU's statistics office, published on 31/05/2013, the unemployment rate rose to 12.2% in April 2013 from the previous record of 12.1% the month before. In 2008, before the worst of the financial crisis, it was around 7.5%. Unemployment across the 17 European Union countries that use the 'Euro' hit another record high in April 2013 –and appears to hit 20 million this year in what would be another gloomy landmark for the currency block. A net 95000 people joined the ranks of the unemployed, taking total to 19.38 million. At that pace, unemployment in the currency block __ which has a population of about 330 million __ could breach the 20 million mark by the end of the year.

In India, the problem of unemployment and underemployment is very serious and disturbing as the number of affected people is increasing year after year. The latest data also shows growing disenchantment among the youth as unemployment surges to 11 per cent. Each year almost one crore or 1.2 crore youth join the job queue. With an alround slow down, it is not just the youth who are unemployed, even mid-career professionals are jobless, as industries fire workers for a slimer workforce. Consumer inflation is a concern, says RBI Governor Raghuram Rajan. A 11.24% rise in consumer inflation and almost 18% food and vegetable inflation combine to give an average inflation increase of 41% in three years. **This shows that the poor are the worst hit, forcing the Government to come out with a food security law and accept that over 67% or 81 crore people remain hungry.** This has not only increased the subsidy bill of a weak Government but also led to direct confrontation at World Trade Oeganisation's Bali meet.

Expansion of industrial sector in India is possible only when agricultural land is transformed into industrial land. Forest cover is to be increased too from the present 22% to 33% in the first phase (as per Govt. of India's forest policy) and then to 40% in the second phase (as per author's view) to absorbe present and future emissions of carbon dioxide. This shall further necessitate transfer of agriculture land to forest cover (where it originally belonged to). Since India's population is already very large and continuously growing, it is practically impossible to transform agriculture land into other uses. This is a catch 22 situation for our planners and Indian economy is caught into a quagmire where it is sinking deeper and deeper. **Our planners and political masters could not visualize the dangers of over population.** Had they foresighted this peril in advance at the time of Independence and acted proactively, as our neighbour China had done, this quagmire-like situation would certainly have been avoided and prosperous, poverty-free, fully and gainfully employed citizens of India could have been found.

India's problem of massive unemployment and underemployment is also creating the problem of wastage of fruits and vegetables and other perishable commodities. Around 40% volume of vegetables/fruits and other perishable items go waste in India on account of unemployment/ underemployment situation. Several unemployed youth in urban centers and a large number of underemployed persons in rural areas migrate to cities to earn some money and take up their own petti-retail business dealing in vegitable/fruit stalls as vendors. Since their numbers exceed in comparison to buyers in the market, they fail to sell all their commodities during the day and a substantial portion of these become stale, fetching either a very low price or no price, worth only to be thrown away. **In this way, these poor vendors suffer economic losses on the one hand and India suffers a national loss of valuable fruits/ vegetables/perishable goods on the other. All this is due to failure on the part of our economy to provide these poor people with any type of gainful employment worth the while.**

There is substantial waste of agricultural produce that India encounters. About 40% of total agricultural produce rots before it reaches the market. Much of the loss is constituted by fruits and vegetables, the primary driver of the recent bout of food inflation.

The problem of unemployment can be gauged from the following fact; In Uttar Pradesh, prospective teachers who qualified the Teacher Eligibility Test, in November 2011, and responded to the advertisement for the recruitment of 72,825 posts of teachers are still nowhere in the line of appointments. The politics in recruitment has played its part. The rules of recruitment that were notified in the times of the last BSP Government were not found appropriate by the present Government. No one cares about those who are in schools without teachers. Who is worried about young persons waiting for the job? **There are 65 lakh (65,00,000) applicants for these 72825 posts.**

The public recruitment examination was one of the biggest-ever recruitment exercises with more than 21 lakh people (2.1 million) taking the examination for the post of 41160 constables. Sources said officials from the Guiness Book of Records contacted the U.P.Police Recruitment Board for details.

The extent of demand for banking jobs is evident from the fact that nearly 10 lack (one million) candidates appeared in the written exams for 19000 vacancies for officers in state-run Banks. Out of 10 lakh, only 57000 will be called for interviews.

Are we not heading towards total anarchy and a horrific holocaust?

Fig-65

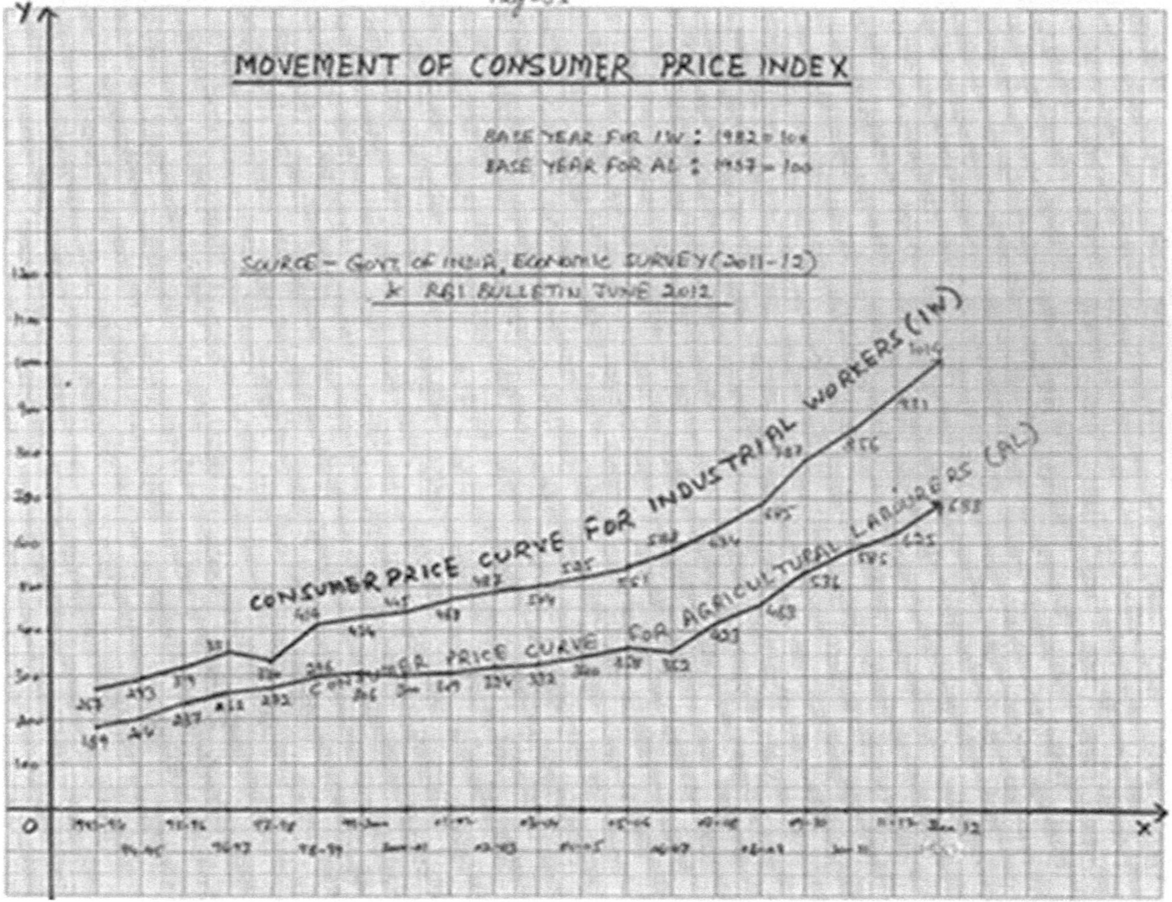
MOVEMENT OF CONSUMER PRICE INDEX
BASE YEAR FOR IW : 1982 = 100
BASE YEAR FOR AL : 1957 = 100
SOURCE - GOVT OF INDIA, ECONOMIC SURVEY (2011-12)
& RBI BULLETIN JUNE 2012
CONSUMER PRICE CURVE FOR INDUSTRIAL WORKERS (IW)
CONSUMER PRICE CURVE FOR AGRICULTURAL LABOURERS (AL)
Y
X
O

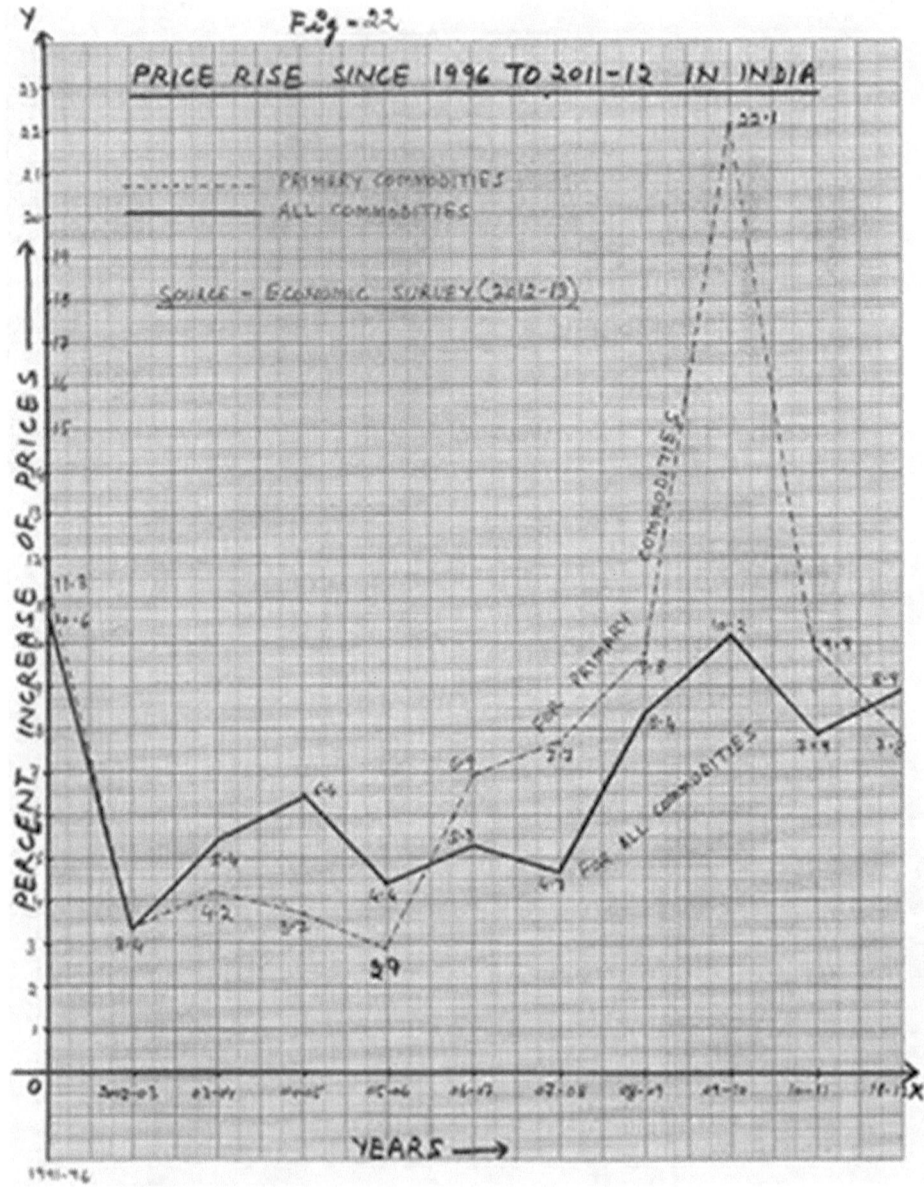

GDP growth
(INDIA)

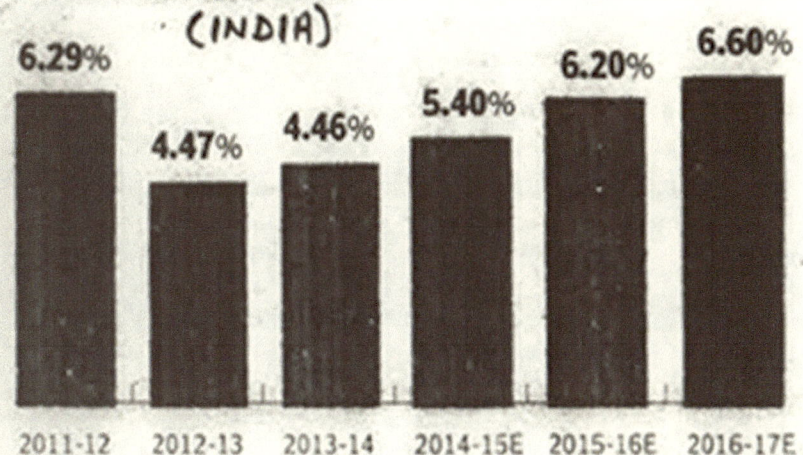

6.29%   4.47%   4.46%   5.40%   6.20%   6.60%

2011-12   2012-13   2013-14   2014-15E   2015-16E   2016-17E

Consumer price inflation (INDIA)

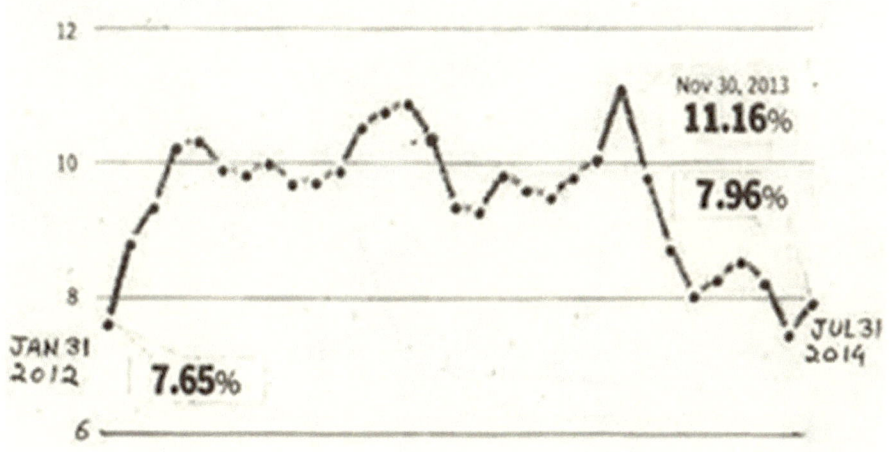

Nov 30, 2013
11.16%

7.96%

JAN 31
2012

7.65%

JUL 31
2014

SOURCE - THE TIMES OF INDIA
SEPT. 05, 2014

Fig. 23

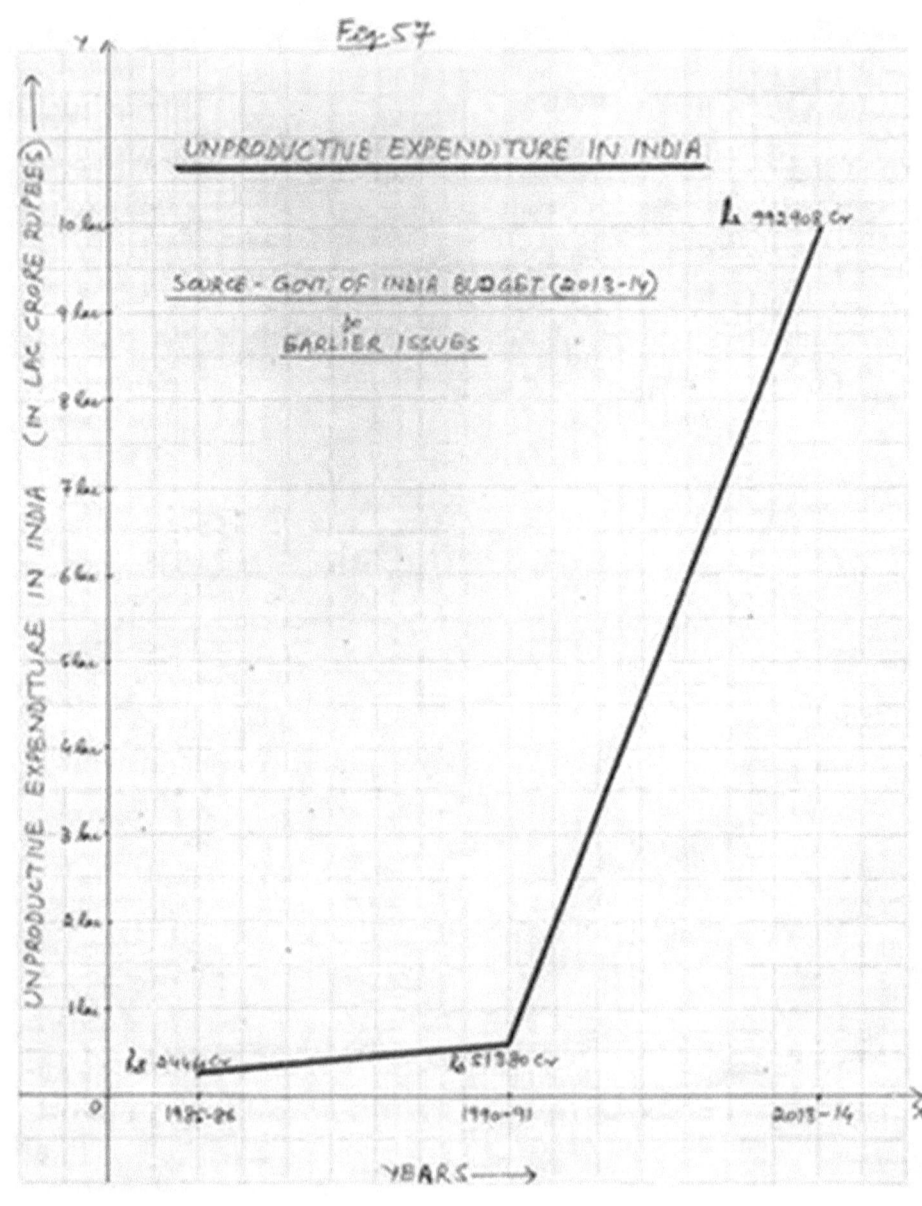

Fig. 57

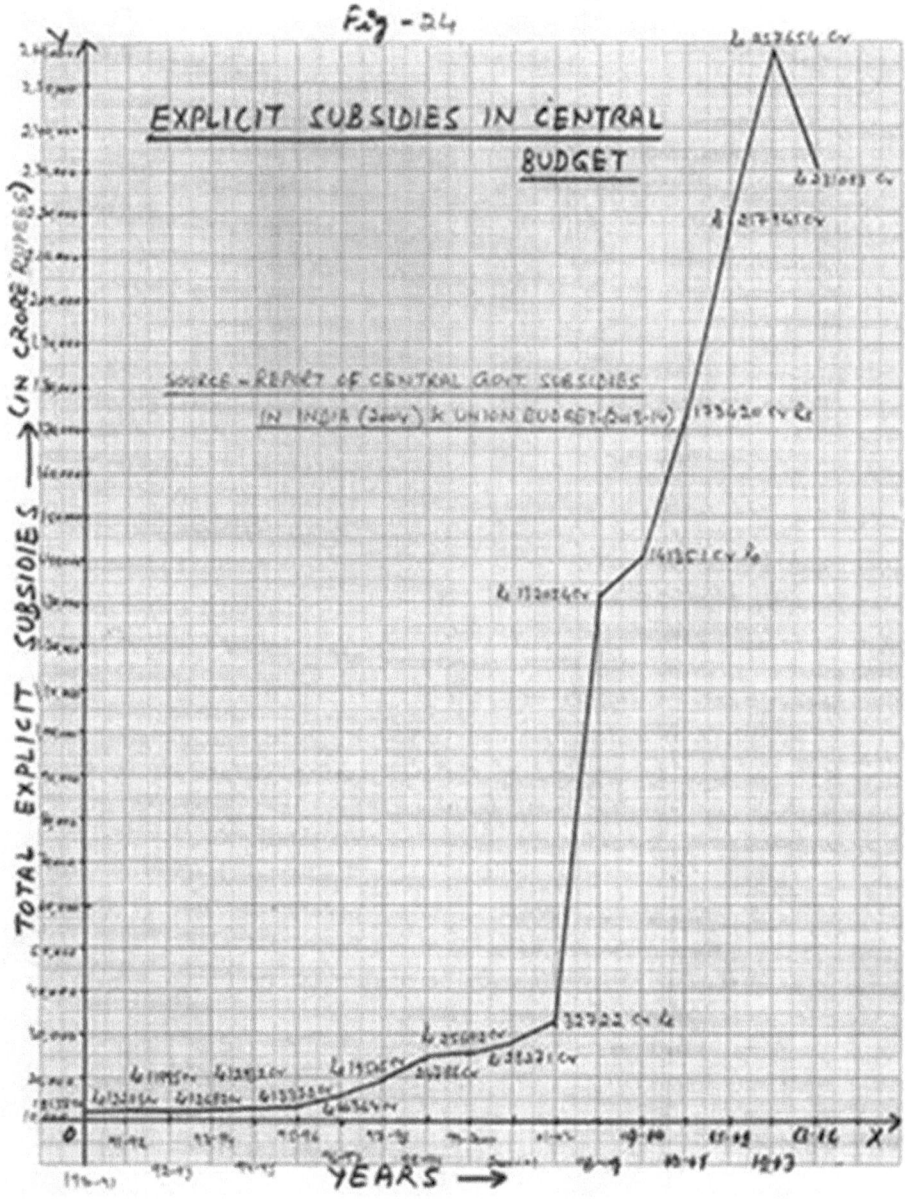

Fig - 24

EXPLICIT SUBSIDIES IN CENTRAL
BUDGET

fig-25

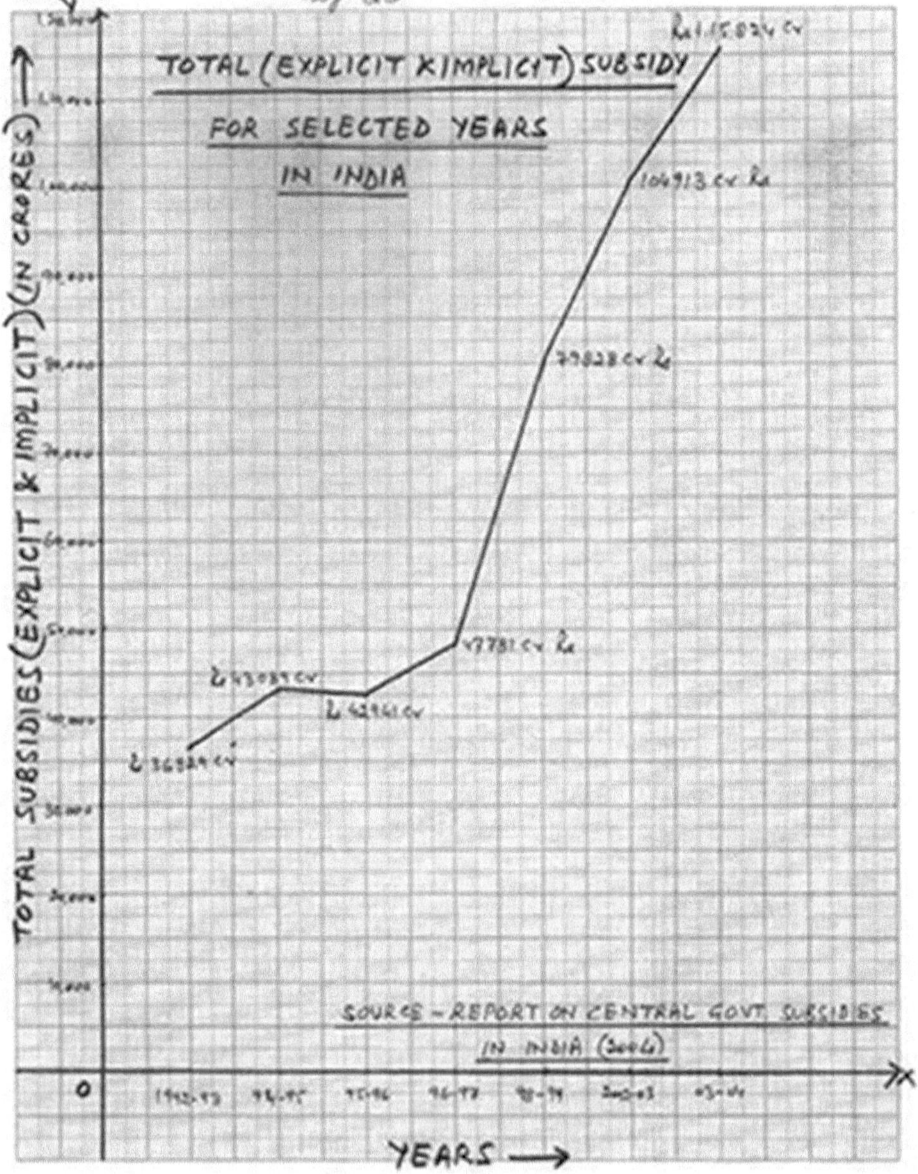

TOTAL (EXPLICIT & IMPLICIT) SUBSIDY
FOR SELECTED YEARS
IN INDIA

Rs.1,15,824 cr

1,04,913 cr. Rs

79,828 cr Rs

57,732 cr Rs

₹ 43,083 cr

₹ 42,961 cr

₹ 36,929 cr

SOURCE - REPORT ON CENTRAL GOVT. SUBSIDIES
IN INDIA (2004)

TOTAL SUBSIDIES (EXPLICIT & IMPLICIT) (IN CRORES) →

YEARS →

1992-93 94-95 95-96 96-97 98-99 2002-03 03-04

Fig - 69

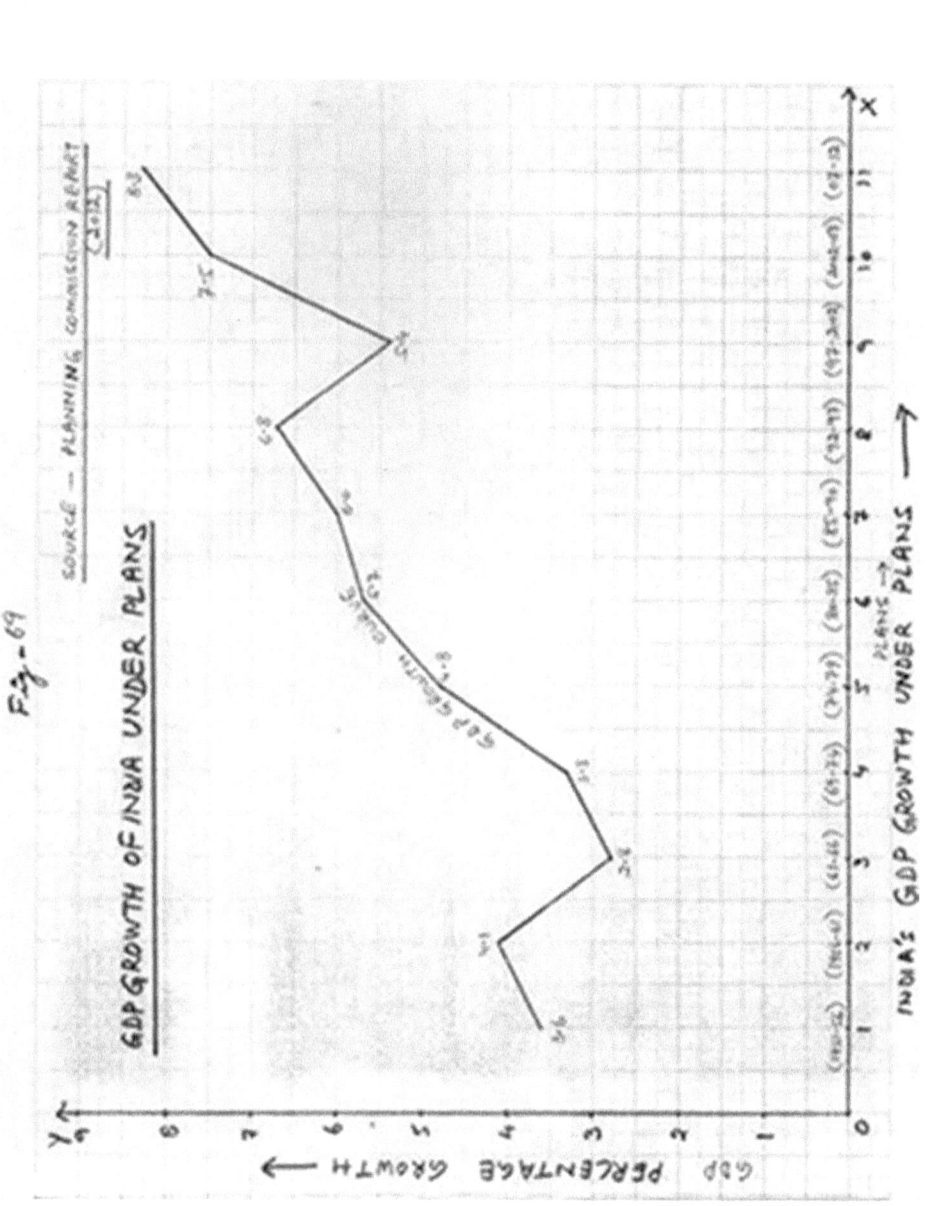

GDP GROWTH OF INDIA UNDER PLANS

SOURCE — PLANNING COMMISSION REPORT (2012)

INDIA'S GDP GROWTH UNDER PLANS

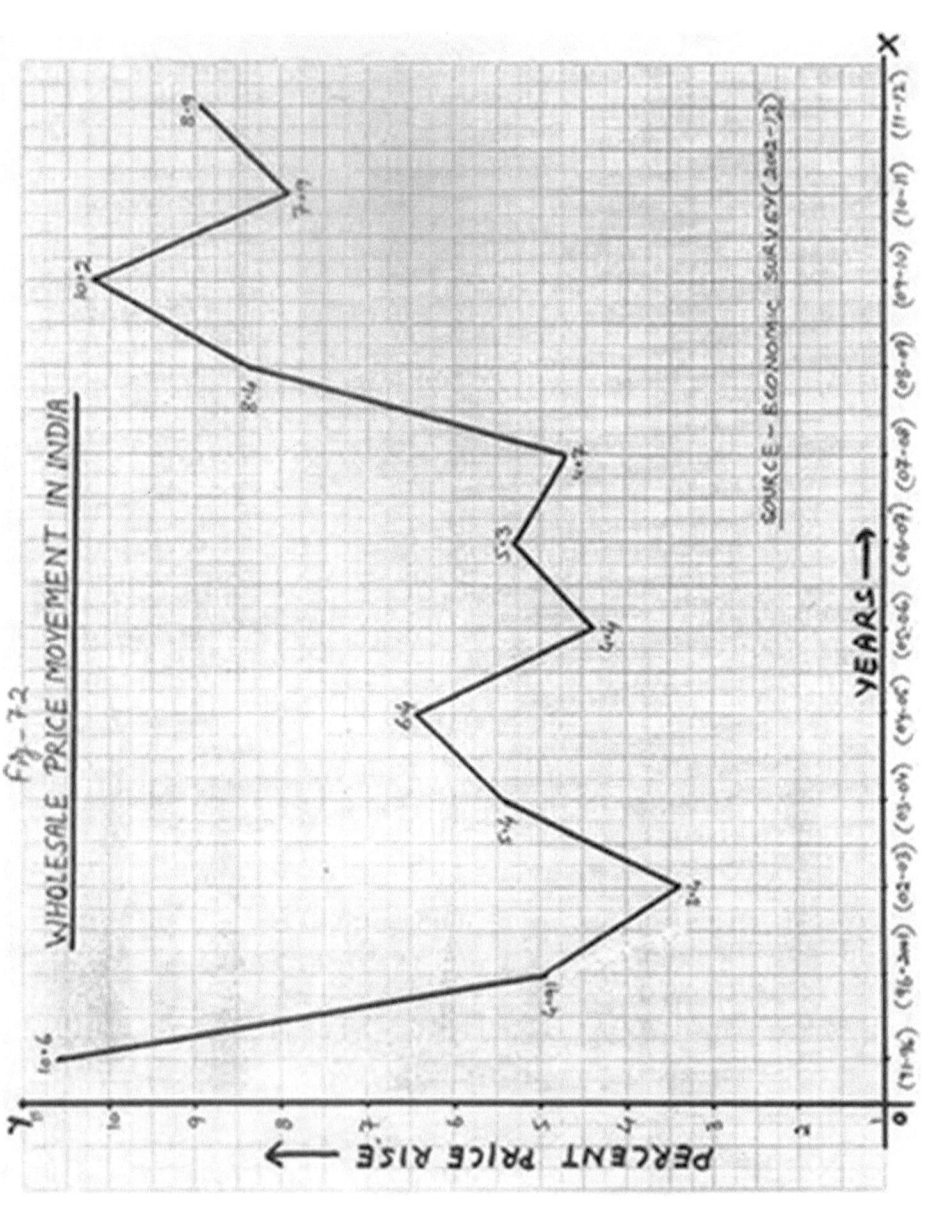

Fig - 7.2

WHOLESALE PRICE MOVEMENT IN INDIA

SOURCE - ECONOMIC SURVEY (2011-12)

YEARS →

PERCENT PRICE RISE ←

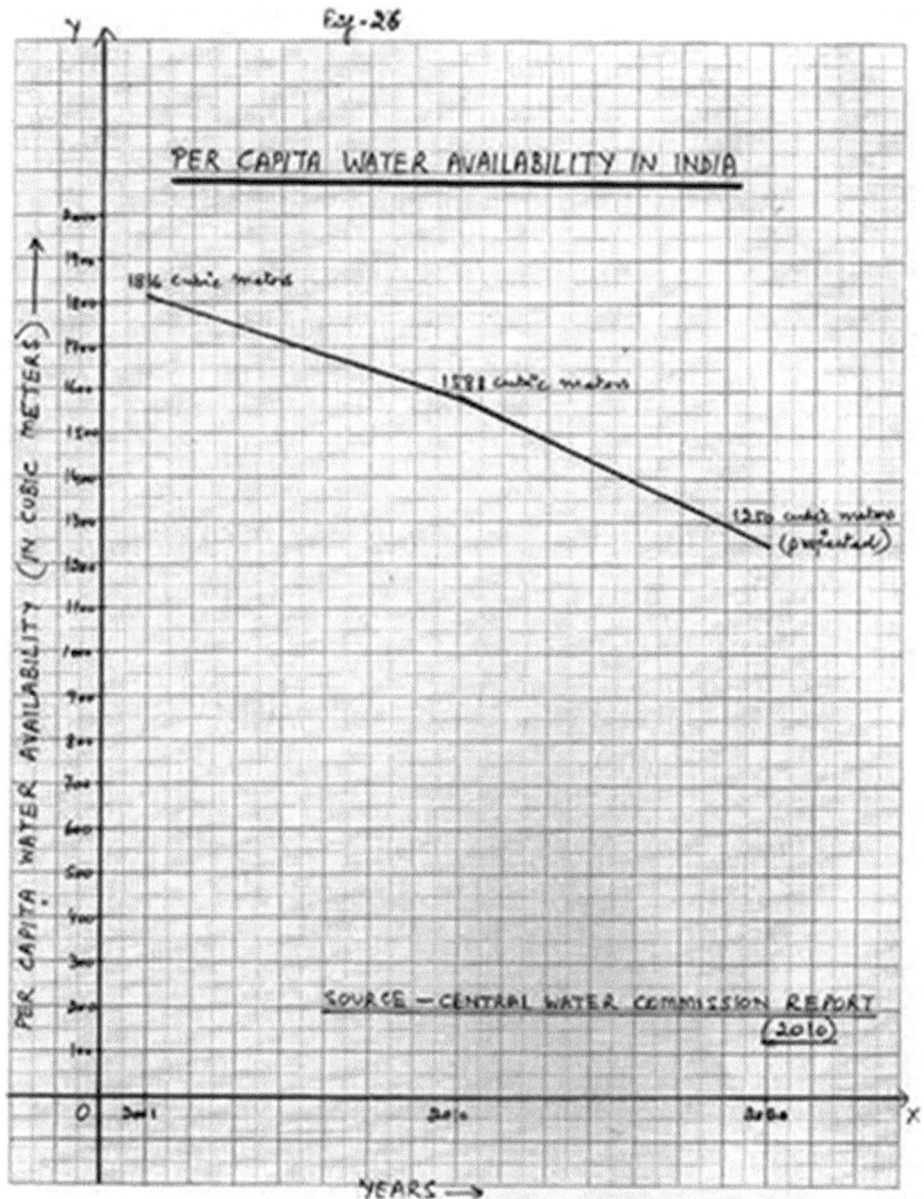

Fig.26

PER CAPITA WATER AVAILABILITY IN INDIA

VICIOUS CIRCLE OF OVER-HEATING OF THE ECONOMY

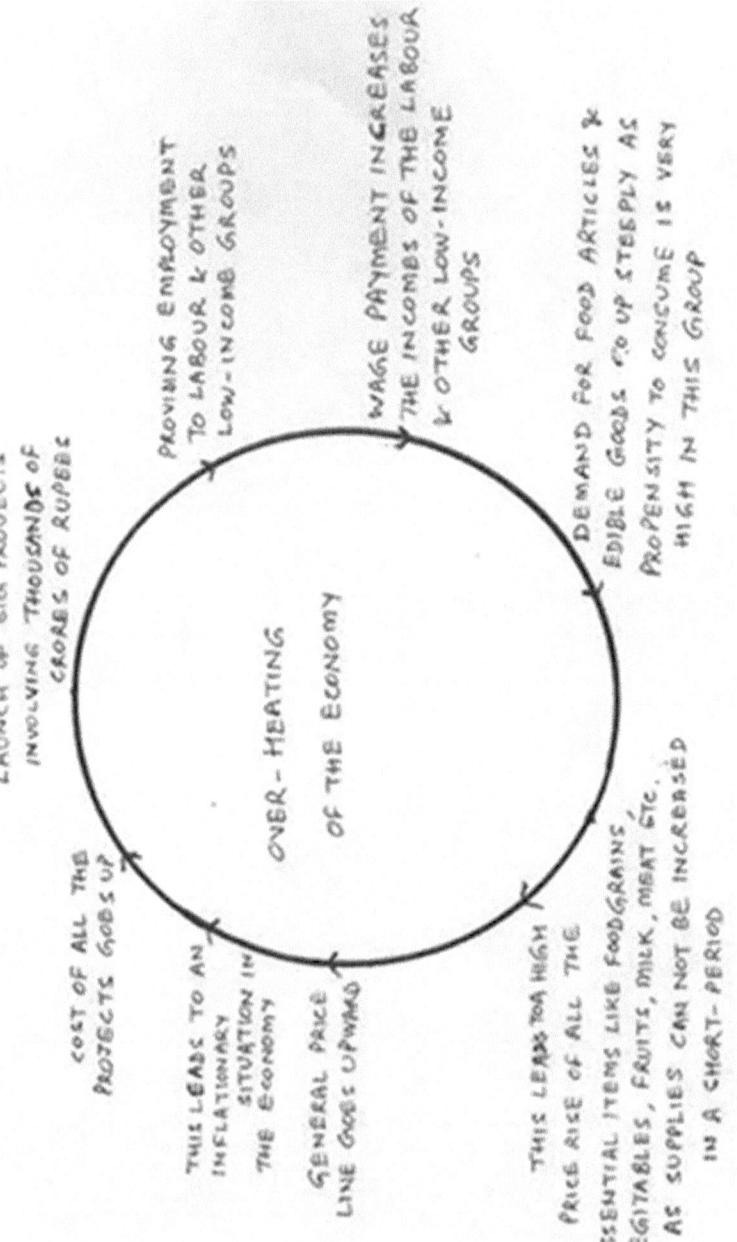

LAUNCH OF BIG PROJECTS INVOLVING THOUSANDS OF CRORES OF RUPEES

PROVIDING EMPLOYMENT TO LABOUR & OTHER LOW-INCOME GROUPS

WAGE PAYMENT INCREASES THE INCOMES OF THE LABOUR & OTHER LOW-INCOME GROUPS

DEMAND FOR FOOD ARTICLES & EDIBLE GOODS GO UP STEEPLY AS PROPENSITY TO CONSUME IS VERY HIGH IN THIS GROUP

THIS LEADS TO A HIGH PRICE RISE OF ALL THE ESSENTIAL ITEMS LIKE FOODGRAINS, VEGETABLES, FRUITS, MILK, MEAT ETC. AS SUPPLIES CAN NOT BE INCREASED IN A SHORT-PERIOD

GENERAL PRICE LINE GOES UPWARD

THIS LEADS TO AN INFLATIONARY SITUATION IN THE ECONOMY

COST OF ALL THE PROJECTS GOES UP

OVER-HEATING OF THE ECONOMY

Fig. 27

General Price Levels During the Plans

Price-rise of goods and services has a direct repercussion on the fixed income groups, salaried class and people employed in the unorganised sector including agriculture. Those who are employed in the organized sector, having strong trade unions, may get some compensation in the form of dearness relief or allowance, but this dearness allowance is calculated on the basis of price-index of some selected essential commodities on average basis which never reflects the factual price-rise in the economy. Consequently, the labour and employees of the organized sector never get the accurate compensation of financial loss due to price-rise and always get lesser relief in the shape of dearness allowance. In other words, workers and employees in organised sector always get cheated in the guise of price-rise calculation. Even the organised sector employees/workers have had to resort to the methods of strikes and other arms-twisting techniques to get increased dearness allowance. Since organized sector is a very small portion of the total economy, the ratio of compensation in the shape of dearness allowance with the total effect of price-rise in the economy remains very small too, as we have shown in fig (21) and a large portion of incomes of other unorganized people is taken away through the mechanism of price-rise, because these people/workers do not get any compensation worth the name on account of their being unorganised. They bear the brunt of the price-rise the most and have had to curtail their expenditure in general. After relatively a long spell, when their employer or government feels it fit to dole out some compensation after much hue & cry, they raise their dearness allowance and farmers get enhanced support price for their produce, known as minimum support price (MSP). In other words, price-rise of goods and services always transfers 'real incomes' of the workers, employees, farmers and all the people in the organized and unorganised sectors to big business tycoons, government and capitalist class. **The price-rise mechanism helps rich grows more rich and poor becomes poorer. It helps concentration of wealth in the hands of industrialists and big business tycoons.** For the fear of industrial unrest and strikes, this industrialist class, government and business tycoons transfer a small portion of this accumulated wealth to the workers, salaried people and farmers in the shape of dearness, bonus, medical help and minimum support price for agriculture produce, but these transfers always form only a fraction of the real price-rise. In this way, capitalism or market mechanism works in liberal capitalist economies like India. What is happening in India since Independence is the above story in toto. We have shown in figs (22 & 23) the trend of price-rise in India since Independence. **Suppose, if we have a GDP growth of 5% per annum and an annual price-rise too is 5% in the same year, then, it means that only transfer of wealth has taken place from the unorganised sector mostly and no economic growth has taken place in the real sense of the term.** Pauperization of peasantry and other unorganised sections is the clear reflection of this price-rise mechanism as we see in India since Independence. Large scale suicides by poor farmers and other poor people are the direct consequences of this hidden loot.

During the NDA rule (1999 to 2004), India posted average annual GDP growth of 5.8% __ ranking 50th in the emerging world __ with inflation of 3.9% __ ranking 70th in the emerging world.' It means, the actual GDP growth during NDA (1999-2004) rule was only (5.8-3.9) 1.9%.

Similarly during the UPAI (2004-2009) rule, 'It's GDP growth rate accelerated to 8% over the next 5 years under the Congress government, but its place in the ranks did not improve much. From 2004 to 2008, India ranked 39th in the emerging world for average GDP growth and 73rd for inflation. India's inflation rate has risen from 6.5% in its first term (UPAI) to 10.5% in the second (UPAII), while its inflation ranking has fallen from 73rd in the world to a bottom decline rank of 130th.

It means, under UPAI, the actual GDP growth was only (8.0-6.5) 1.5% per annum, and, under UPA II, it was only (6.5-10.5) -4.0% (negative) which means that India's economy has gone down in real terms under UPAII.

Here, we shall recall our fig No.11, wherein we have shown India's optimum level of population as 550 million or 55 crore, but our population has crossed 1250 million mark in 2013-14, which means that around 700 million or 70 crore population of India falls under the category of 'surplus'. The work force of 140 million /14 crore among these 700 million / 70 crore 'surplus' people are either unemployed or underemployed (assuming a family of 5 persons). **The secret of the abject poverty in India is nothing but this surplus segment of population, for they contribute nothing or very little to our GDP on account of their being either unproductive or underproductive, while a big chunk of budgetary support is provided to sustain them in the form**

of various subsidies and tax concessions. They have got no element of natural resources to fall back upon and survive only on the hard earned incomes of the gainfully employed workforce (in our case this is only 110 million/11 crore) in the shape of heavy taxes and various other levies. Subsidized food, shelter, clothing, education, medical/ health services, cheap transport, cheap bank loans etc. are being provided to these 700 million people by taxing heavily 550 million gainfully employed people, directly or indirectly through annual budgetary exercises by our Central and State Governments. **This unproductive expenditure is the root cause of inflation. (fig 57)** Economists have struggled to understand why India's consumer prices have been rising 10% a year for the past five years when prices in the world have been reasonably steady. Even in poor emerging economies, prices have risen at half the rate as India's. Inflation is complex but it has become clear that India's inflation is the result of the same bad policies that brought down our growth. Huge government spending without commensurate production has meant that too much money has been chasing too few goods.

Subsidy

The concept of subsidy which came from Western countries in the form of 'welfare economics' whereby the people, affected by unemployment caused due to the great economic crisis of the nineteen thirties in the U.S.A, the U.K. and other Western nations, have been provided with cheaper or free food and other essential services and goods for life to minimise their sufferings. When the economic crisis was over, and economy began to function as usual as before, the governments of these countries gradually reduced or withdrew the subsidies from these essential goods and services and brought back the prices as per the prevailing market rate. This application of subsidies was a temporary measure to help the poor and unemployed and as soon as they had been provided with their lost gainful employment, the subsidies gradually reduced or withdrawn and commodities were made available to them on the prevailing market rates once again.

But in India, the situation is entirely different. Here, we have a permanent 'leg-support' of subsidies since Independence and its volume is regularly growing with the growth of population or, in other words, with the growth of poverty-ridden population, as we have already crossed the level of optimum population in 1970. As shown in figs 24&25, the volume of explicit and implicit subsidies have been growing with every annual budget and reached Rs 1,15,824 crore in 2003-04 which was 2.3% of our GDP. As per budget estimates for 2013-14, the total amount of subsidies will be Rs 2,31,084 crore! This shall continue to grow further as our population grows continuously. This is a big burden on the shoulders of the gainfully employed persons who are heavily taxed directly and indirectly to provide for subsidies. In India, our Central Government has passed a 'Food Security Bill 2013' in Parliament, according to which our 81 crore people shall get food grains at a highly subsidized rate, i.e., rice at Rs 3 per kg, wheat at Rs 2 per kg, coarse grains (sorghun, pearl millets, finger millets) at Re 1 per kg! Households under Antyodaya Anna Yajana are already being protected by making availability of 35 kg of food grains per month through fair-price shops. In this way, our Central Government has increased food subsidy three times from the pre-Food Security Bill.

Apart from food subsidy, subsidies on health services and medicines, education, fertilizers, petroleum products, housing, irrigation, transport, gas, clothing etc. are some of the examples of cheap subsidised good and services which are being provided by our Central and State governments alike. Interest subsidy and capital subsidy are being provided to poor borrowers through public sector banks. In addition to this, various debt waiver and debt relief schemes have been introduced to help poor farmers and artisans. Rs 70, 000 crore have been doled out to poor farmers and artisans through Banks by the recent Debt Waiver and Debt Relief Scheme 2008. These are explicit subsidies which are discernible in annual budget. Instead, there is no indication that after the passage of 67 years of Independence, subsidies are to be reduced or removed. Conversely, implicit subsidies in various forms continue to grow both at Central and State levels. For example, large number of tax exemptions on setting up Special Economic Zones (SEZs) is granted by the government. They imply a big loss to exchequer in the shape of tax revenues. The Times of India dt. Nov. 24, 2014 reports; 'Exposing systemic weaknesses in tax administration, a performance audit on SEZs by the CAG revealed that ineligible tax deductions were extended to companies, some of which diverted land allotted to them to other uses. There was overall decline in manufacturing in these zones, says the report, likely to be tabled in the winter session of Parliament. "Tax concessions to SEZs for the period 2007 to 2013 works out to Rs 83,104 crore on account of direct taxes and customs," sources said, adding that this revenue foregone did not include loss to the exchequer on account of central excise and service tax that could have accrued if these companies were brought out of the SEZs. The audit also found that more than 50% of the land allotted remained idle even though the approvals dated back to 2006. The revenue foregone, or loss to the exchequer, could be many times more considering other concessions availed by these companies such as stamp duty, VAT, CST etc could not be quantified in the absence of any monitoring mechanism, sources said.' Another example of implicit subsidies are __ land acquisition from land owners on a large scale at a price and then handing over to industrial houses free of cost. In this way, our planners are taking away the employment and livelihood of our farmers, sharecroppers and other associated persons dependent on land on the one hand and providing heavy subsidies of several kind __ land acquisition and its development by the government on behalf of the industry, subsidised power, generous tax holidays, financial support for purchase of equipment, subsidised credit and exemption of import and export duties to industrialists etc on the other. It has been estimated that various kinds of tax exemptions have resulted in revenue foregone to the tune of Rs 2,78,644 crore by the year March 2009. According to experts' estimate, only the subsidy on food, fertilizers and petroleum products is likely to go up to 4 to 5% of GDP which indicates the seriousness of the situation we have been landed in.

As we have shown in fig (12), economy of any country is well sustainable and stable when its population is around optimum level, and as soon as this moves ahead of optimum level, economy begins to develop strains and bottlenecks and starts heating up. This heating-up is not felt much up to 10% increase of the population from the optimum level, but after crossing 10% limit, every incremental increase in population produces strain symptoms, like price-rise of goods and services, deficit financing by the governments, inflation, cropping up of unemployment and underemployment, governments resorting to heavy taxation on gainfully employed work-force, heavy public debt, heavy foreign debt, introduction of subsidy on food, fertilizers and other essential items etc. The governments generally resort to deficit financing to bridge the gap between ever growing expenditure and its limited resources of revenues, which further push the general price-level upward and a vicious circle of inflation and deficit financing starts up. **Exactly this is happening in India since Independence. Our learned planners did not foresee the impact of growing population beyond the optimum level; even they never**

bothered to calculate India's optimum population whereat they should have targeted to halt. None nation, except China in the Third World, foresighted the impact of population growth beyond the optimum level and now we see almost the identical economic situation every where. Even developed countries of the world never bother to ascertain their respective optimum population.

India's present level of population, which has already crossed 1250 million or 125 crore mark at the end of 2013, has pushed demand for all the goods and services to such a high level that it has now become very difficult to satisfy the genuine needs of the people at large. Everywhere we are confronting scarcity; even potable water has become scarce and people are suffering all over India. The water scarcity is fast becoming urban India's number one woe, with government's own data revealing that residents in 22 out of 32 major cities have to deal with daily shortages. The worst hit city is Jamshedpur, where the gap between demand and supply is a yawning 70%. The crisis is acute in Kanpur, Asansol, Dhanbad, Meerut, Faridabad, Visakapatnam, Madurai and Hyderabad __ where supply fails to meet almost 30% of the demand __ according to data provided by states which was placed in the Lok Sabha during the recently concluded Parliament session by the urban development ministry.

New Delhi is the seat of the Union Government and even here, water supply is not only dismal but grossly inadequate and largely contaminated. The day the Bill was sent to the States for their views, in Delhi, half a dozen people died and over 50 were hospitalised due to water-borne infection. In fact, in some Delhi colonies, the water and sewerage pipes run parallel, and leakage from one or both renders the water unfit for drinking. There are some schemes of the Government which are bottomless pits where any amount of money can be siphoned off. In October 2012, the Supreme Court posed a question on clearing the Yamuna and other rivers. It asked what had been achieved after putting in so much money. Where has all this money gone? We don't see any improvement in the water of the river. Yet nearly Rs 12, 000 crore have been spent in the last 18 years by the Union Government and the State Governments of Delhi, Haryana and Uttar Pradesh to clean up the river. There is no accountability on the part of those who make skewed policies or those who are responsible for implementing them.

Ruthless exploitation of ground water has also posed serious consequences. Since ground water withdrawal is greater than the recharge, the ground water table is declining rapidly. This problem is assuming serious proportions in many states especially in Maharashtra where there has been a major shift in cultivation from rain fed coarse grains to water-intensive sugarcane. Over exploitation of groundwater can also lead to the intrusion of saline water, making the water unfit for drinking or irrigation. There is another danger to ground water resources. In recent years, certain cases of dangerous pollution of groundwater have been reported from different parts of the country, for example, pollution of groundwater by the effluents of tanneries in Tamil Nadu, by the textile printing and dyeing units of Tamil Nadu and Gujrat etc. While pollution of rivers and lakes is easily detectable, pollution of groundwater is rather difficult to detect and to rectify.

As we have shown in fig. (26), the per capita water availability in 2010 was 1588 billion cubic meters (BCM), which was 1816 billion cubic meters in 2001. This indicates fast declining per capita availability of water in the country. It is reported by the Central Water Commission that total estimated utilisable water was 1123 BCM per annum, out of which 690 BCM was surface water and 430 BCM was ground water. The nation has been witnessing acute water shortages which are being experienced year after year by most parts of Tamil Nadu, Rajasthan, Gujrat, Orissa etc. The problem of scarcity is assuming crisis proportions with unlimited growth of cities and constantly growing urban population. In rural areas, the rising demand for water for irrigation deepening the crisis further.

Due to excessive exploitation of ground water, and increasing pollution of fresh water resources, we are at the brink of a global water crisis. Today we are living in an environmentally unsustainable world and its repercussions have already become visible. Global warming and climate changes have a debilitating impact on the existing water resources, affecting millions of people around the globe. With India likely to have a shortfall of about 324 BCM of water going by present per capita water consumption per year by the year 2050, the government will have to take immediate steps to prevent a crisis situation. Experts feel that with the present rate of water consumption, India is poised to have more Cauvery-like disputes among states.

Subsidies, therefore, are always taken as a temporary remedy in any economy meant to protect the poor and other vulnerable sections of society. **The planners of the polity must plan the economy in such a fashion that the subsidies are gradually withdrawn.** This is possible only when the poor and other vuthnerable sections of society are made economically strong and stable with the help of 'economic planning', for, whereas the subsidies play the role of paliative balm for the poor and destitute, it prove a great burden on the incomes of the people who are employed gainfully in the shape of heavy taxation. In India, only in the First and Second Five Year Plans, the subsidies should have found a place in our budgets and from Third Five Years Plan and onward, this should have been gradually reduced and become zero in the Sixth Plan. But this did not happen. **Conversely, the subsidy amount kept on growing to unprecedented level and has become a monster who is now roaring and leaping to devour the whole economy and polity as well.** Gradual reduction of subsidy was possible only when our 'learned planners' had taken the task of limiting our nation's human population to optimum level seriously since 1947, just after Independence, as Nehru was well aware of the problem. Had they done this, then by the end of Fifth Plan (1974-79), the target of optimum population of 550 million could have been achieved, as China did. Now we have lost that opportunity and are too late to do anything in this direction at present and can not face & tackle the problems of price rise, massive unemployment/underemployment, high rising subsidies, heavy taxation and deficit financing in India. **Actually, the whole population of India is paying a heary price for being over-populated.**

Over-Heating of the Economy

The term 'over-heating of the economy' is often used by the economists now-a-days. What is meant by over-heating of the economy? In India, (the term was used by our erstwhile Prime Minister Dr. Manmohan Singh) when there happened a very high price-rise of every article of use, especially foograins, vegetables, fruits and other edible items in a relatively short period, say in 2/3 months and government could do nothing to maintain the price-line by all means, this is termed as over-heating of the Economy.

This phenomenon can be explained with the help of establishing a co-relation between the overpopulation syndrome and heavy public expenditure on some big projects like, big dam construction, construction of national highways or laying down of new railway lines and other very big infrastructural projects, involving thousands of crores of rupees. When these big projects are undertaken, a largs sum of money is received by the labour and lower middle class people whose propensity to consume remains very high. They, having got the money, immediately rush to consumer market and satisfy their wants by purchasing essential items for their immediate use. Since supply of these essential items can not be increased in a short or medium period, their prices go upward steeply. This situation is more pronounced when country's population has crossed the optimum level long ago and reached now to more than double of it, inhabiting a very large number of unemployed and underemployed populations, starved of income. (India's optimum population is estimated at 55 crore only). (Fig 27)

Dr. Manmohan Singh's government sensed the syndrome and immediately halted all the developmental projects of large expenditure and sat standstill. Whenever any government, in future, wants of restart these big projects, the same situation of steep price-rise of essential food items shall recur in India. This situation is unavoidable in a highly over-population economy like India. **Therefore, in India, no government can hold the price-line of essential edible goods and other essential services while undertaking big developmental projects, which no responsible government can withhold for a long period for fear of price-rise. This is a situation wherein India's economy lands today, better call it as 'between devil and the deep sea'.**

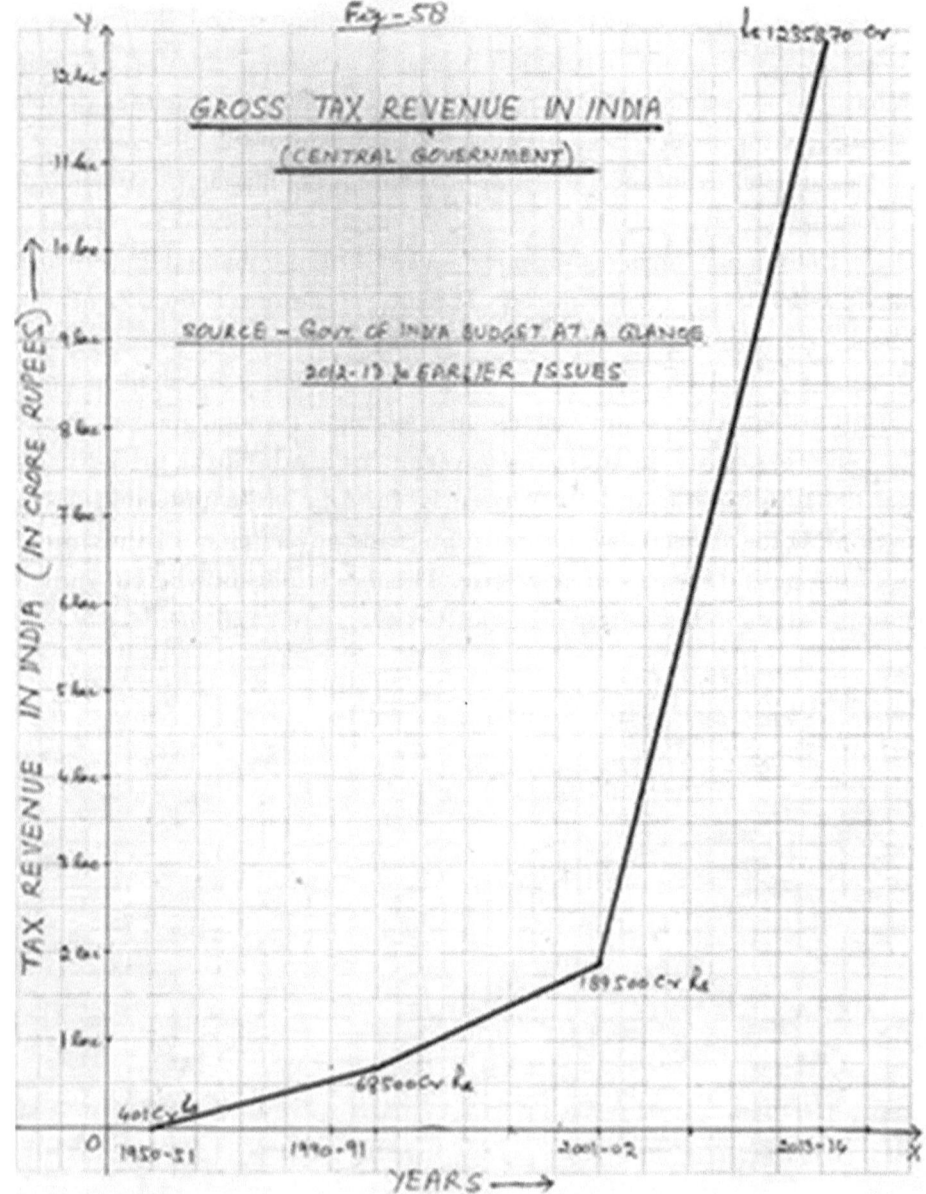

Fig - 28

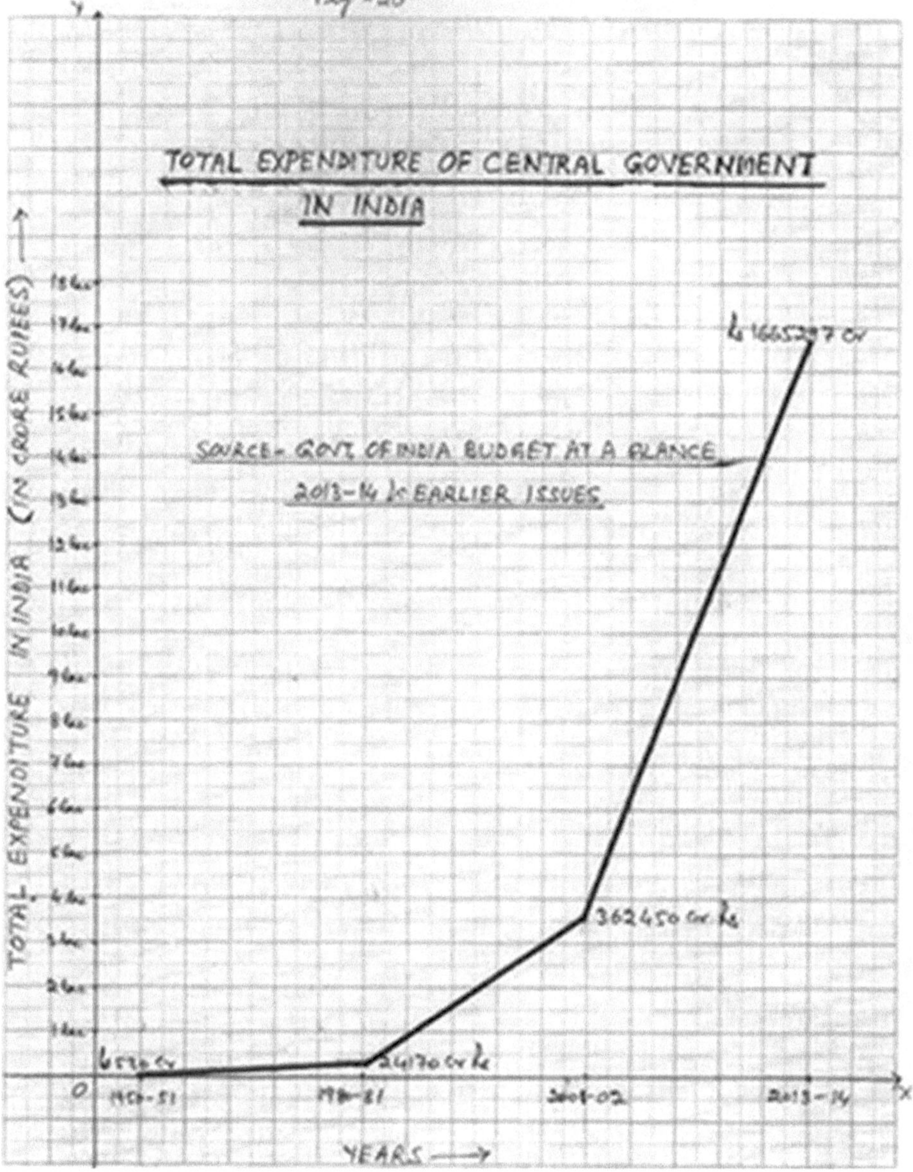

TOTAL EXPENDITURE OF CENTRAL GOVERNMENT IN INDIA

SOURCE- GOVT. OF INDIA BUDGET AT A GLANCE 2013-14)& EARLIER ISSUES

Y axis: TOTAL EXPENDITURE IN INDIA (IN CRORE RUPEES) →

X axis: YEARS →

16655757 cr

362450 cr. Rs

650 cr

24170 cr Rs

1950-51   1980-81   2001-02   2013-14

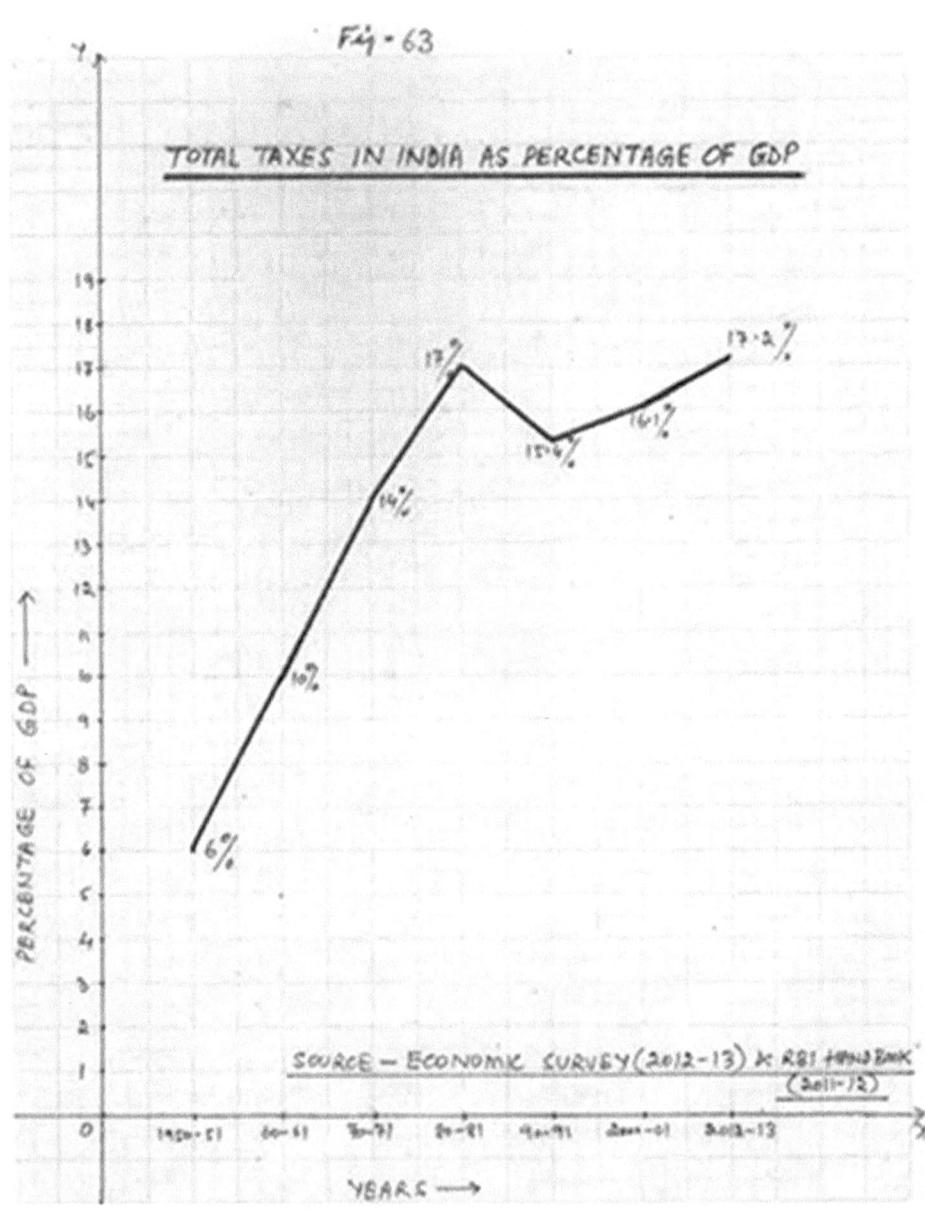

Fig - 63

Fig-62

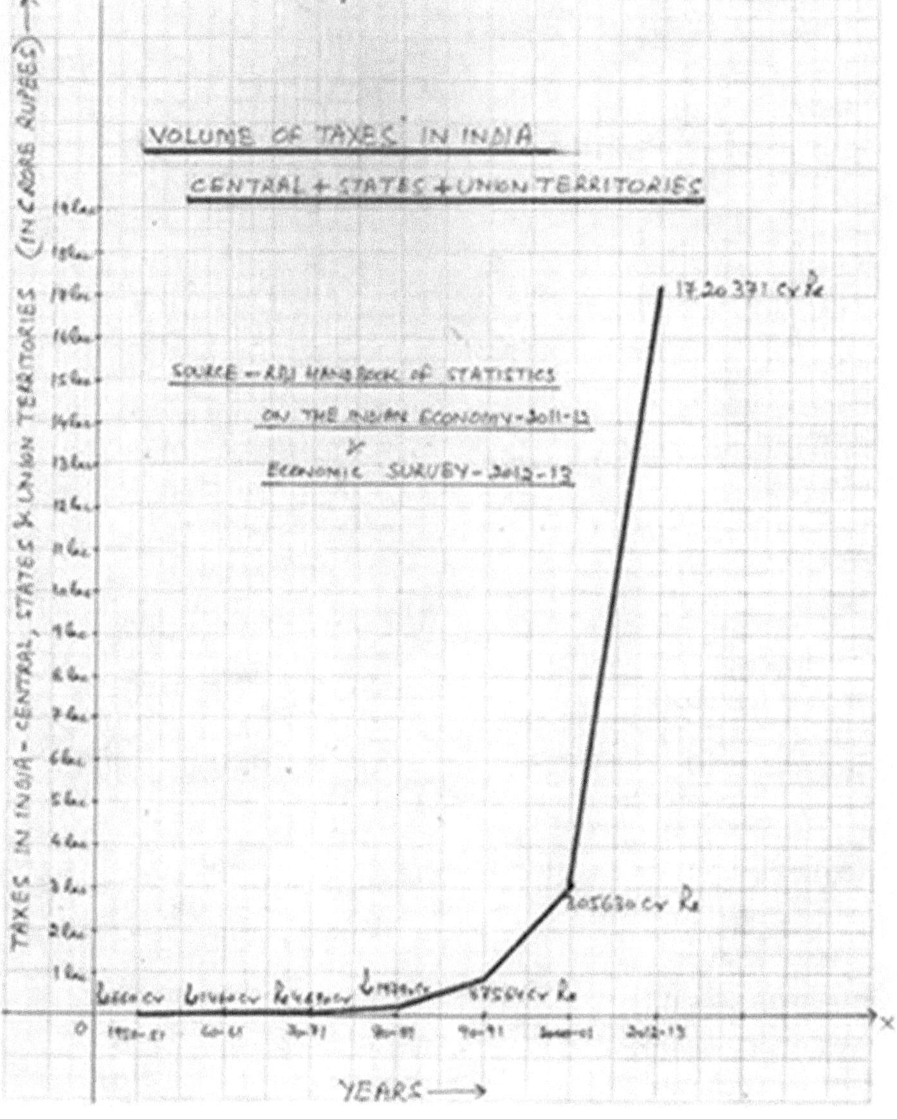

VOLUME OF TAXES IN INDIA

CENTRAL + STATES + UNION TERRITORIES

SOURCE — RBI HANDBOOK OF STATISTICS
ON THE INDIAN ECONOMY — 2011-12
&
ECONOMIC SURVEY — 2012-13

17,20,371 Cr Rs

2,05,630 Cr Rs

67,50 Cr Rs

TAXES IN INDIA — CENTRAL, STATES & UNION TERRITORIES (IN CRORE RUPEES) →

YEARS →

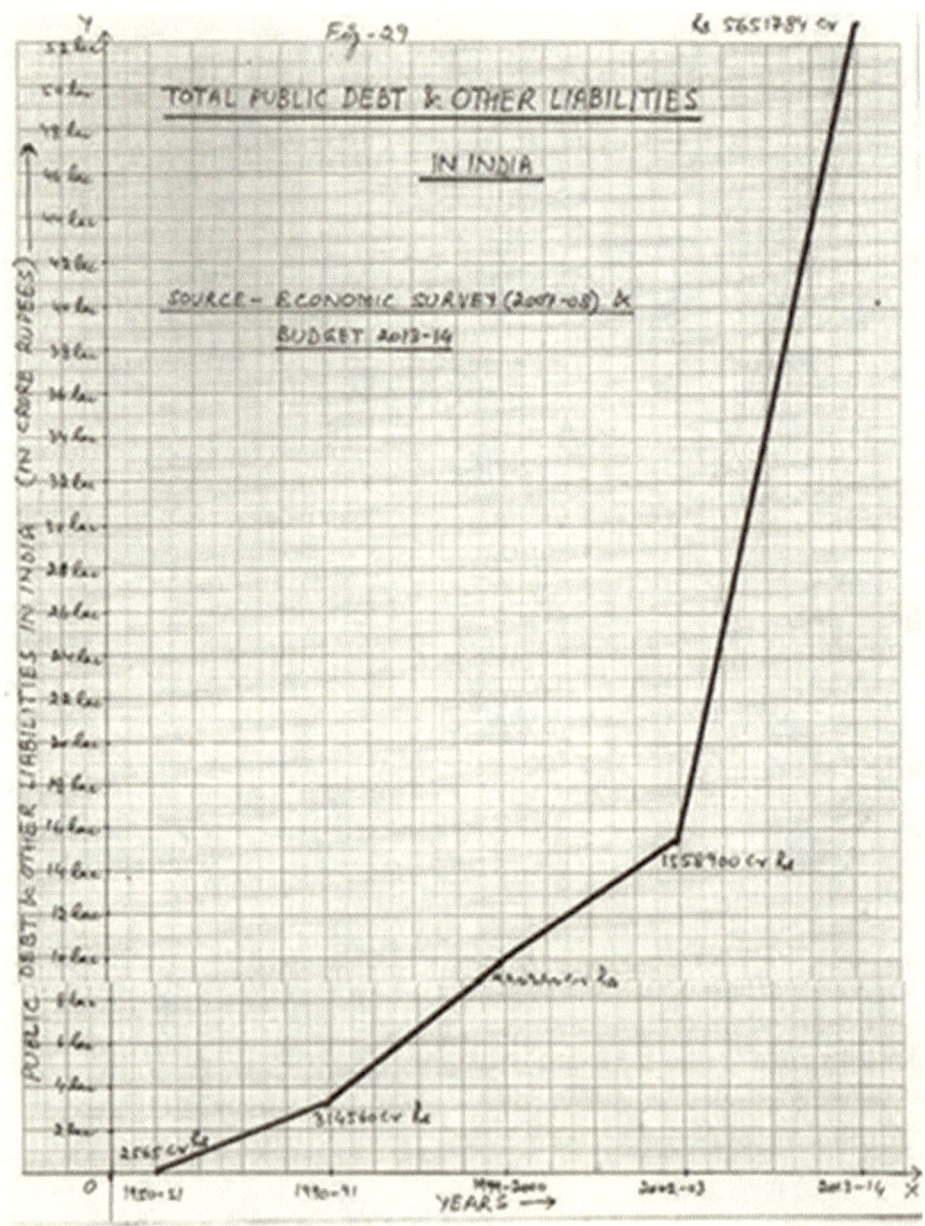

Fig-29

TOTAL PUBLIC DEBT & OTHER LIABILITIES

IN INDIA

SOURCE - ECONOMIC SURVEY (2007-08) &
BUDGET 2013-14

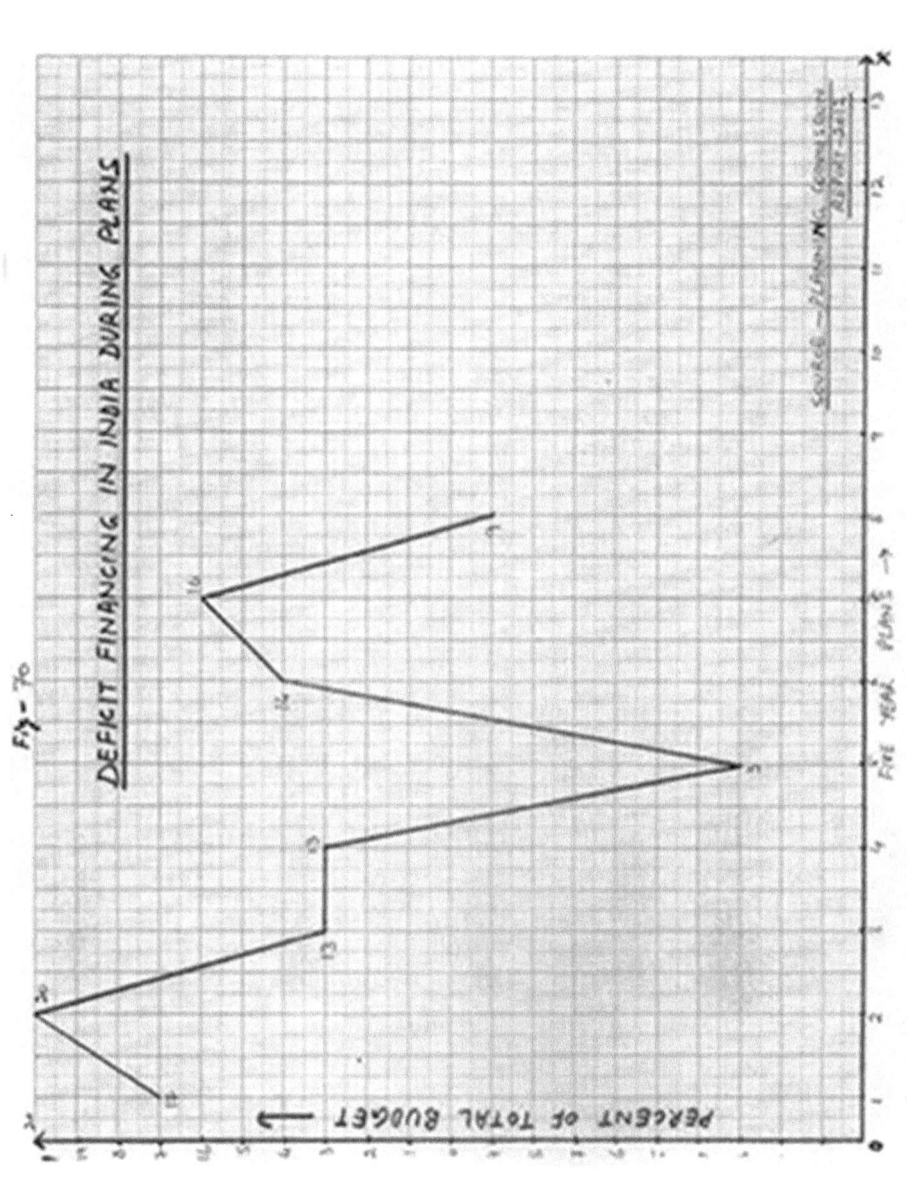

Fig – 70

DEFICIT FINANCING IN INDIA DURING PLANS

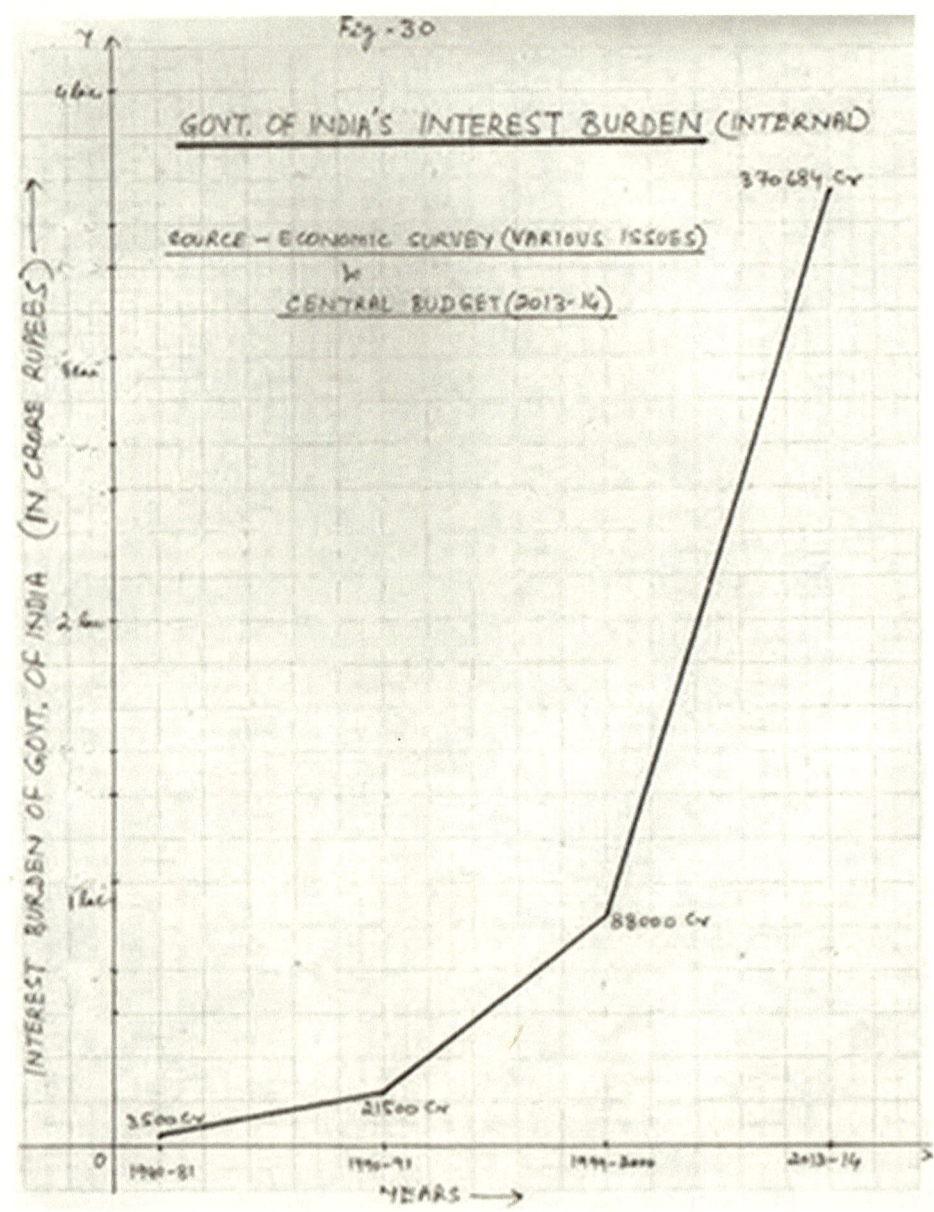

Fig-30

GOVT. OF INDIA'S INTEREST BURDEN (INTERNAL)

SOURCE - ECONOMIC SURVEY (VARIOUS ISSUES)
&
CENTRAL BUDGET (2013-14)

370684 Cr

88000 Cr

21500 Cr

3500 Cr

INTEREST BURDEN OF GOVT. OF INDIA (IN CRORE RUPEES) →

0   1980-81   1990-91   1999-2000   2013-14

YEARS →

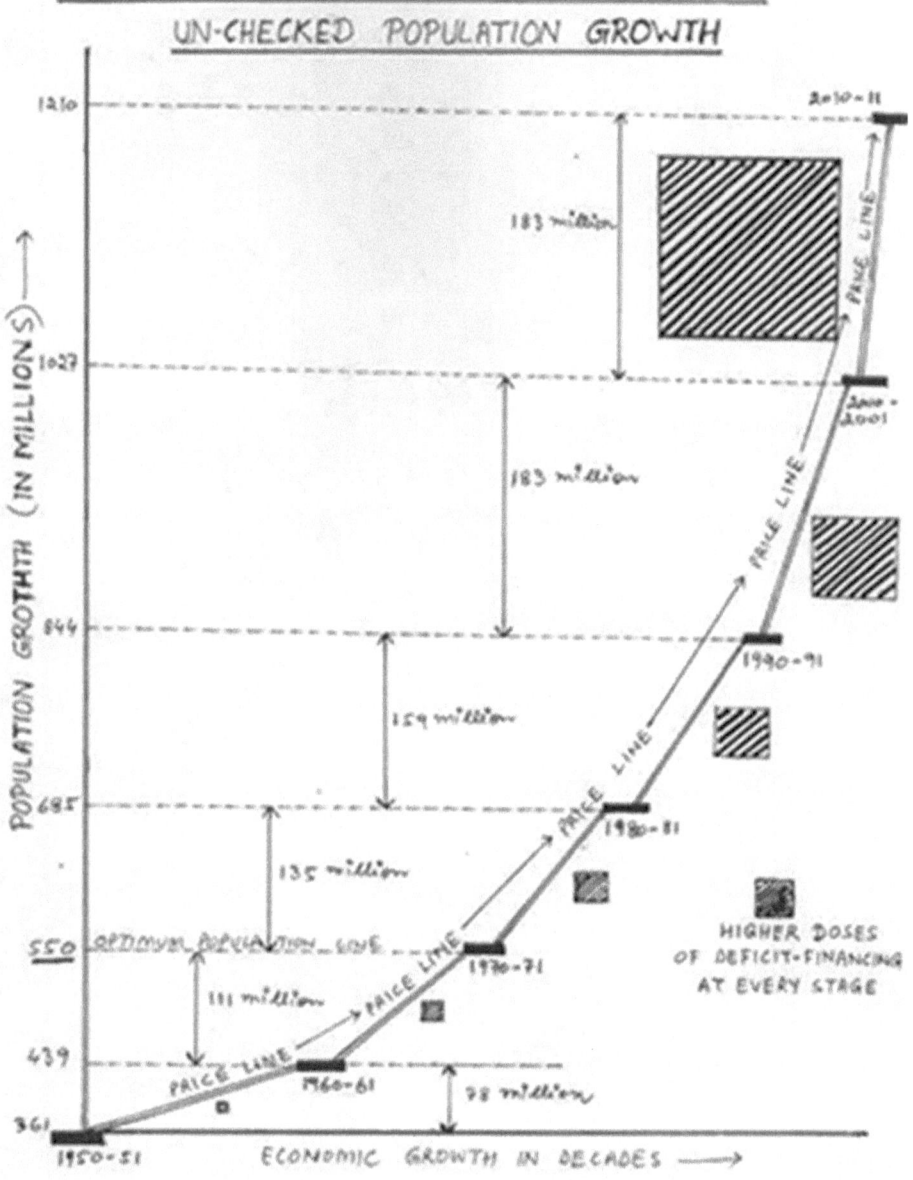

Fig - 76

GROWTH-MODEL OF INDIAN ECONOMY WITH UN-CHECKED POPULATION GROWTH

POPULATION GROWTH (IN MILLIONS) →

ECONOMIC GROWTH IN DECADES →

1210   2030-11

183 million

1027   2000-2001

183 million

844   1990-91

159 million

PRICE LINE

685   1980-81

135 million

PRICE LINE

550 OPTIMUM POPULATION LINE

111 million   PRICE LINE   1970-71

439   1960-61

PRICE LINE   78 million

361

1950-51

HIGHER DOSES OF DEFICIT-FINANCING AT EVERY STAGE

Fig-75

GROWTH-MODEL OF INDIAN ECONOMY WITH POPULATION STABILIZATION

AT OPTIMUM LEVEL

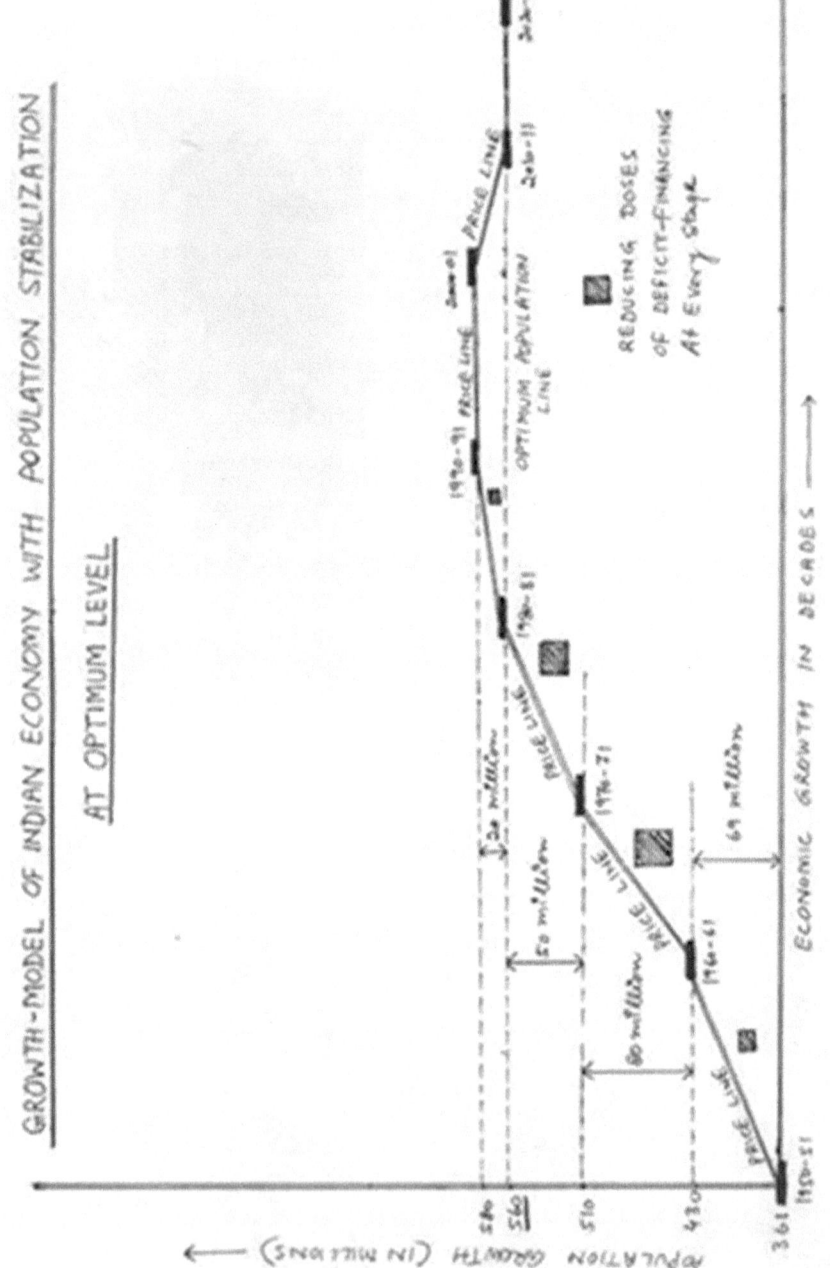

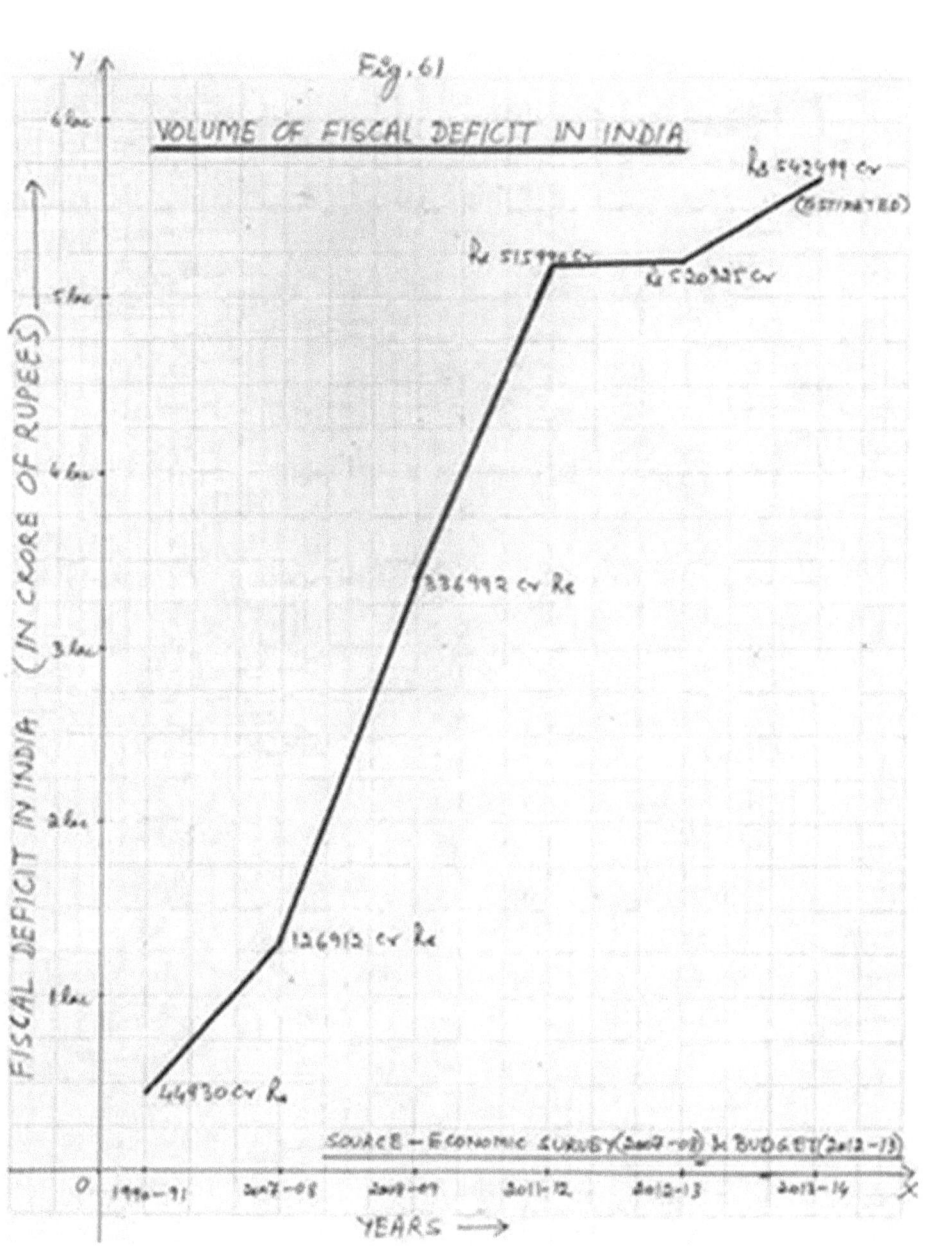

Fig. 61

VOLUME OF FISCAL DEFICIT IN INDIA

Rs 542499 Cr
(ESTIMATED)

Rs 515990 Cr

Rs 520925 Cr

336992 Cr Rs

126912 Cr Rs

44930 Cr Rs

SOURCE — ECONOMIC SURVEY (2007-08) & BUDGET (2012-13)

1990-91   2007-08   2008-09   2011-12   2012-13   2013-14

YEARS →

FISCAL DEFICIT IN INDIA (IN CRORE OF RUPEES)

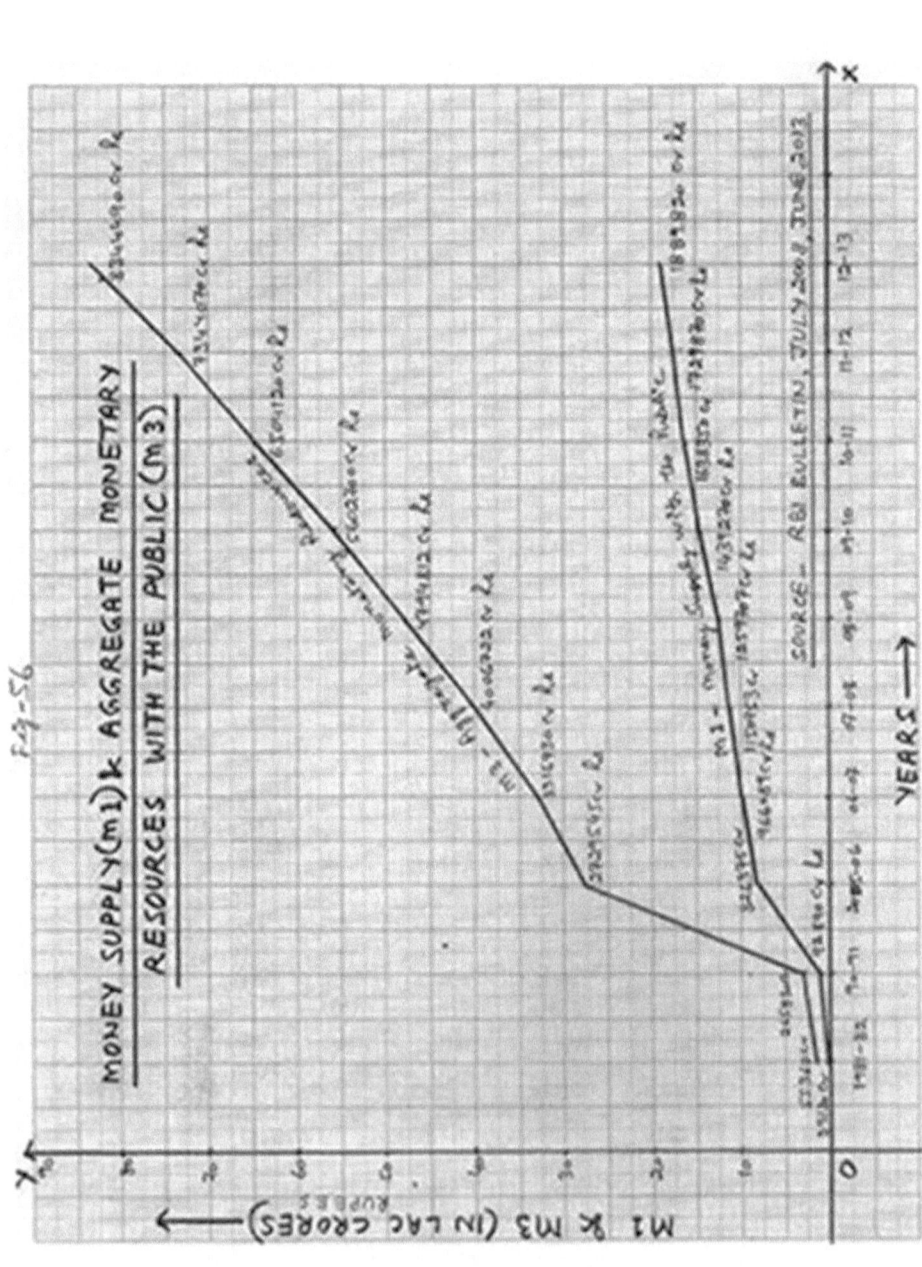

Fig-56

MONEY SUPPLY(m1) & AGGREGATE MONETARY
RESOURCES WITH THE PUBLIC (m3)

M1 & M3 (IN LAC CRORES)
RUPEES

YEARS

SOURCE- RBI BULLETIN, JULY 2008 & JUNE 2013

CHAPTER – 6

Taxation, Expenditure, Deficit Financing & Public Debt in India

Taxation

It is believed that India is the highest taxed country in the world. As shown in fig (58), India's direct and indirect taxation not only growing rapidly during every annual budget, but its percentage to GDP is also growing. While in 1950-51, the direct tax was Rs 230 crore, it jumped to Rs 6, 57, 317 crore in 2012-13. Similarly our indirect taxes grew from Rs 430 crore in 1950-51 to a staggering high of Rs 10, 63, 054 crore in 2012-13. Total taxes jumped from Rs 660 crore in 1950-51 to as high as Rs 17, 20, 371 crore in 2012-13. On the other hand, the percentage of total taxation to our GDP is also growing. While it was only 6% in 1950-51, it went as high as 17.2% in 2012-13, which clearly shows that India is a highly taxed country.

Ironically, the share of indirect taxes in the total tax collection is 46% in 2013-14, which constitute nearly half of the total collection. The incidence of indirect taxation generally falls on the shoulders of lower and middle income groups, working in the organised as well as in the unorganised sector. The organised sector, most of the times, gets compensated in the form of dearness allowance (though not fully), but the unorganised sector bears the brunt of the burden of indirect taxes. India's labor force had 465 million workers in 2010, of whom only 6% (27.9 million) were in the organised sector including state-owned companies. The rest (447.1 million) were in the unorganised sector with little protection.

Thus, unorganised sector, which constitutes farmers, agriculture labors, urban workers of medium & small industries, shop workers and petti-shopkeepers, small road transporters and other poor people pay the government most for the welfare expenditure meant for them. **This is like first taking out blood from a dying patient in order to infuse the same into his body to save his life.**

On the other hand, direct taxes are levied on income and property of an individual. They are called direct, as the assessees have to pay them and cannot shift on to others. In other words, direct taxes are levied on those people who are employed gainfully in the economy and have surplus incomes to part with as taxes (though unwillingly). The share of direct taxes to total tax-collection is 54% in 2013-14. In recent years, the Government of India has been widening the base of income tax (direct tax) to cover as many people as possible in order to collect more and more taxes. This resulted in catching the middle and lower middle class in the tax net, as regular increase in dearness relief due to constant price-rise index pushes their money-income upward and they fall into income tax net. Middle class and lower middle class people are not gainfully employed, instead, they come under the category of underemployed. This shows that our government is now trying to extract income tax from underemployed persons also. All this exercise on the part of the government of India is nothing but to collect more and more taxes in order to expend them on the ever growing amount of subsidies, explicit and implicit both, and other welfare measures for those sections of the population which fall under the category of over-population i.e. beyond the level of optimum population (700 million). In the case of India, this number is (1250-550) 700 million as at March 2013. Indians are among the most heavily taxed people in the world, if you take into account all the hidden taxes, like sales tax, and actroi, and VAT. While India's tax net catches all the small fish __ you and me ____ who willy-nilly pay all these taxes on a daily basis, often without even realizing it, the big fish find loopholes in the net and siphon their untaxed wealth onto foreign shores. India has one of the most complicated tax systems in the world, which is also the most inefficient. Simplifying the system by doing away with multiple taxes would increase efficiency in collection.

As shown in fig (63), total tax collection in India has reached 17.2% of the GDP in the year 2012-13 from 6% in the years 1950-51. This clearly shows that Indian people are very heavily taxed. **The volume of total tax collection of Central and State governments plus Union Territories has gone up from Rs 660 crore in 1950-51 to Rs 17, 20, 371 crore in 2012-13.**

Expenditure of Govt. of India

As shown in fig (28), the expenditure of the Central government has been increasing year after year. It was Rs 530 crore in 1950-51 which has been raised to Rs 16, 65,297 crore in 2013-14. Similarly, out of this expenditure, the unproductive expenditure rose from Rs 24460 crore in 1985-86 to Rs 9, 92, 908 crore in 2013-14. This high level expenditure, especially its unproductive part clearly reveals that a large number of India's population is either unproductive or underproductive which is being sustained through this nature of expenditure.

At least Rs 2 lack crore (Rs 2000 billion) is estimated cost of building a new capital of the residuary State of Andhra Pradesh. The estimate was prepared by the senior State officials __ including Chief Secretary IVR Krishna Rao on the direction of Chief Minister-in-waiting N.Chandrababu Naidu. Sources said that Naidu wanted the officials to prepare detail proposals to seek the financial aid from the Centre for building a new capital city. Naidu was keen to start work at the earliest as he does not want to depend on Hyderabad as a joint capital for a long time. He promised to develop the capital as a world class city.

According to an assessment of the ruling Telugu Desam Party (TDP), Rs 5 lakh crore will be required to build a city like Hyderabad. The Modi Government has said it will provide all support to Capital of the State.

Similarly, Modi Government's commitment to build 100 new ultra-modern cities all over India is a fit case of unproductive expenditure which will increase inflation tremendously on the one hand and diversion of public funds from productive to unproductive channels on the other.

Deficit Financing & Public Debt

Since our government's expenditure level is very high in comparison to the revenue collected through the taxes, direct and indirect, Govt. of India resorts to deficit financing and public debt. As shown in fig. (29), the total public debt and other liabilities of the Government have risen from Rs 2565 crore in 1950-51 to Rs 56, 51, 784 crore in 2013-14, which is colossal. In a matter of just last 22 years, the volume of public debt and other liabilities of the Central Government has risen nearly 15.97 times or 1597 per cent. As a direct result of this growth of Government's total liabilities, the annual interest burden of the Government is also mounting dangerously which is bound to force the Government to land into a debt trap. As shown in fig (30), the interest burden of the Govt. of India has risen from Rs 3500 crore in 1980-81 to Rs 3,70,684 crore in 2013-14. Even to pay the interest component, our government is resorting to further borrow from the public, which clearly shows that it has landed itself in a severe debt-trap. Nearly 47% of the current tax revenue of the Central Government goes towards the payment of interest burden only. No wonder, the Government of India has to borrow heavily to meet revenue deficits. This is the dangerous aspect of the situation since it is bound to force the Government to land into a debt-trap.

Similarly, Govt. of India, since 1950-51 resorted to deficit financing to boost the development process, as its people were very poor and resources very scarce. Year by year, the volume of deficit financing grew regularly and it has reached to Rs 542499 crore in 2013-14 (as per interim budget estimates). (fig 61) Owing to deficit financing of this level, the money supply with the people increased menacingly. As show in fig (56), the money supply with the people (M1) was Rs 23120 crore in 1981-82 which grew up to Rs 18, 89, 820 crore in 2012-13 and aggregate monetary resources (M3) grew from Rs 55360 crore in 1981-82 to a colossal Rs 83, 44, 490 crore in the year 2012-13. Since production of goods and services did not grow at the same rate (especially food grains and other edible goods), it caused general price-rise to an unprecedented level and people of India, especially unemployed, underemployed and earners under unorganized sectors suffered the most.

The most serious disadvantage of the deficit financing is the inflationary rise of prices. Deficit financing increases the total volume of money supply in the country and therefore, raises the aggregate demand for goods and services. In the absence of a corresponding increase in aggregate supply of goods and services, deficit financing leads to rise in the general price-level. It has been argued that deficit financing has been adopted in India for the purpose of development and that, therefore, increase in production will eventually check the price-rise, but this did not happen in India; because, production of goods and services takes some time to occur, say 3 or 4 years which is called gestation period. This gestation period may even be longer for some specific industries, say 5 to 8 years and during this period, human population continues to grow rapidly, making demand for goods and services more enhanced and what is produced after completion of the gestation period in the form of new goods and services is instantly demanded by the new in-comers in the market. Hence, the immediate money-supply pushes prices to rise on account of deficit financing done prior to gestation period, and this never comes down at the arrival of the newly produced goods and services in the market. As we have shown in fig (74), the above said explanation of price-rise in India can be understood easily. This model of economic growth is highly inflationary and never attains its objective of 'growth with stable prices'. On the other hand, it is not only self defeating model which leads our economy toward anarchy and chaos, but it makes the economy unmanageable too. Conversely, as shown in fig (75), the fall of price-level would have been possible to the pre-deficit financing level, had our population remained constant at the pre-deficit financing level. Although, initially, efforts in the direction of population control bear little fruits and population continues to grow, yet its growth-rate can be checked successfully with vigorous efforts and after 30 or 40 years, our planners might become successful in stabilizing the population, as our Chinese neighbor has been doing. **Now Chinese population is around 1320 million in March 2011. Since China's land area is three times to that of India, its 'actual' population comes out to only 440 million (1320 / 3), when we compare it with India's land area. It means China has achieved the level of optimum population in March 2011. This is the secret of China's prosperity and power in the world.** We Indians only boast of being a 'super-power' in the world, whereas our 810 million people do not have even the basic necessity of food security, as per Govt. of India's own declaration; see fig (37).

Our unchecked population growth beyond the level of 'optimum population' (550 million) has been the basic reason behind the failure of our deficit financing thesis and has landed our economy into a debt-trap from where, it is now almost impossible to get out and retrieve it.

Industrial & Services Sector Growth

As we have already mentioned above, Indian economy at the time of independence in 1947 was predominantly agriculture and 75% of its population was engaged in Agriculture and allied activities contributing 55% to our GDP (fig 31 & 32). Whereas, in 1948-49, the share of industry/ manufacturing sector was only 17% of our GDP, employing only around 10% of the workforce. Thus India was industrially backward at the time of independence and it was in the fitness of things to concentrate on industrial development through Five-Year Plans to catch up with the advanced nations of the world. With this view in perspective, the Govt. of India launched a process of industrialization as a conscious and well-planned policy in the early fifties and recognized the significance of industrialisation in the economic development of the country. Our planners characterised the process of industrial development "as a base for the growth of the primary sector (agriculture & allied activities), as a catalytic agent for the development of infra-structure, as a stimulant to generation of technologies through Research & Development effort and as a growth multiplier."

The initial endeavour for industrialization has been made in our Second Five-Year Plan (1955-60) which was based on the Industrial Policy Resolution of 1956, and aimed at a big expansion of the public sector. Under this policy, a base of heavy industry was sough to be created through public sector and a total investment of Rs 870 crore was to be done for this purpose. Rs 675 crore were to be invested by the private sector and a sum of Rs 265 crore was to be invested in village and small industries by private and public sectors both. Thus total investment in industrial sector was to the tune of Rs 1810 crore or 27% of the total investment during the Second Five-Year Plan.

Thus, the beginning was impressive and first of all, three steel plants in the public sector were established during the Second Plan. First was Rourkela Steel Plant in Odissa (Orissa), second was Bhilai Steel Plant in Madhya Pradesh and the third was Durgapur Steel Plant in West Bengal. The other programmes of industrial development included the manufacturing of heavy electrical equipments (BHEL), expansion of Hindustan Machine Tools (HMT), expansion of Sindri Fertilizer factory and the establishment of a fertilizer plant at Nangal, expansion of Hindustan Shipyard and Chittarnjan Locomotive Factory. Most of the investments in the Second Plan were in heavy and basic industries. There was also rapid expansion of machine-building industries for use in agriculture and transport, industries such as chemicals, textiles, jute, cement, tea, sugar, flour and oil mills, paper, mining etc. Quite a number of new industrial items, for example, industrial boilers, milling machines, tractors, motor cycles, scooters etc were also produced in large quantity.

In subsequent Five-Year-Plans, further progress has been made and now India has become almost self-reliant in the manufacturing of consumer goods. As shown in fig (33), India's industrial growth rate was 8% during 1951-60 (average) and lowest was 4% in 1971-80 (average) decade. In the 64 years of planning since 1951, our average growth rate is only 6.12% and now it is stagnating at around 5% per annum. Since our agriculture sector growth is also stagnating at around 2% to 3% per annum only on an average, whereupon around 60% of our population depends, we can not expect much from our industrial sector whose large chunk of products are consumed by the men in agriculture sector. **Actually, fragmentation of agriculture land into very small pieces and existence of a large number of poor small and marginal farmers hamper the growth of agriculture and so the low level of their incomes and consumption.** Further, there is a tough competition for consumer goods in international markets where we can export. China's cheap and better quality goods are competing with our goods in international market and we lag behind China in this respect. Thus our manufacturing sector finds expansion neither in domestic market nor in international market. Even our industrialists are now investing abroad and foreign direct investment in our industry is sluggish.

India's core sector growth slowed to 2.5% in March 2014 from 7% in the same month a year ago as output of crude oil, natural gas and fertilizer declined. The eight core industries __ fertilizer, cement, steel, electricity, crude oil, coal, petroleum refinery products and natural gas __ have a combined weight of about 38% in the index of Industrial Production. For 2013-14, core sector growth slowed to 2.6% from 6.5% in 2012-13, according to data released by the Ministry of Commerce and Industry.

The questions now arise as to why this poor growth of manufacturing sector did happen? and what is going to happen in the years to come? As shown in fig. 31&32, the contribution of manufacturing sector to our GDP as of now is around 26.7% and employing nearly 21.5% of our workforce, while our services sector is contributing around 60% to our GDP and employing nearly 25.4% of our workforce. Since agriculture sector is contributing only 13.7 to our GDP and employing around 53.1% of work force, which is on a very high level and is surplus. This surplus work force in agriculture needs to be transferred to manufacturing and services sectors. This is possible only when our manufacturing sector and services sector grow at a much faster rate in order to employ not only surplus stock of agriculture sector but also the growing number of urban unemployed and underemployed, which include educated unemployed and underemployed in our cities, towns and big urban centers.

But the figures of employment in manufacturing and services sectors show that their capacity to absorb the surplus work force of India is very limited and these two sectors want to produce goods and provide services more and more through automation and computerisation. They are not interested in employing the needy workforce in general. This is so, because our government and planners now want to promote our private sector in manufacturing and services sector to have a high standard of efficiency and quality control as per international standards, and earn more and more profits. **This promotion of private sector has generated a near job-less growth in our economy.**

This is evident from the fact that during the 19 year period from 1990-91 to 2009-10, whereas, there is a sharp increase in capital investment from Rs 1,94,913 crore in 1990-91 to Rs 23,94,711 crore in 2010-11 (which is nearly 12.3 times), the total employment figure has increased from 81.6 lakhs to 126.3 lakhs only (nearly 1.55 times) during the same period in the manufacturing sector. This clearly shows that the manufacturing sector, dominated by the 'private sector', is pursuing a capital intensive path of development, which is nearly job-less. In the last 20 years, total employment increased by nearly 44.7 lakhs. Although, the net value added by the manufacturing sector has shown a growth rate of 16.3% per annum, the employment growth during the same period is negligible at 1.9% per annum. Further, the profit per unit of investment has gone up from 5.8% in 1990-91 to 16.6% in 2010-11. From these facts, it follows that there can be little hope from the manufacturing sector of absorbing new additions to labour force due to its inherent limitations.

Similarly, our services sector shows the same growth path as the manufacturing sector. Here, whereas the contribution of services sector turned double to our GDP from 30% in 1950-51 to 60% in 2012-13, the employment grew only nearly 13%, from 12% in 1950-51 to 25.4% in 2009-10.

Another major problem which the industrial sector is facing now – a –days, is land acquisition at competitive rates. Indian Parliament has passed a law in 2013 regarding land acquisition, according to which the farmers are free to sell or not to sell their land to government agencies / industrialists subject to the approval of their respective village committees which need at least 70% majority for PPP projects and 80% for private entities. No farmer can now be pressurised to sell his/her land under duress. The farmer is now entitled to demand up to four times rate of his land from the market rate. In this way, the land acquisition has now become not only quite cumbersome exercise but expensive too. This will further restrict the growth of manufacturing sector in the coming years. **The author visualizes a dark future for the manufacturing sector as well as its capacity to generate sufficient output and employment in the economy, without which our economy can not grow any further.**

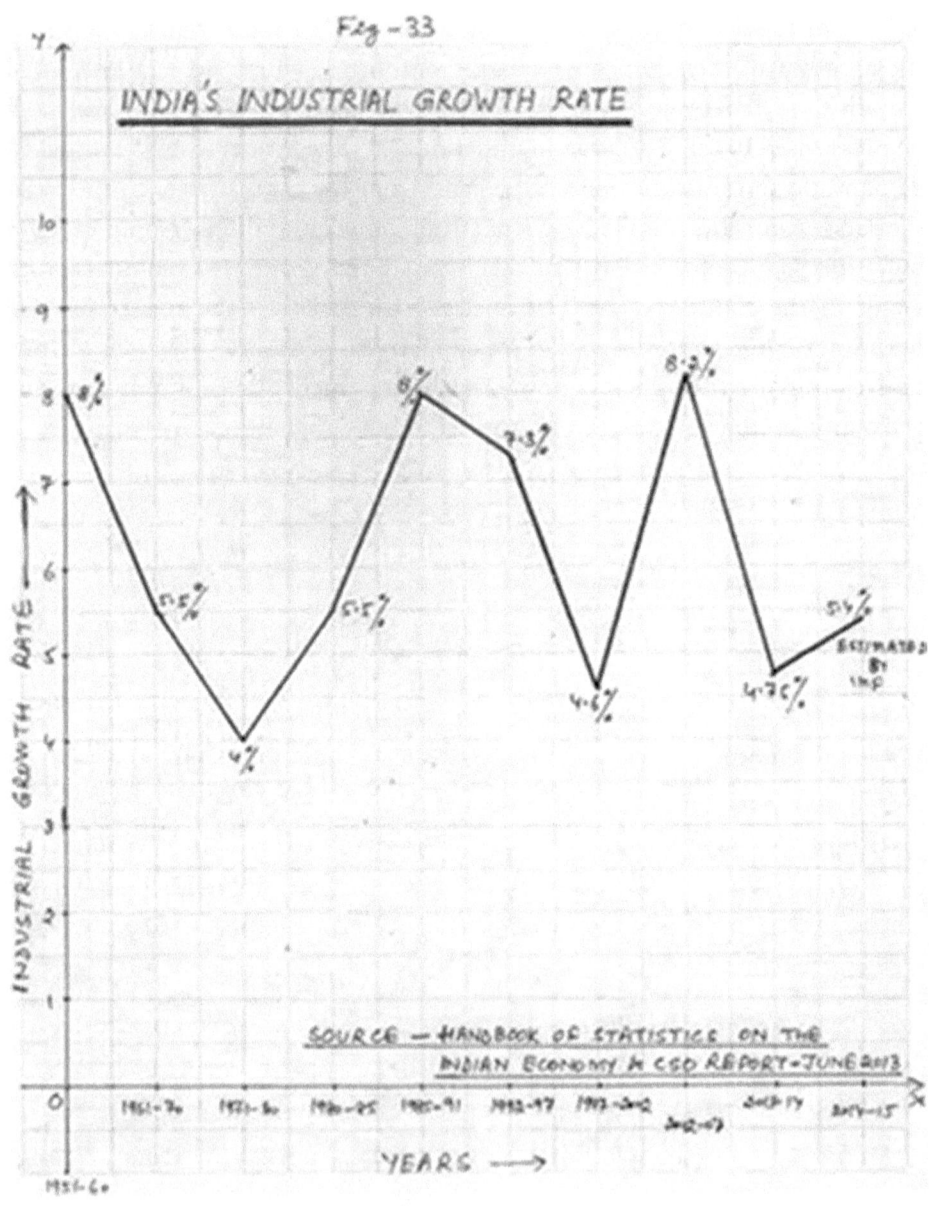

Fig - 33

INDIA'S INDUSTRIAL GROWTH RATE

SOURCE — HANDBOOK OF STATISTICS ON THE
INDIAN ECONOMY & CSO REPORT - JUNE 2013

YEARS ⟶

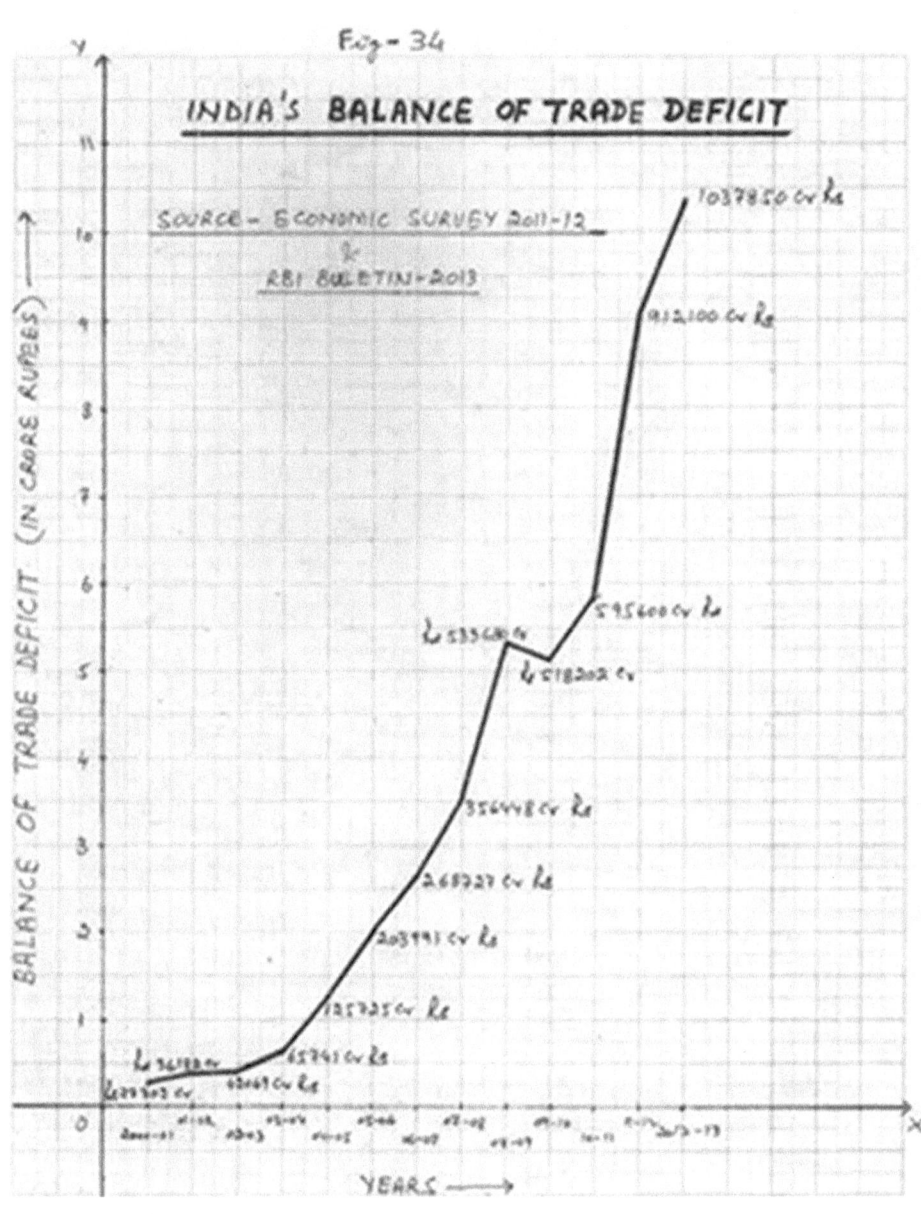

Fig - 34

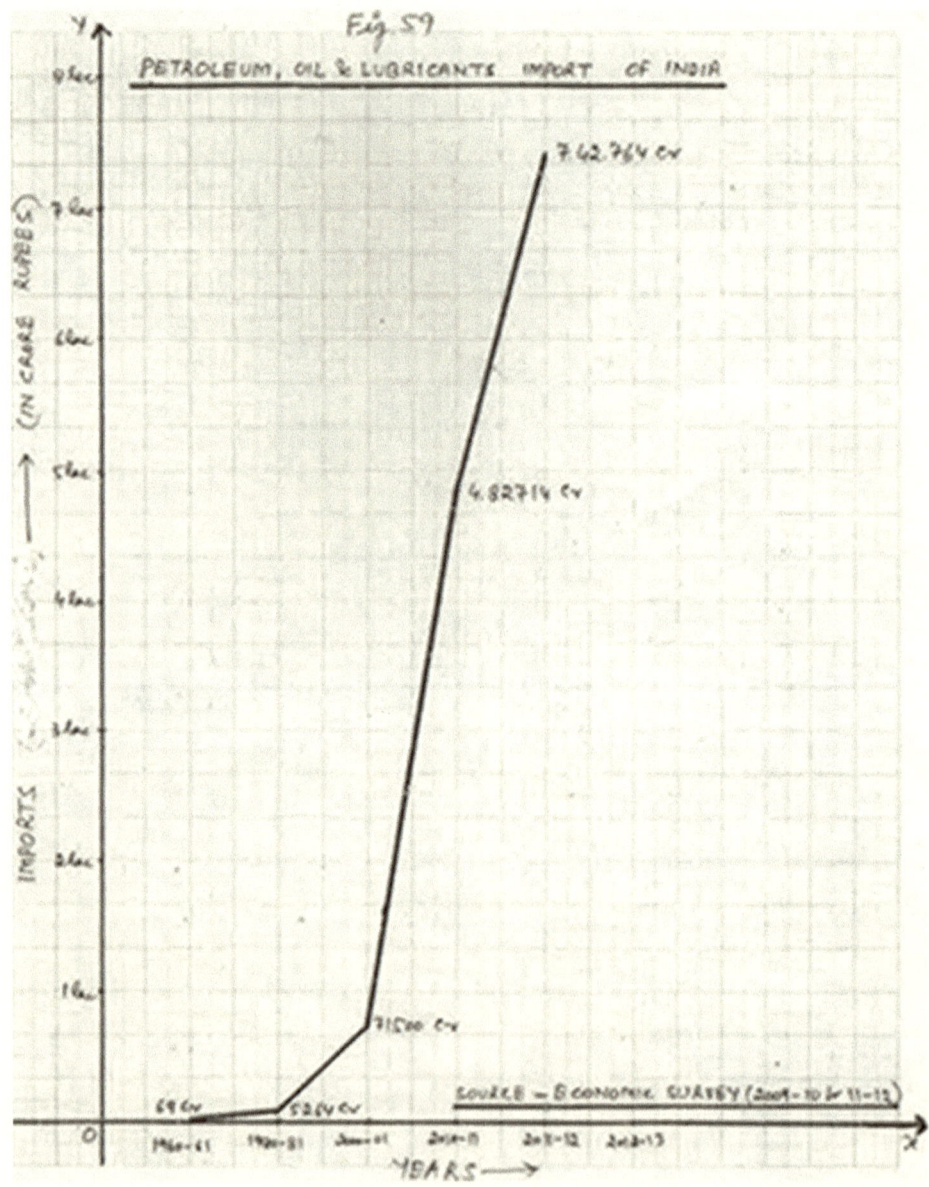

Fig. 59

PETROLEUM, OIL & LUBRICANTS IMPORT OF INDIA

7.62.764 cr

4.82714 cr

71500 cr

69 cr   53.64 cr

SOURCE — ECONOMIC SURVEY (2009-10 & 11-12)

1960-61   1980-81   2000-01   2010-11   2011-12   2012-13

IMPORTS (IN CRORE RUPEES)

YEARS

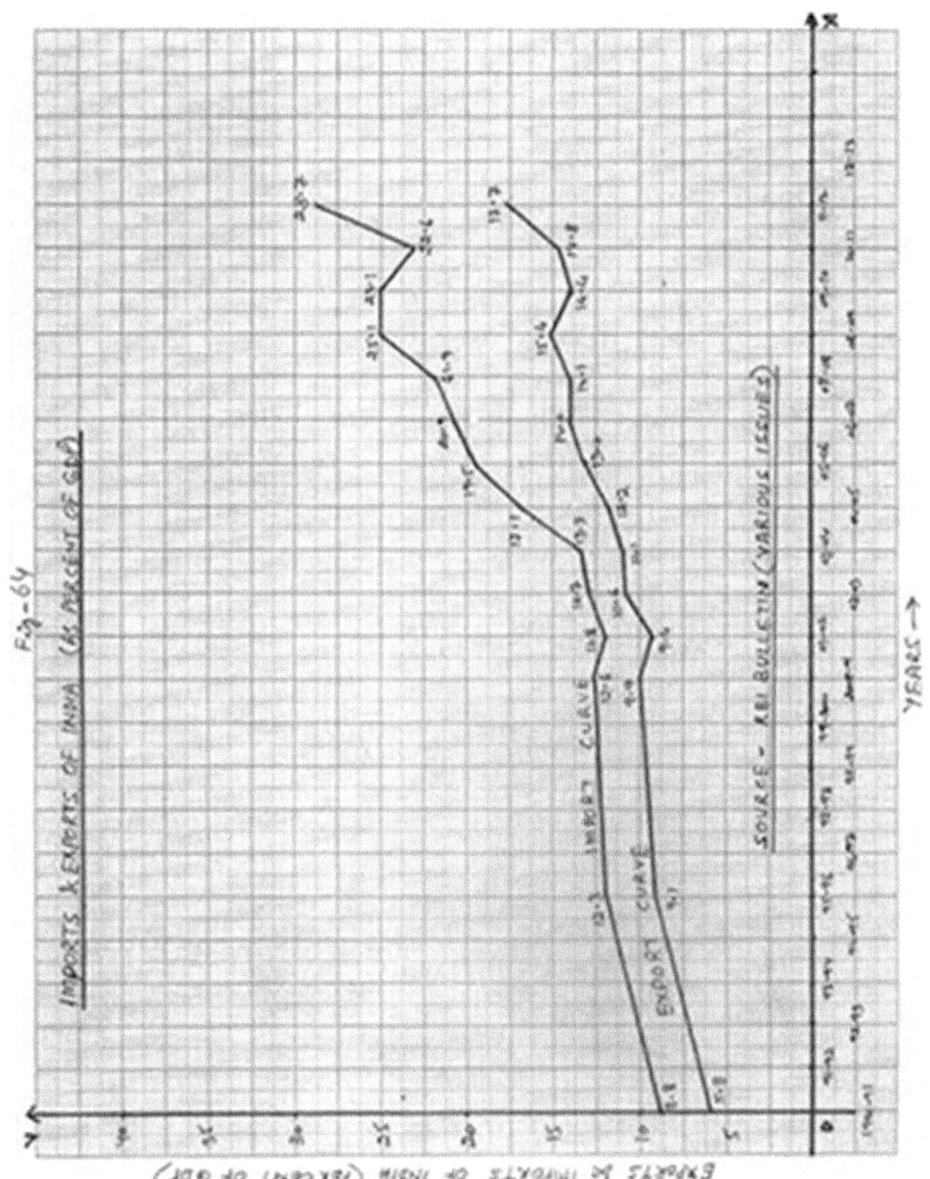

Fig - 6.4

IMPORTS & EXPORTS OF INDIA (As PERCENT OF GDP)

SOURCE - RBI BULLETIN (VARIOUS ISSUES)

YEARS →

EXPORTS & IMPORTS OF INDIA (PERCENT OF GDP)

Fig-35

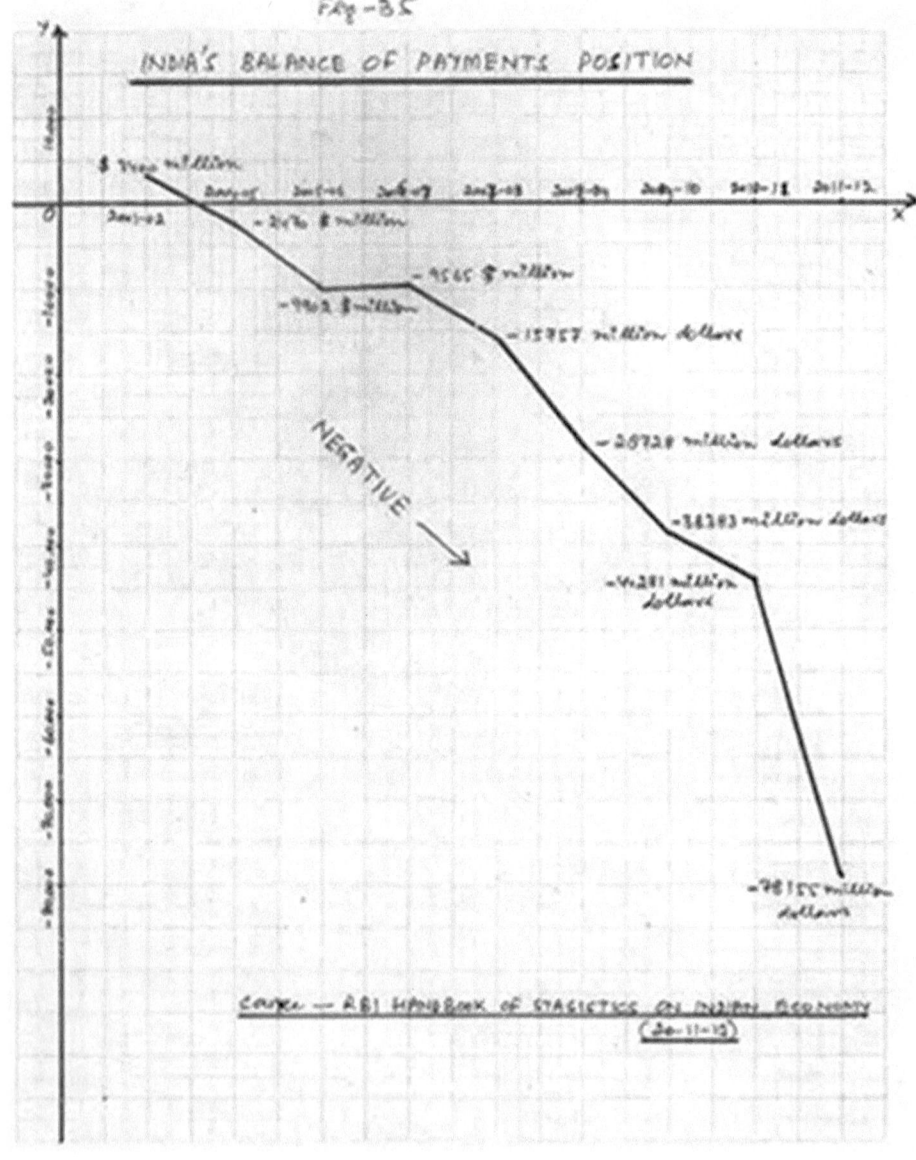

INDIA'S BALANCE OF PAYMENTS POSITION

Fig - 54

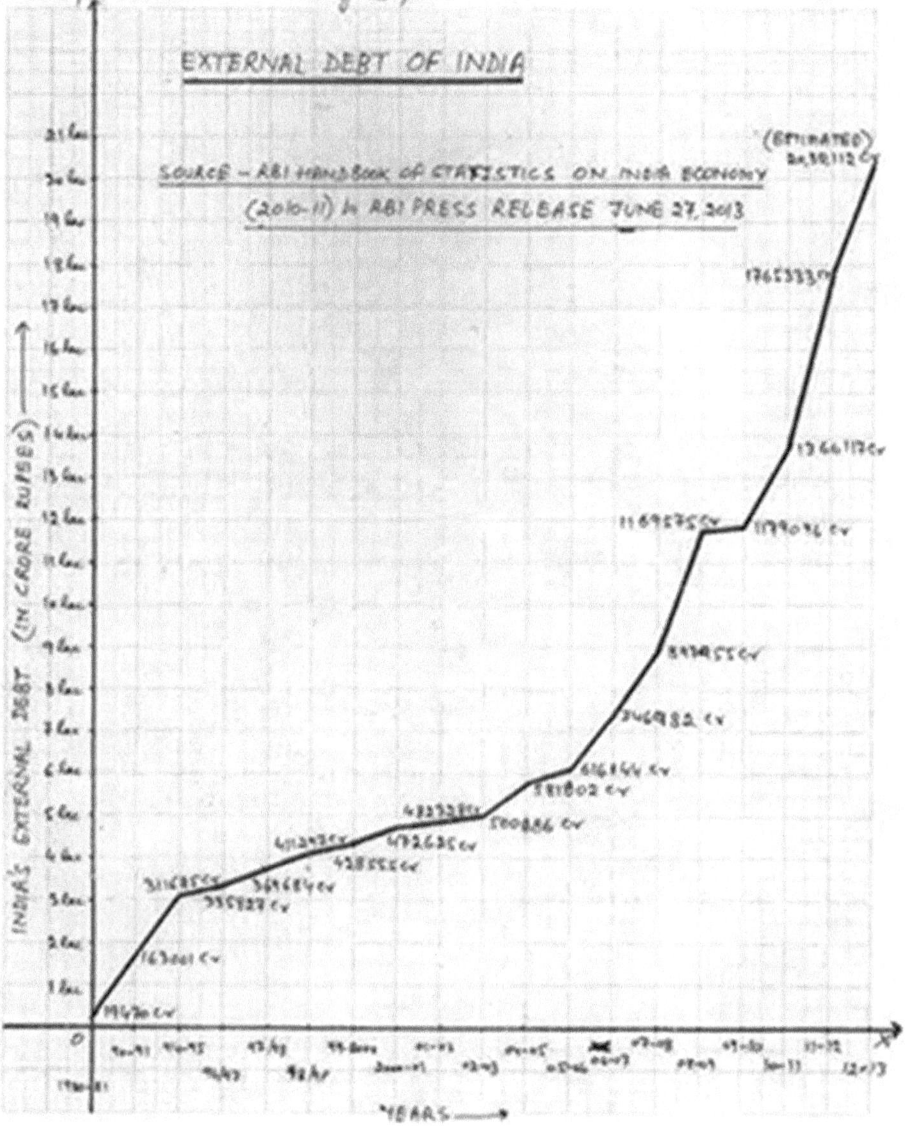
EXTERNAL DEBT OF INDIA
SOURCE - RBI HANDBOOK OF STATISTICS ON INDIA ECONOMY
(2010-11) & RBI PRESS RELEASE JUNE 27, 2013
(ESTIMATED)
INDIA'S EXTERNAL DEBT (IN CRORE RUPEES)
YEARS

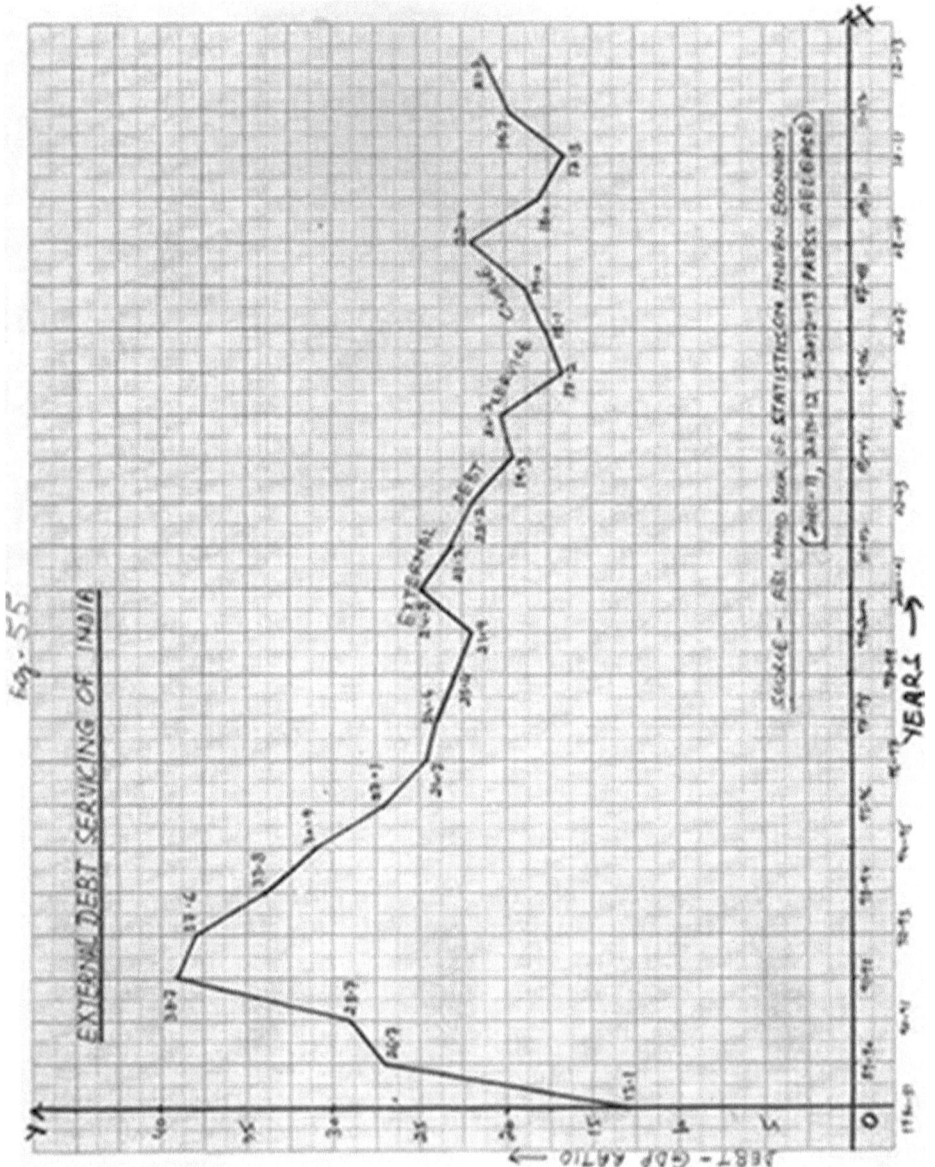

Fig. 55

EXTERNAL DEBT SERVICING OF INDIA

SOURCE – RBI HAND BOOK OF STATISTICS ON INDIAN ECONOMY
(2010-11, 2011-12, & 2012-13 /TABLE AEL67056)

Fig-36

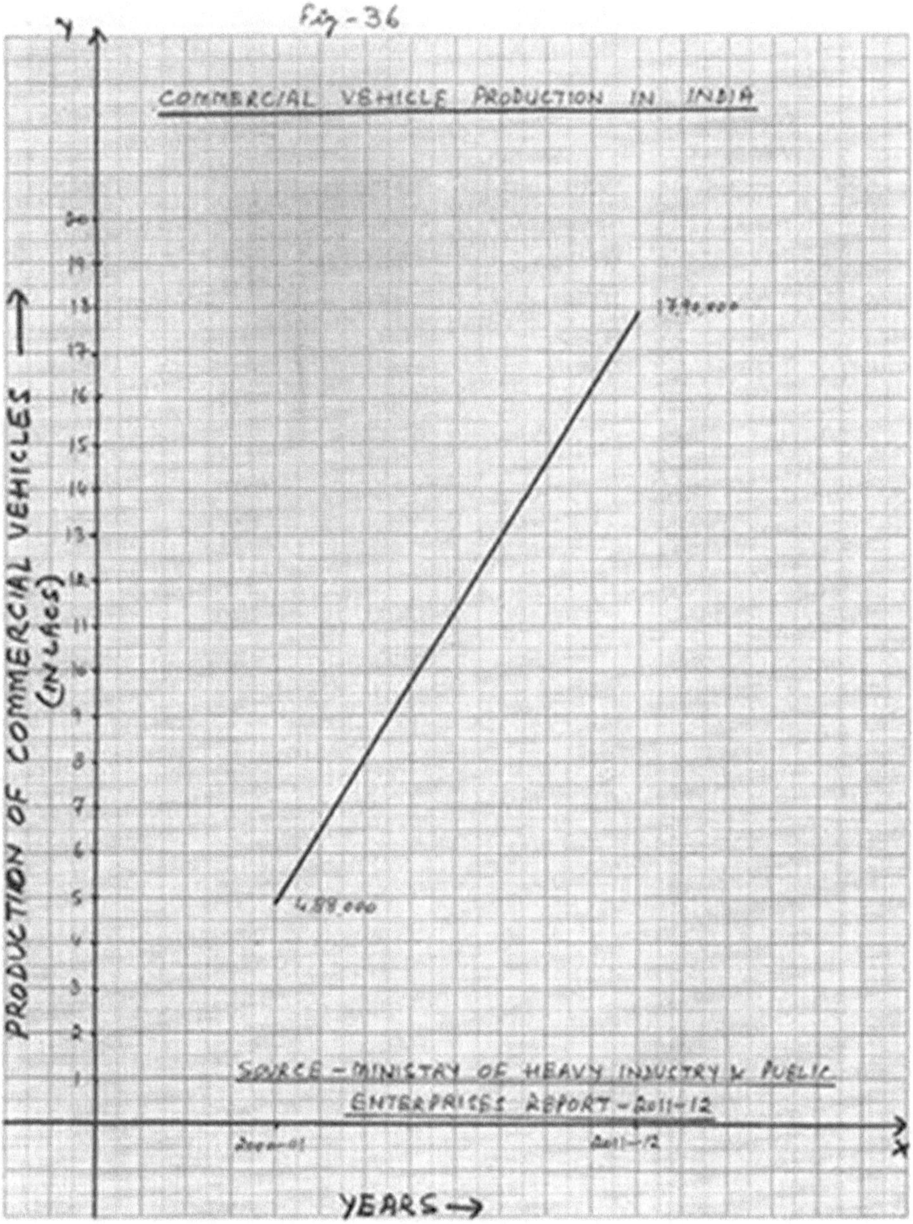

COMMERCIAL VEHICLE PRODUCTION IN INDIA

17,90,000

4,88,000

SOURCE - MINISTRY OF HEAVY INDUSTRY & PUBLIC
ENTERPRICES REPORT - 2011-12

2000-01   2011-12

YEARS →

PRODUCTION OF COMMERCIAL VEHICLES (IN LACS) →

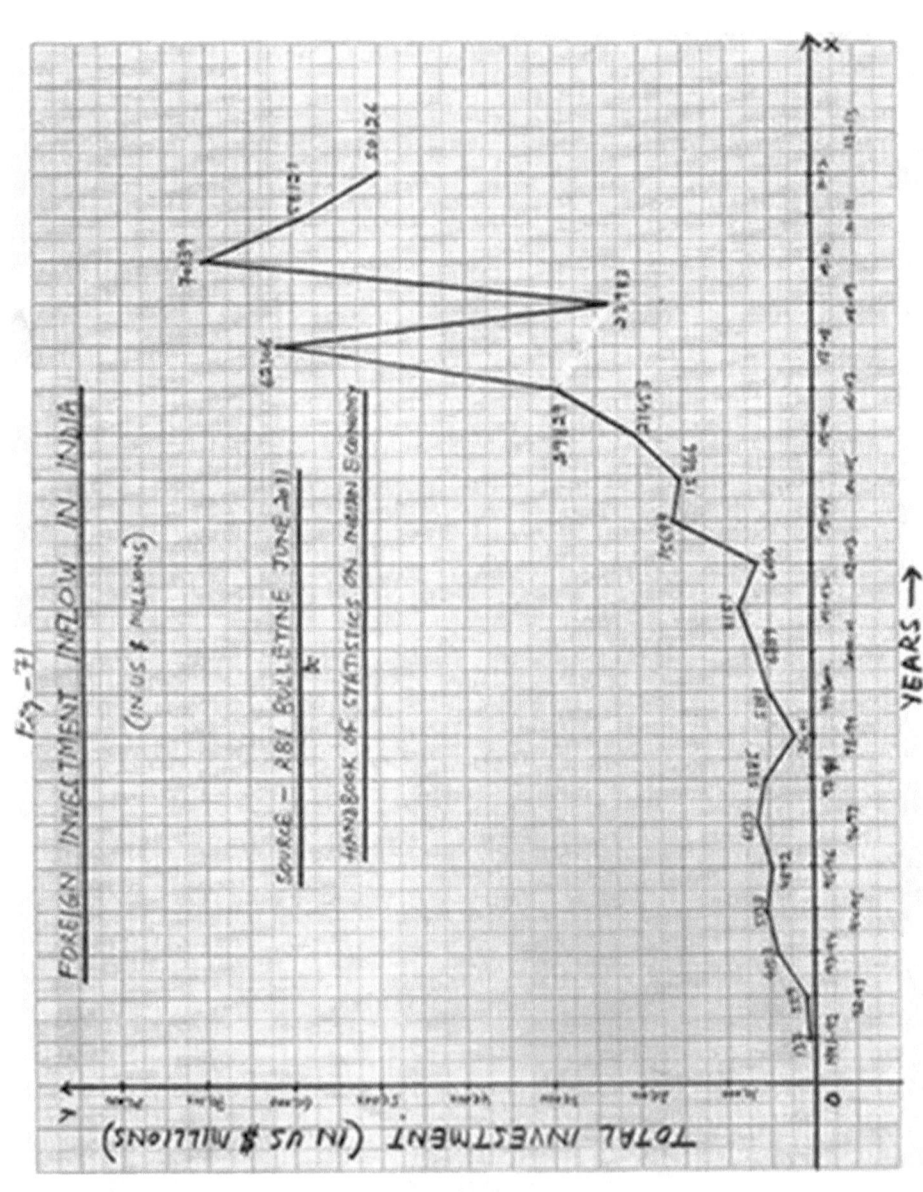

Fig.-71

FOREIGN INVESTMENT INFLOW IN INDIA

(IN US $ MILLIONS)

SOURCE - RBI BULLETINE JUNE-2011
&
HANDBOOK OF STATISTICS ON INDIAN ECONOMY

TOTAL INVESTMENT (IN US $ MILLIONS)

YEARS →

Fig - 37

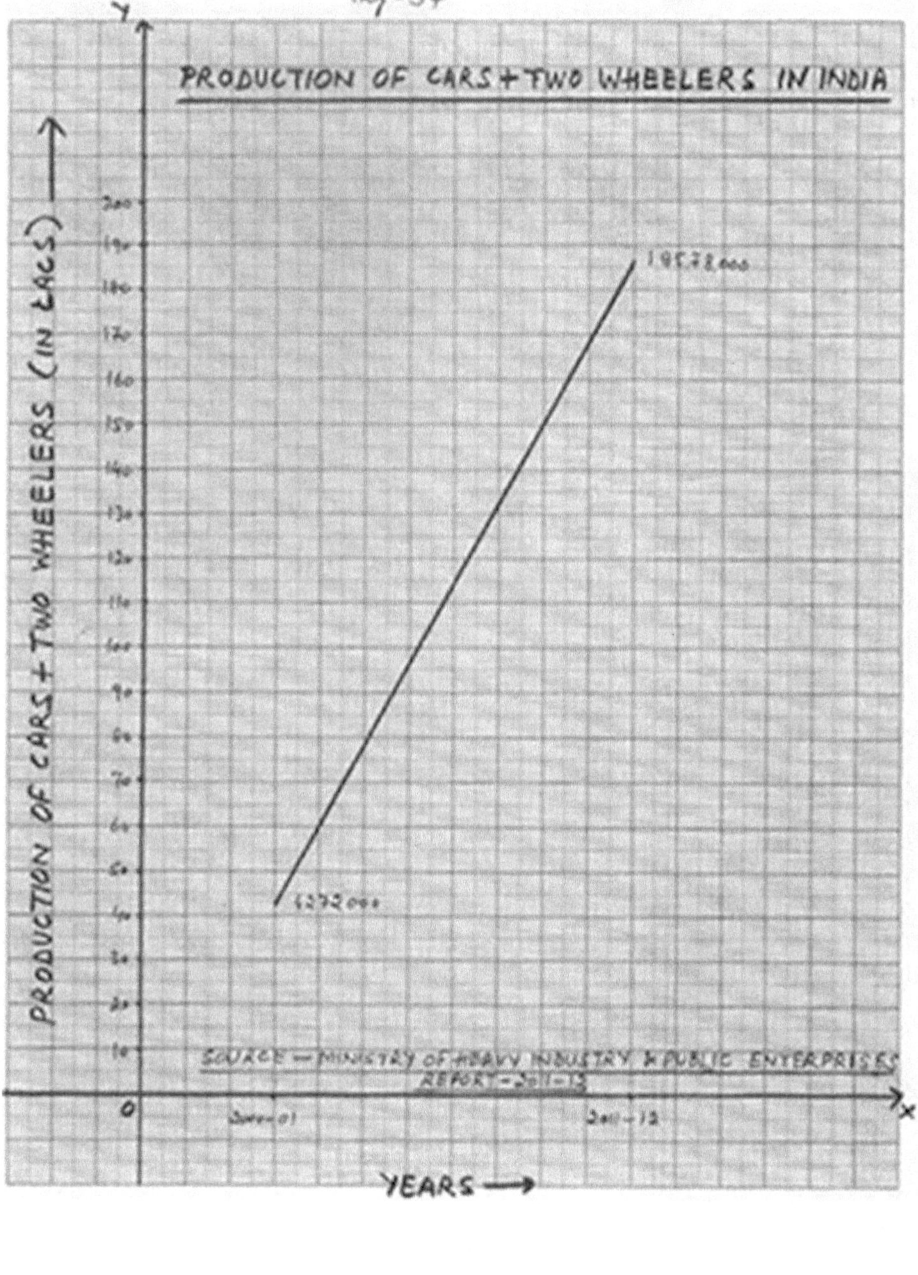

PRODUCTION OF CARS + TWO WHEELERS IN INDIA

Y-axis: PRODUCTION OF CARS + TWO WHEELERS (IN LACS)

X-axis: YEARS →

18578000

6272000

SOURCE — MINISTRY OF HEAVY INDUSTRY & PUBLIC ENTERPRISES
REPORT — 2011-12

2000-01   2011-12

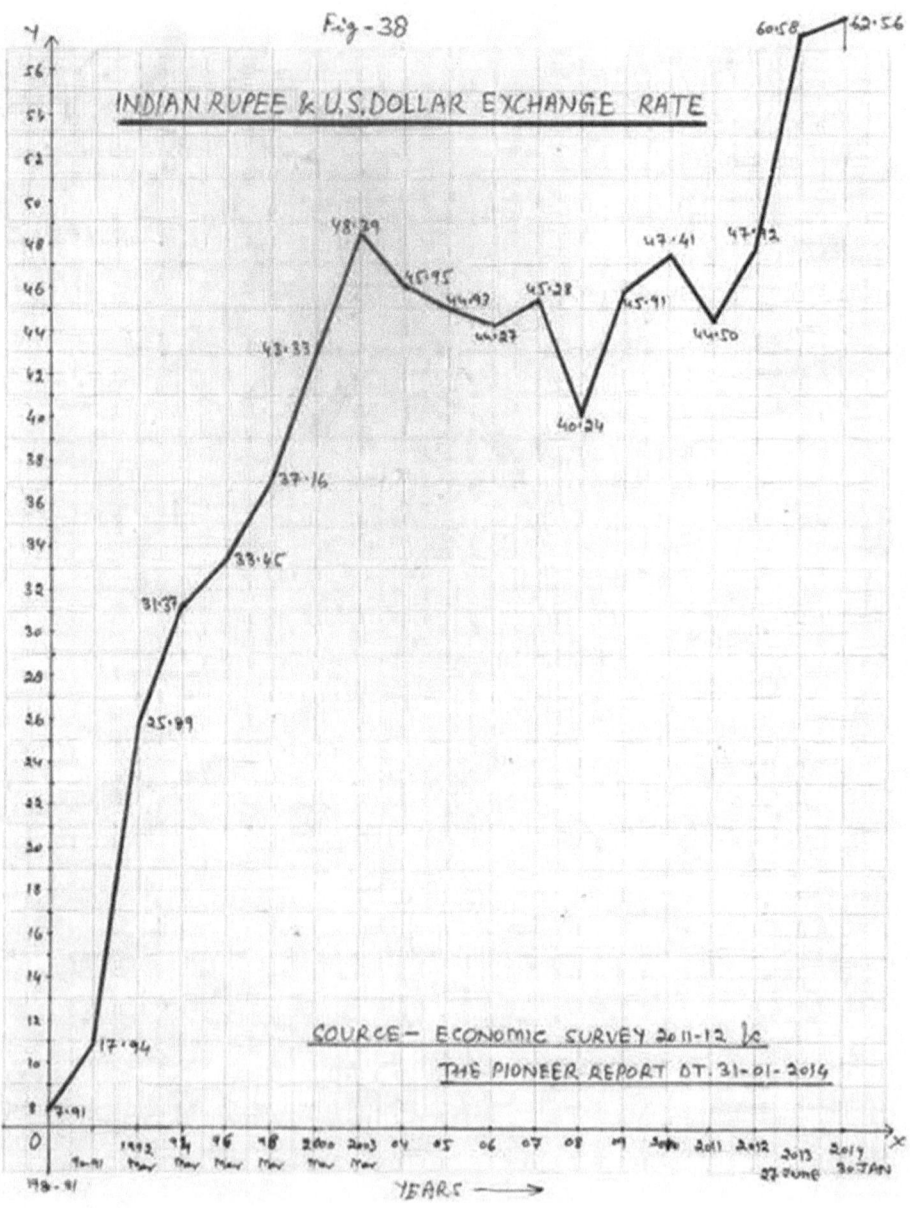

Fig - 38

INDIAN RUPEE & U.S. DOLLAR EXCHANGE RATE

SOURCE— ECONOMIC SURVEY 2011-12 &
THE PIONEER REPORT DT. 31-01-2014

YEARS ——→

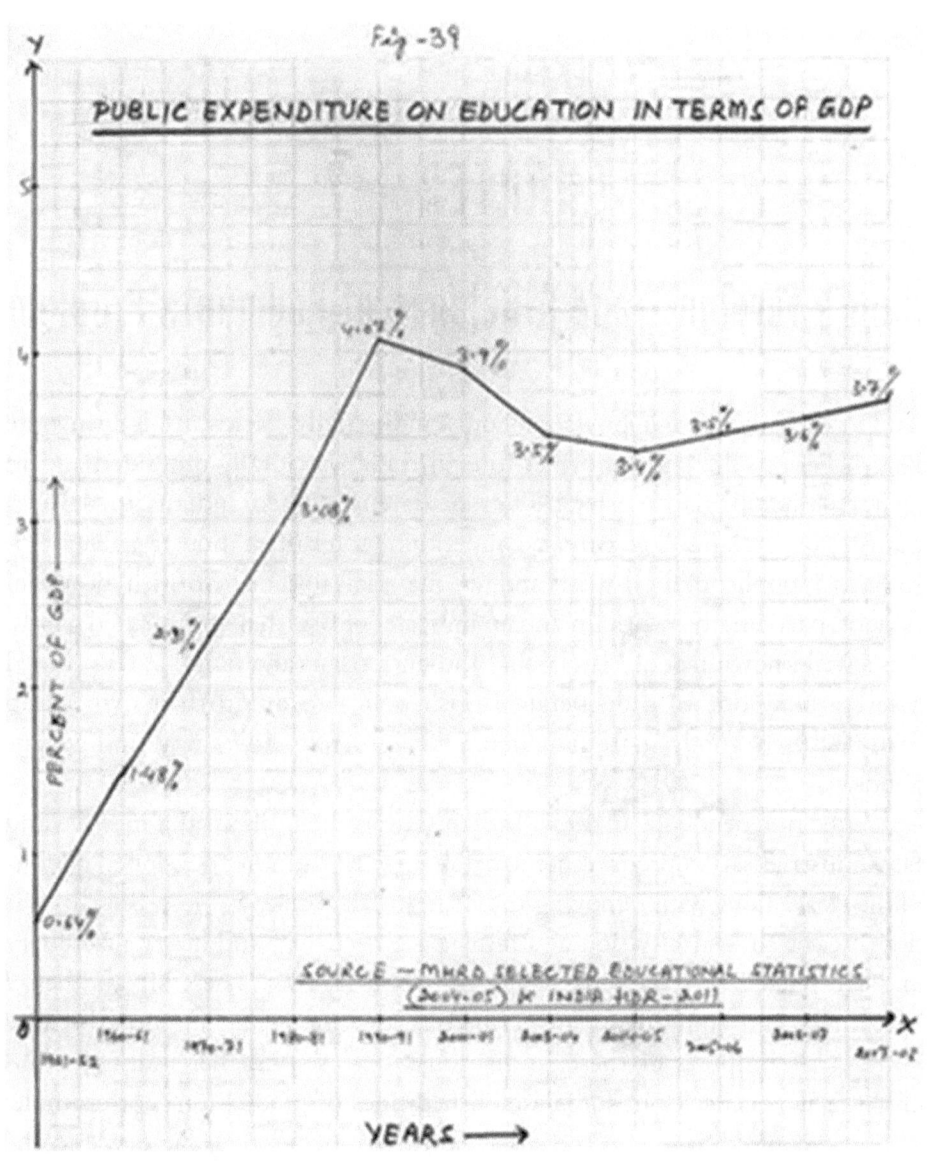

Fig -39

PUBLIC EXPENDITURE ON EDUCATION IN TERMS OF GDP

CHAPTER - 7

India's Foreign Trade & Balance of Payments Problem

India's colonial past kept its economy industrially backward. During the British Period, the pattern of her foreign trade was totally one sided and in favour of her British masters. They never encouraged Indians to develop industry on Indian soil to avoid a competition with British industry. They kept India as a supplier of food-stuffs and raw materials to the pro-British industrial nations, particularly to Britain and an importer of British manufactured goods. It is a well known fact of history that Indian artisans and handicrafts suffered a severe blow due to a deliberate British policy to dump their own cheap manufactured goods in Indian market in order to drive away indigenous goods.

After Independence in 1947, Indian Government planned a massive and fast industrialisation programme to catch up with the other developed nations of the world along with removing India's industrial backwardness. But this was not so easy. Industrialisation at a faster pace needs big and heavy machinery and equipments to start with, which India was lacking. These big and heavy machinery and equipments are termed as 'developmental imports' because without the imports of these, India could not establish her industries and enhance new capacity in some established lines of production. For example, imports required to set up the steel plants, the locomotives factory, and the hydroelectric projects which were of a developmental nature. Similarly, a developing country like India, which urgently needed to set in motion the process of industrialisation at home, required to import the necessary raw materials and other intermediate goods so as to properly utilize the capacity in full, already created in the country. These types of imports are known as 'maintenance imports'. The 'maintenance imports' are as essential as the 'developmental imports', because many of the industrial projects are held up for lack of maintenance imports. For a developing nation like India, the developmental and maintenance imports both are equally important and they set the limits for the industrialisation stage which can be carried out in a given time-frame.

Apart from it, sometimes, some consumer goods which are in scarcity in India, also need to be imported to keep price-line low in indigenous markets. Such imports are anti-inflationary because they reduce the scarcity of consumer goods. For example, India had had to import food grains in post-Independence period to arrest the price-rise and scarcity at home owing to its shortage in domestic market. It is, therefore, inevitable and but-natural that during the initial years of development, imports have to be increased at a very fast rate. It was natural that the balance of trade in such a situation would turn heavily against the developing countries, like India. But, as far as the imports of consumer goods were concerned, steps should have been taken to curtail our domestic demand on the one hand and produce the same in India itself. This would have facilitated first to stop imports of such items and then gradually step-up exports of the same. But this did not happen in India. In the year 2011-12, India's 12.3% import were either consumer goods or other goods which could be produced in India itself, which we could not do even after a lapse of more than 67 years of Independence. These items include cereals and pulses, edible oils, fertilizers, non-ferrous metals, paper and paper boards, metallic ores, iron & steel etc. Further, India's 31.7% imports in 2011-12 constituted Petroleum, crude oil and petroleum products, which could have been curtailed by suppressing the demand of the same. India's import of petroleum, oil & lubricants (POL) was only Rs 69 crore in 1960-61 which went up to Rs 7.42.764 crore in 2011-12 (fig-59), which speaks itself our dependence on POL imports. Since, POL is a non-sustainable source of energy and one day this will exhaust, its prices are regularly being increased by the OPEC, fuelling inflation.

Instead of curtailing its demand at home, Indian government encouraged its consumption by imitating luxurious life-styles of the developed nations, like importing and manufacturing big oil guzzling cars and SUVs and examples of this imprudent imitation of developed countries and imbecile conspicuous consumption. Also, we did not check our population growth to maintain at a reasonable level or at optimum level, due to which, demand for every item, consumer or otherwise, steeped many fold, resulted in imports of the same, for we could not produce them at home so soon. 'In can be noted that gold imports has been the second biggest bill after crude leading to higher CAD (Current A/C Deficit), which had touched 4.8% of GDP in FY 13. However, with curbs on gold import, CAD had been brought to about $ 35 billion in FY 14.

The immediate consequence of this imprudent imitation of developed nations along with a big population-pushed demand for consumable goods is the creation of a huge gap between our value of exports vis-à-vis our value of imports and this gap kept on growing every year since Independence. As shown in fig (34&64), our trade-deficit in 2000-01 was Rs 27302 crore which mounted up to Rs 10, 37, 850 crore in 2012-13 and this created a foreign exchange crisis. We have had to borrow foreign exchange from the IMF to sustain our foreign trade. IMF aid is always subject to conditions, which we shall have to bear. **External aid can help share the burden of growth in the short run, but ultimately, the developing country has to bear and manage the burden of development itself. It has to plan its economy including its human population in such a fashion as to make it self-reliant in due course. Every prudent individual as well as country seeks the same course, but our planners could not manage our economy on correct lines.** In fig (35), we have shown India's balance of payments position; it was favorable ($ 3400 million) only in the year 2001-02, but in subsequent years, this has been regularly unfavorable and turned negative up to the extent of U.S. $ 78155 million in 2011-12. External debt also mounted manifold since Independence, and our economy is landed now in the trap of foreign debt. In the year 1980-81, our foreign debt was Rs 19470 crore, which steeped up to Rs 17, 65, 333 crore and is expected to touch the figure of Rs 20, 30, 112 crore in the year 2012-13.

Persistent adverse balance of trade since 1951 and consequent adverse balance of payments, acute foreign exchange shortage, extensive borrowing by India from IMF and other international agencies to overcome balance of payments problems ___ all these factors induced India to devalue her Rupee by 36.5% in June 1966. It is a well-known saying in economics ___ **Flag follows the foreign Capital.** IMF, World Bank and other developed countries always put conditions before India in lieu of 'aid' and we have had to accept them on account of our weak position. Devaluation of Indian Rupee was done to achieve the under noted objectives;

1- to reduce the volume of imports, for, the imports become costly due to devaluation;
2- to boost exports, for, the exports become cheaper due to devaluation; and
3- to create a favorable balance of trade and balance of payments position.

But none of the above objectives could be achieved as India could not control over her imports. Since devaluation was done during a year of drought and the following year again happened to be a bad weather year, the imports continued to increase. Further, Govt. of India announced its policy of import liberalization in case of 59 industries, the immediate effect of devaluation was further aggravation of our trade deficit and much more gap in balance of payment position on account of devalued Rupee. This all was done under pressure from IMF and World Bank. Although after devaluation of the Rupee, exports increased during 1966-67 and 1967-68, but on account of ever increasing imports, the import bill soared from Rs 1.992 crore in 1966-67 to 2043 crore in 1967-68, and consequently, the balance of payments situation worsened further. **Actually, Indian government behaved like an imprudent customer who ignores expenses on conveyance, say of Rs 100 to travel a long distance market to purchase a commodity cheaper by only Rs 10 from his nearby market.**

India's external debt was a little just over $ 100 billion in 2004; by March 2013, this had grown to $ 390 billion. More worryingly, the short term debt payable within a year, an indicator of immediate vulnerability, has ballooned to $ 172 billion in 2013, from $ 54 billion in 2008. Consequently, India has to pay back $ 172 billion to foreign lenders by March 2014. This is nearly 60 per cent of its current foreign exchange reserves. In the four years after 2008, India's own experience has been one of losing its export competitiveness relative to other developing countries. This has decelerated our export earnings, added to this is our mounting import bill, largely led by rising oil prices. The massive increase in gold imports further added to our woes. The double whammy of decelerating exports and rising imports has resulted in India becoming one of the highest current account deficit nations, at nearly 5 per cent of GDP annually. India needs at least $ 90 billion of fresh capital inflows a year to meet its current account deficit.

Our foreign debt burden has become enormous during the last decade and so its repayment was also an arduous task, apart from facing undue pressure from the IMF and the World Bank. All these negative factors have arisen because of our planners' lack of farsightedness and their inability to adjudge the impact of our unproductive population growth and its demand-generated problems in the economy. For example, take the figures of automobiles production in India since Independence. As shown in fig 36 & 37, the commercial vehicles production in 2011-12 was 17,90,000 while only 10 years ago, in 2000-01, there were only 4.88.000 vehicles on the Indian roads. Similarly, the production of cars and two-wheelers reached to 1,85,78,000 vehicles in 2011-12, while it was only 42,72,000 in 2000-01. Total automobile production in 2000-01 was 47,60,000 vehicles and it went up to 203, 68, 000 vehicles in 2011-12, which is more than four times in a decade only. All these vehicles are consuming petroleum, diesel and gas, polluting the atmosphere along with increasing our import bill. This all is due to our unlimited population growth which constitutes primary reason for almost all the ills, India is facing. Our leaders and planners have got no time to pay any attention to this. They also do not pay any attention to develop a pollution free public transport system which may replace pollution-generating private transport vehicles and bring about a reduction in its numbers on our roads. Traffic jams and fatal accidents are now a very common feature in major cities, towns and on highways of India. We failed to widen our roads for want of space and money to cope with a mountainous growth of auto-vehicles on the roads, resulting in traffic jams and fatal accidents alike, wasting public money in insurance claims in addition to loss of precious human lives and property.

A report from National Crime Records Bureau (NCRB) for 2013 shows that a total of 4,00,517 people died of accidental deaths in 2013, an increase of 1.4% over the previous year; Road accidents continue to be the major cause of unnatural accidental deaths recording 34.3% of all deaths, followed by 'sudden deaths' (7.8%), drowning (7.5%), 'poisoning' (7.3%), 'railway accidents' (7.2%) and 'fire accidents' (5.5%).

Falling Value of India Rupee vis-a-vis U.S. Dollar

The value of India rupee has been on the downhill since Independence. As we have shown in fig-(38), the exchange value of one U.S. Doller was Rs

7.91 in the year 1980-81, which went down to Rs 48.39 in March, 2003 and further lowered to Rs 62.56 on January 30, 2014. This fall of exchange value of Indian Rupee vis-à-vis U.S Doller is all due to under noted two factors;

1- unprecedented demand for U.S Dollars by Indian importers since Independence on account of mountainous jump of imports; and
2- a continuous price-rise of India's goods and services since Independence which affects adversely the exchange value of rupee measured through the Purchasing Power Parity Theory in Economics.

Since the purchasing power of Indian Rupee is regularly going down in the face of a regular price rise of indigenous goods and services in India, it can not withstand against the U.S.Dollar whose value is relatively constant in the U.S. economy. Since we have failed to control our price-line as well as our imports, the value of rupee was bound to fall rapidly and this trend shall continue as long as this type of situation persists in India. The latest Rupee-Dollar exchange rate was Rs.64.24 per U.S. Dollar on 07/05/2015.

Poor Condition of Education & Health in India

A glaring feature of an underdeveloped economy is the poor quality of human capital. Most of the underdeveloped countries suffer from mass-illiteracy and poor educational standards which is the main factor behind the all round backwardness of Indian polity. Illiteracy not only retards economic growth, but keeps people's outlook and thought-process in negative direction too. They waste there time, energy and hard-earned money on frivolous, superstitious and unproductive rituals/channels which further keep them poor and ignorant. A minimum level of scientific education is necessary to acquire skills as well as to comprehend social and economic problems. Literacy and scientific education widen the outlook of humans and they can acquire skill to distinguish between what is good for them and what is bad. In the rural areas of India, where illiteracy, malnutrition and disease-prone life are common features, are the back-waters of civilization and the citadel of superstition, social taboos and conservatism. Prevalence of fatalism and acceptance of misery and backwardness an inherent part of life are the direct outcomes of illiteracy and unscientific mindset. These people believe that all this is because it is a pre-destined fate due to their 'Karmas' (doings) in the 'previous life' and none can change it. If India is to develop fast, then its human capital (at present human garbage) i.e., its all people shall have to acquire scientific knowledge, skill and training of a high order; and for this to achieve, they are to be made not only literate, but well educated too, having a scientific bent of mind.

As a result, the expenditure on education, (specially upto primary level), skill development, research and innovation along with improvement in health and sanitation are to get top priority in India's economic planning. Around 40 crore people of India are still illiterate and further 20 crore are literate only nominally i.e. they can only read and write and can not be termed as educated. Thus India's nearly half population is practically illiterate or semi-literate. Actually, when all the people of India become educated, only then this nation shall get a necessary human capital base needed for development. Merely literate or semi-literate will not do any good as far as our break from the backwardness is concerned, let alone progress and development.

Despite being among the top five countries with most children out of school, India experienced the largest cuts in aid to basic education. Its aid to the sector fell by $ 278 million between 2010-12. While global aid to education is seriously declining, for India, it fell by 10% in this period. These figures are released by UNESCO's Education for All (EFA) Global Monitoring Report ahead of the Global Partnership for Education's Replenishment Pledging Conference in Brussels on June 25-26, 2014. Basic education which enables children to acquire foundational skills and core knowledge ____ is receiving the same amount of aid as it was in 2008. As funds diminish, and just one year before the deadline for achieving the global EFA goals, 57 million children and 69 million adolescents are shill out of school. When so many girls and boys are still out of school and not learning, the continuing drop in funds for education is cause for concern.

India's public expenditure on primary to higher education and research and development in 2002-04 was only 3.3% of its GDP, while the same for the U.S.A. was 5.9% of its GDP. Under the United Nations Development Programme (UNDP), countries have been ranked on the basis of Human Development Index (HDI). This index is based on life expectancy, adult literacy, combined enrolment ratio ____ first, second and third level and real GDP per capita (on purchasing power parity basis) in U.S. Dollars. In the year 2012, India has been ranked at 136 on the HDI basis while Chine was at 101 mark. The U.S.A., Japan, Canada, France and the U.K. were at 3, 10, 11,

20 and 26 respectively. Can we still call ourselves an 'economic power'? The constitution of India resolved to provide elementary education for every one within 10 years of its adoption. It states in Article 45;

"The state shall endeavour to provide, within a period of ten years from the commencement of this constitution, for free and compulsory education for all children until they complete the age of fourteen years."

Even after 65 years of its adoption. India's 50% population is still either illiterate or nominally literate. The Government of India had set up an Education Commission in 1966 under the chairmanship of Dr. D.S.Kothari, and eminent educationist to determine the need and give an estimate of Gross Domestic Product (GDP) required for promoting education. Dr. Kothari emphasised the critical relationship between education and productivity and underlined the role of education in India's national and economic development. It stated very categorically;

"Education as investment in human resources plays an important role among the factors which contribute to economic growth." It also stated that during the next 20 years, expenditure on education should be stepped up to 6% of the GDP. As shown in fig (39), the maximum public expenditure on education was 4.07% of the GDP in the year 1990-91, and in all the other years, it was less than 4% of the GDP. For a healthy and true democracy, literacy and education is a must which India lacks. **Hence calling India as the 'largest democracy' of the world is a sham. India's 'largest democracy' may be called as the' 'largest democracy of the illiterates and the ignorant' people of the world.** Actually, it is deliberately being kept uneducated and illiterate to perpetuate the corrupt and exploitative character of the polity. Nehru was a democrat and a socialist. He championed universal franchise when this was by no means a foregone conclusion among newly independent nations. **This turned India into the world's first largely illiterate democracy.** That in a way, is a measure of the man. **Historically, for most democracies, universal education came before universal franchise. But when the first Indian election look place in 1952, 85% of eligible voters could not read or write. At the same time, this also illustrates the dark side of Nehru's legacy. Democracies do not function well without education.** But India's strides in education have been very slow. It's not something that Gandhi or Nehru stressed very much and to this day India remains one of the most poorly educated nations in the world.

Our learning standards are also going down, as per a World Bank study. High enrolment but low learning level characterises school education across South Asia. According to the World Bank study __ 'Students learning in South Asia' __ released on Monday, June 30, 2014, the number of out-of-school children in the age group of 8-14 between 1999 and 2010 fell from 35 million to 13 million in Afghanistan, Bhutan, Bangladesh, India, Maldives, Nepal, Pakistan and Sri-Lanka. In India enrolment went up from 79% to 92%. Girls enrolment also improved from 60% in 1990 to 74% in 2010. The number of 'out-of-school' girls in the region dropped from 23 million to 9.4 million.

Here, the author's view-point is that, while the 6% of GDP minimum public expenditure is a must, to get any tangible improvement in India's education and literacy landscape, as demanded by Dr. Kothari, unless India's population growth is checked strictly, the monster of illiteracy, backwardness and ignorance can never be killed. **It has got no use of expending hard-earned public money on half-hearted literacy / educational programmes without controlling population growth strictly.** Even we would not get land for opening new schools/colleges/universities for want of land availability. The position of education in U.P., the most populous state of India, tells its story;

As per rough estimates, there are approximately 18.6 lakh seats in U.P. universities and colleges, which includes technical and medical, for over 34 lakh aspirants in U.P, U.P, Board alone accounts for 28 lakh students followed by around 1.20 lakh of CBSC and ISC Board. Around 3 lakh students who could not get admissions in the past two years would again be trying their luck in various colleges and universities. Further, four major institutions of learning __ Banaras Hindu University, Aligarh Muslim University, Allahabad University and Lucknow University attract students from different states like Bihar, Assam and Manipur.

'Another interesting aspect of the students is that about 9.5 million are 'marginal workers'. That is, they are working on an irregular or part time basis, not more than six months in a year. About 60% of these working students are male and the remaining female. This reflects the pressure families face in making ends meet, and the costs of education.

This clearly shows our lackadaisical and directionless attitude towards this very important field of education and literacy.

Health Scenario

Indian people's mass poverty and ignorance resulted in the prevalence of illness and diseases which causes poor heath and low productivity, apart from wastages on expenses on doctor's fees, medical tests (often manipulated), medicines etc. Heavy expenses on hospital establishment and maintenance on the part of the Government should also be added as a tax burden on the Indian people at large. Medical and health bear a direct relationship with the state of poverty, level of ignorance/awareness about hygiene and sanitation, including availability of pure drinking water in the wake of all round pollution. Water-borne diseases are the main fountainhead of poor heath and illness in India. Malnutrition among the abject poor people of India pushes them towards an easy prey to illness, as their body resistance remains so weak that they can not bear even a mild infection. Their failure to secure a healthy & balanced diet manifests in the low calorie intake and a low level of protein consumption in India. In 1999, the average calorie intake of food is only 2496 as compared to over 3400 calories per day in most of the developed countries. This is slightly above the minimum intake for sustaining life estimated at 2100 calories per day for a person. **When India's 810 million people (81 crore) or 67% of the total population do not have even the basic need of food-/security, how we expect of them to have a balanced/healthy diet full of proper calories and proteins therein? We have every reason to believe that these 810 million people, having no food-security, do not get even the minimum level of intake of 2100 calories a day!**

According to World Development Indicators, India's 46% child population suffers from malnutrition. The average protein intake of an Indian is only 59 gms per day as against 145 grams per day in developed countries. India's around 60% mothers are malnourished. According to 2001 Census, India's 64% households had no access to safe drinking water. All these shortcomings, if taken together, constitute a strength-less, stamina-less and disease-prone Indians, who are poor and ignorant too. This is responsible also for a low level of efficiency and sturdiness in Indian workforce, resulting in low productivity. Shall we ever be able to construct a powerful economy and polity in India whose 67% population is physically weak and disease prone? The answer is ____ certainly not.

The magnitude of the sanitary problems is particularly severe for children aged below six years. The latest report released by 'Child Rights & You' states that 52 per cent children living in Delhi's slums and unauthorised colonies defecate in the open. In addition, these children also lack safe drinking water facilities, and that leads to the frequent prevalence of water-borne diseases. Given this scenario and coupled with the fact that India's slum population is expected to surge to 104 million (10.4 crore) or 9 per cent of the total population by 2017, there is an urgent need to take corrective measures so that the basic right to clean drinking water and sanitation is assured. The problem of lack of clean drinking water and inadequate sanitation facilities has a global scale to it. The United Nations estimates that there are nearly 2.5 billion people (250 crore), or 37 per cent of the world's population, who still do not use an improved sanitation facility, over one billion (100 crore) practice open defecation even today. In fact, 80 per cent of diseases in developing countries are caused by unsafe water and poor sanitation. According to a study conducted by the National Council for Applied Economic Research, nearly 50% of the Indian population will be living in the cities by 2050. This will put enormous pressure on urban infrastructure. The state of sanitation remains a powerful indicator of the state of human development in any community.

India's Central and State Governments together spend only around 1% of nation's GDP on health, as shown hereunder;

Year 2003-04   ____   0.99% of the GDP
Year 2004-05   ____   1.03% of the GDP
Year 2006-07   ____   1.13% of the GDP
Year 2009-10   ____   1.1% of the GDP

The budgetary allocation for healthcare in 2015-16 is Rs. 33,152 crore, a little over Rs. 30,645 crore for 2014-15. Significantly, last year, in order to meet its fiscal deficit target, the government had abruptly cut the health budget to Rs. 24,400 crore, which reflected the fiscal challenge the sector faces. The total health spend in the first three years of the 12th Five –Year Plan has been about Rs. 70,000 Crore, way below the Rs. 2,68,000 crore budgetary allocation in the year 2012-17 period. It is no surprise, then, that public healthcare spending in India, at about 1% of GDP, is the lowest when compared to China's 3%, Brazil's 4.1% and 8.3% of the U.S.

The importance shown by our Central and State Governments in sparing their resources for the needs of Indian people's health and medical facilities is clear from these figures. Although, India has achieved significant improvement in various health indicators like life expectancy, infant and maternal mortality rate, yet countries in similar stage of development as China, Indonesia, Sri Lanka etc. have performed much better. India's around 43 million people live in slums in our cities and urban centers which account for around 15% of the urban population. Lack of sanitation and poor quality of drinking water lead them to high incidence of diseases and deaths. There is a need to provide clean drinking water and proper sanitation especially in slums and backward/remote rural areas so that these poor people can be saved from water-borne diseases. In this way, there hard-earned money may be saved to augment their protein rich diet. We have only 33% population in India who has access to improved sanitation.

But the real question is, how is this to be done? Our hard pressed governments of resources are not in a position to do much towards this end. Now they have allowed private sector to step in the health and medical field, but their primary motive is profit, not service. Their target groups are rich and prosperous sections who can pay the high fees of the private hospitals. The poor and downtrodden even shudder to think about them, let alone their entry into them. Corruption is very high in our government hospitals and dispensaries. Doctors and other helping staff are short vis-à-vis the number of patients visit there and a total anarchy and mismanagement prevail all over this sector. Recently big scams came into light in U.P. and other States in NRHM and NUHM. Thousands of crores of rupees have been plundered by the authorities in the form of bogus billing and an enquiry is going on by the Central Bureau of Investigation (CBI). What little is provided to health/medical sector, did not even reach the needy and poor, and they are left high and dry.

The Society for Less Investigative Medicine initiated by All India Institute of Medical Sciences doctors, fights unnecessary tests prescribed to patients. This is commendable and urgently required, India's healthcare sector, potentially a revenue source via medical tourism, is instead gaining the reputation of being one of the most dishonest in the world ___ Transparency International even ranks healthcare as the second most corrupt institution Indians encounter after police. Prescribing unnecessary tests at facilities giving doctors commissions in cash or kind is a powerful symptom of how deep this malaise has spread.

A recent article in the British Medical Journal finds a range of tests for X-rays to MRIs, sonographies to ECGs, often boxed under package health checks, routinely prescribed to patients with no need for these. Patients endure such stress only to enrich testing centres, and doctors callously consigning them to expensive, often dangerous tests. This practice reflects a crisis of deliberately squeezed supplies. With huge gaps in doctor numbers____ India has only 387 medical colleges and an average of one doctor per 1,700 people, when WHO recommending a minimum of one per 1100 ____ the pressure is immense.

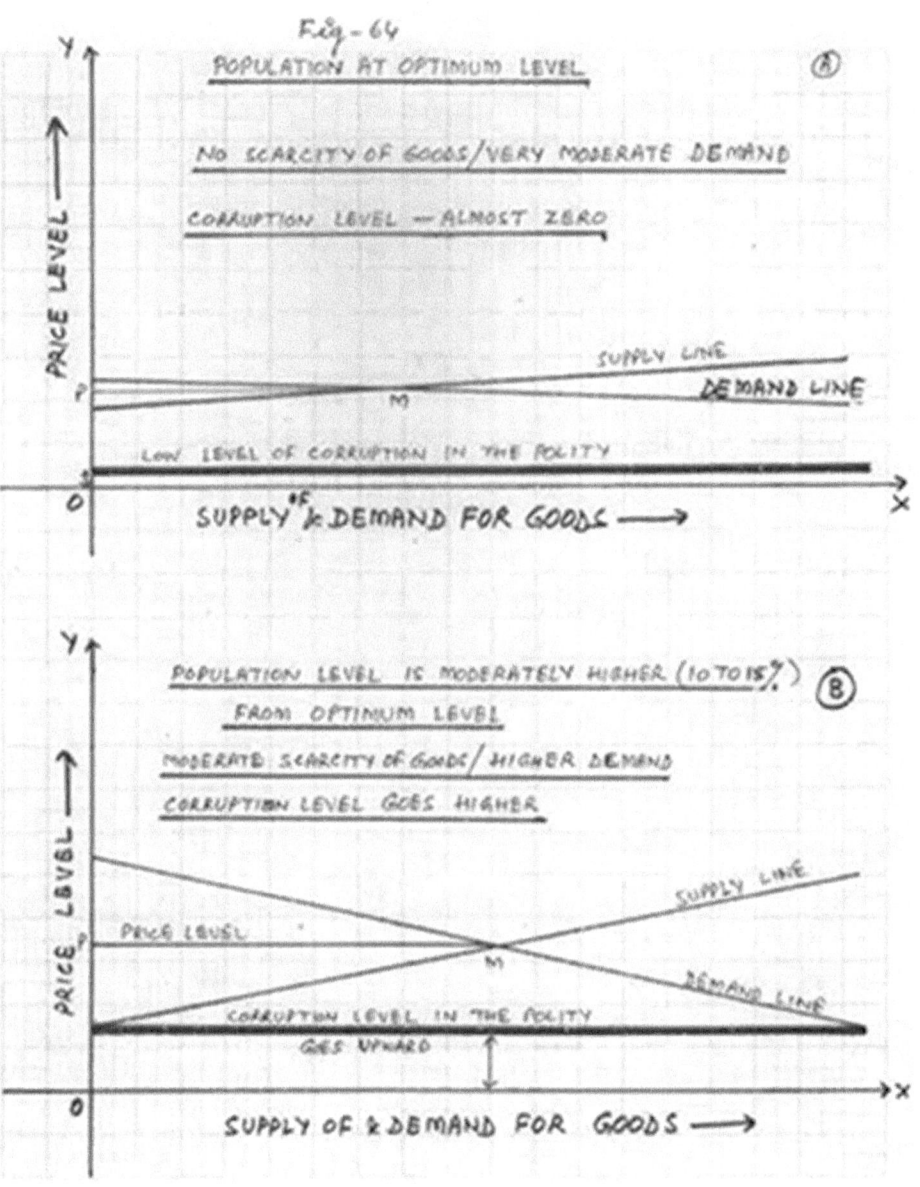

Fig - 64

A

POPULATION AT OPTIMUM LEVEL

NO SCARCITY OF GOODS/VERY MODERATE DEMAND

CORRUPTION LEVEL — ALMOST ZERO

SUPPLY LINE

DEMAND LINE

M

LOW LEVEL OF CORRUPTION IN THE POLITY

PRICE LEVEL

SUPPLY & DEMAND FOR GOODS →

B

POPULATION LEVEL IS MODERATELY HIGHER (10 TO 15%)
FROM OPTIMUM LEVEL

MODERATE SCARCITY OF GOODS/ HIGHER DEMAND

CORRUPTION LEVEL GOES HIGHER

SUPPLY LINE

PRICE LEVEL

M

DEMAND LINE

CORRUPTION LEVEL IN THE POLITY
GOES UPWARD

PRICE LEVEL

SUPPLY OF & DEMAND FOR GOODS →

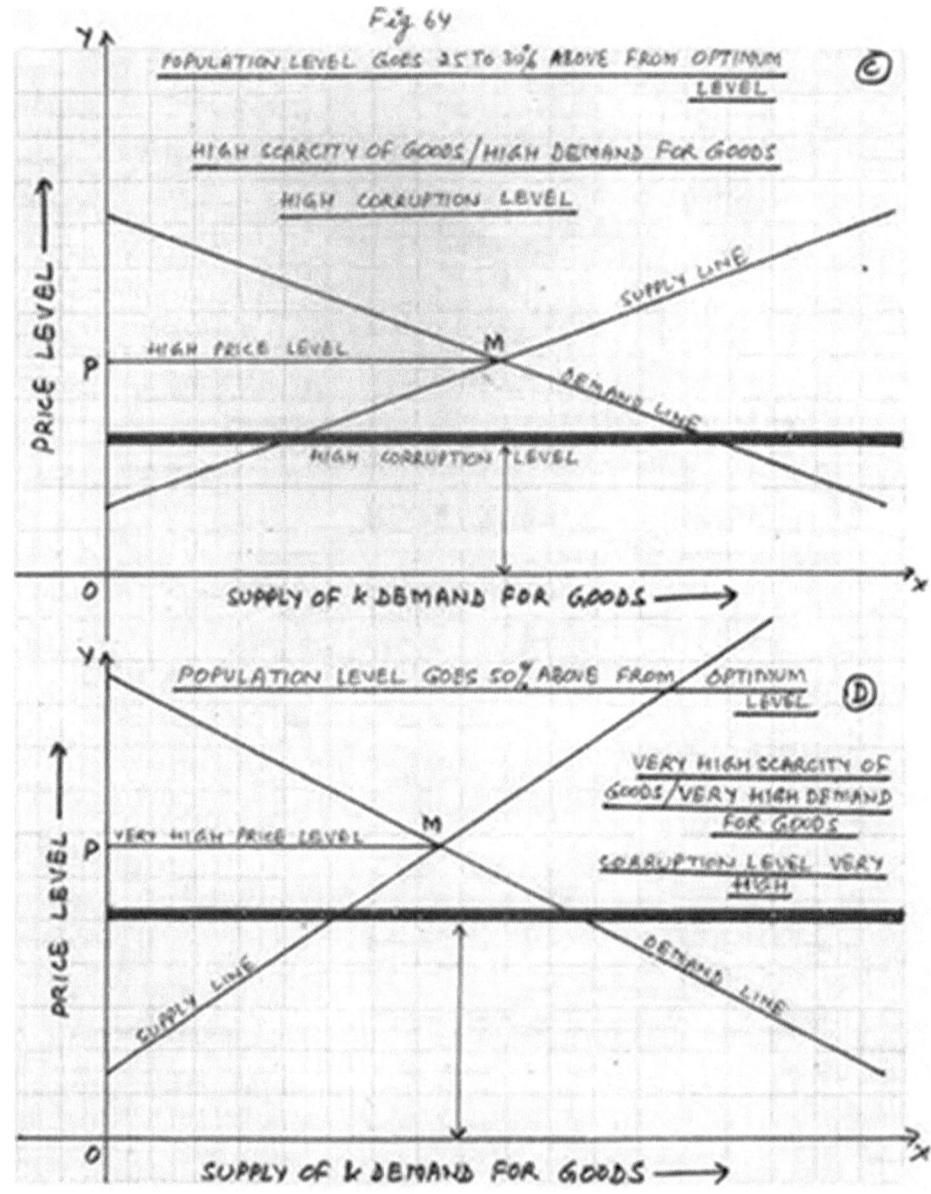

Fig 64

Fig 64

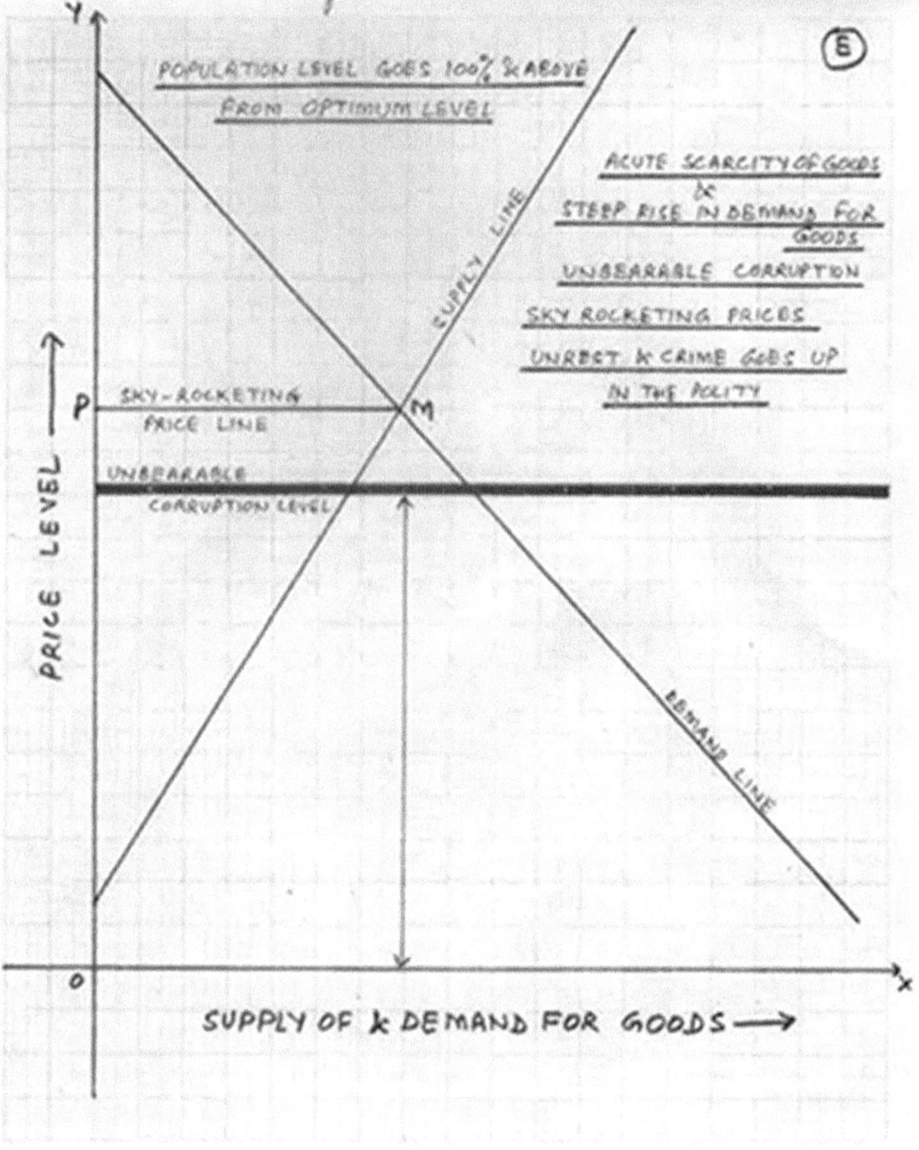

POPULATION LEVEL GOES 100% & ABOVE FROM OPTIMUM LEVEL

ACUTE SCARCITY OF GOODS
&
STEEP RISE IN DEMAND FOR GOODS
UNBEARABLE CORRUPTION
SKY ROCKETING PRICES
UNREST & CRIME GOES UP
IN THE POLITY

SKY-ROCKETING PRICE LINE

UNBEARABLE CORRUPTION LEVEL

SUPPLY LINE

DEMAND LINE

PRICE LEVEL →

SUPPLY OF & DEMAND FOR GOODS →

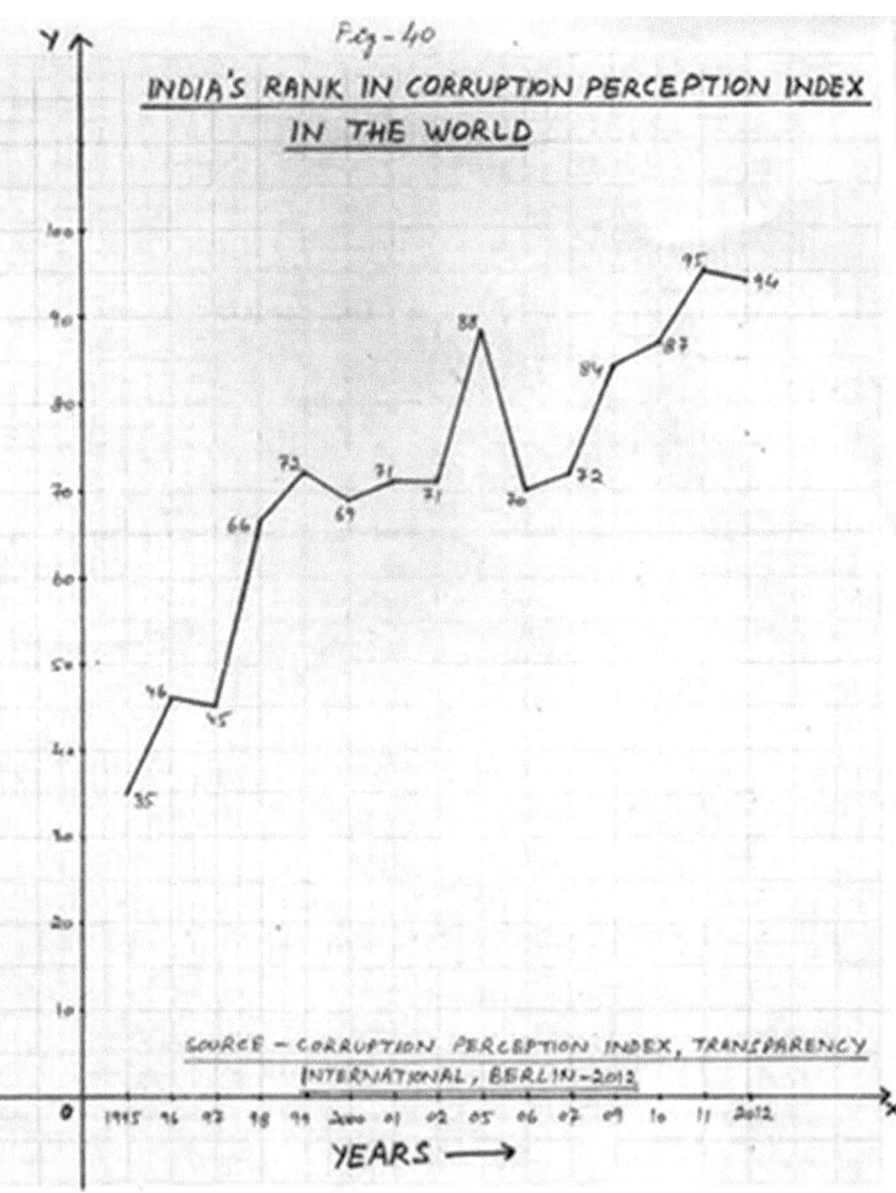

Fig-40

INDIA'S RANK IN CORRUPTION PERCEPTION INDEX IN THE WORLD

SOURCE — CORRUPTION PERCEPTION INDEX, TRANSPARENCY INTERNATIONAL, BERLIN-2012

YEARS →

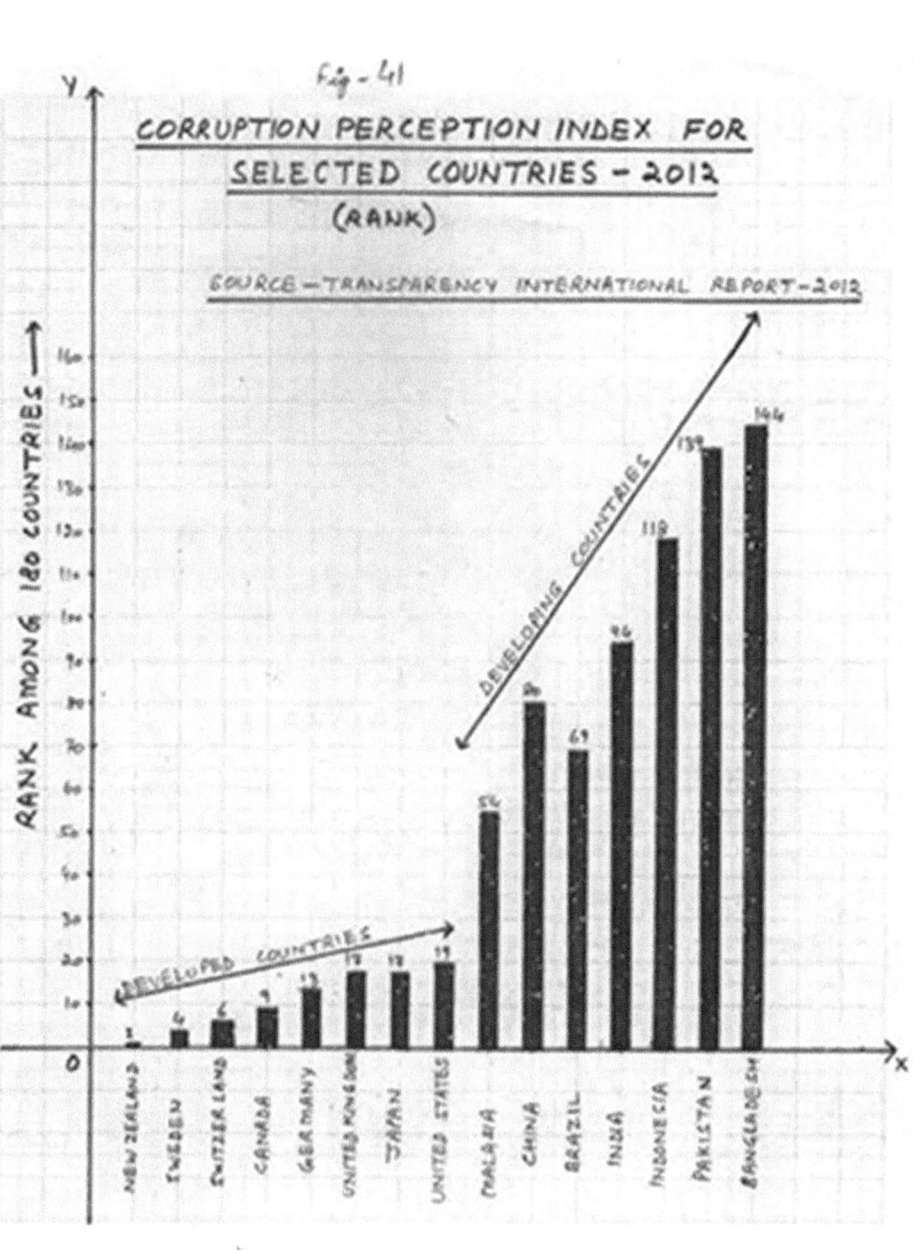

Fig - 41

CORRUPTION PERCEPTION INDEX FOR
SELECTED COUNTRIES - 2012
(RANK)

SOURCE - TRANSPARENCY INTERNATIONAL REPORT - 2012

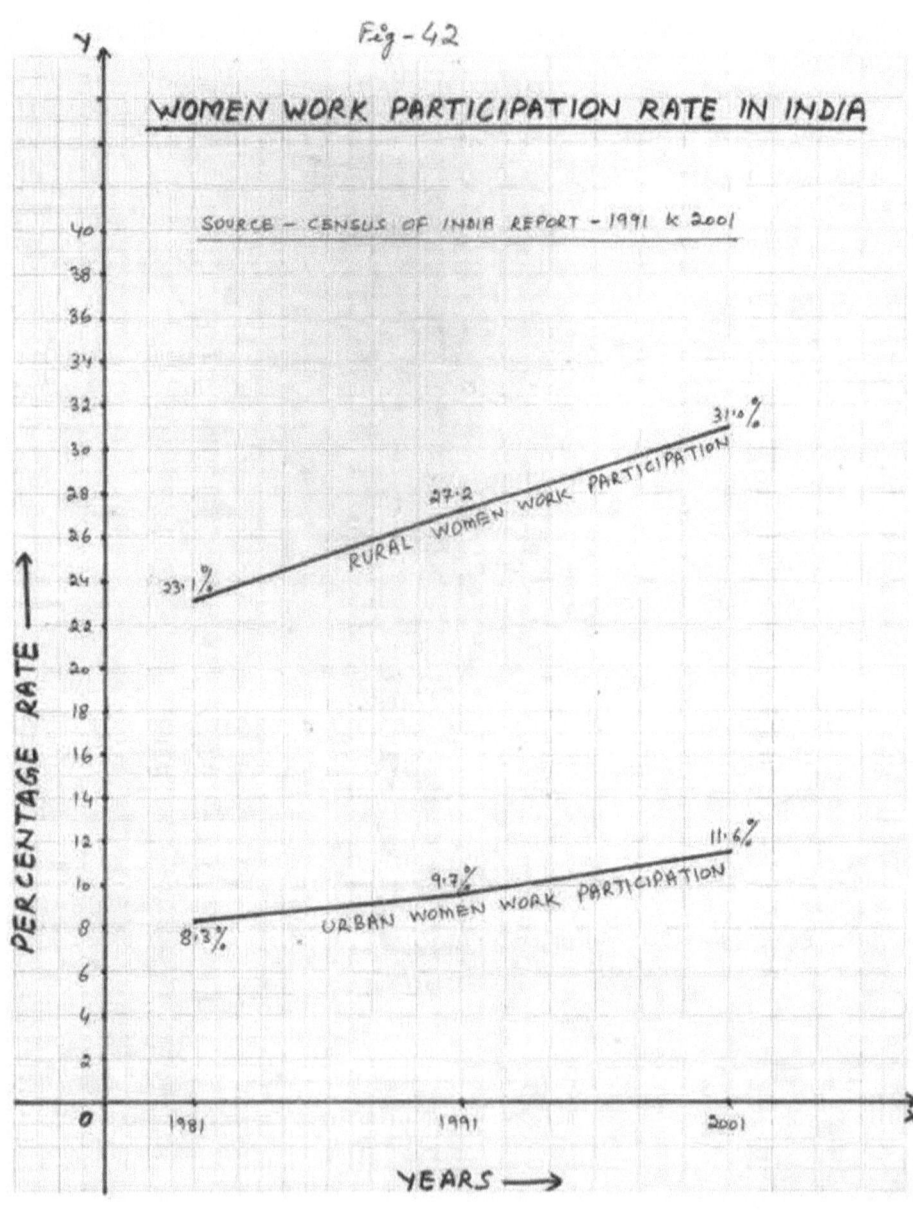

Fig - 42

WOMEN WORK PARTICIPATION RATE IN INDIA

SOURCE - CENSUS OF INDIA REPORT - 1991 & 2001

VICIOUS CIRCLE OF CHILD-LABOUR

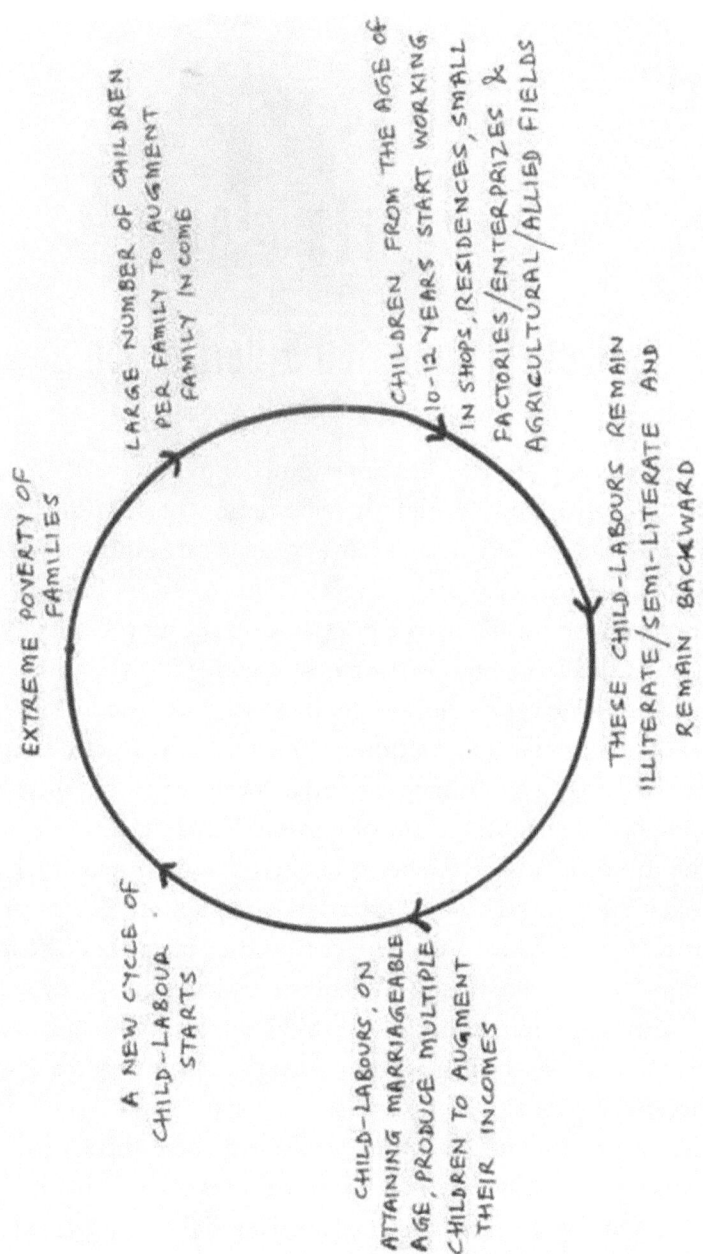

EXTREME POVERTY OF FAMILIES

LARGE NUMBER OF CHILDREN PER FAMILY TO AUGMENT FAMILY INCOME

CHILDREN FROM THE AGE OF 10-12 YEARS START WORKING IN SHOPS, RESIDENCES, SMALL FACTORIES/ENTERPRIZES & AGRICULTURAL/ALLIED FIELDS

THESE CHILD-LABOURS REMAIN ILLITERATE/SEMI-LITERATE AND REMAIN BACKWARD

CHILD-LABOURS, ON ATTAINING MARRIAGEABLE AGE, PRODUCE MULTIPLE CHILDREN TO AUGMENT THEIR INCOMES

A NEW CYCLE OF CHILD-LABOUR STARTS

Fig. 43

CHAPTER – 8

Over – Population & Corruption

Scarcity of goods and services and uncertainty about financial and economic security breed corruption. When the population of a country crosses its optimum level, the level of corruption also goes up simultaneously, for the simple reason, the natural resources get exhausted to its fullest extent and their further demand pushes up the price-line on account of scarcity of goods and services. At this level, now, in economy, it increasingly becomes more and more difficult to match the supply of goods & services vis-à-vis their demand. This situation gives birth to government controls, quota/permit regime, lure of profiteering through hoarding of essential goods, and other illegal practices such as adulteration, manufacturing of spurious items etc. As the mass poverty spreads, the government resort to heavy taxation on the rich in order to finance various welfare schemes through subsidies and support prices for essential commodities, the tax evasion also comes into the picture and the monster of black-money comes into existence. All this necessitates greater dependency on the middlemen and bureaucrats. These middlemen and bureaucracy want to take full benefit of the shortages and resort to corrupt practices by denying the benefits to the poor and needy and sidelining the goods for black-marking which were meant for the poor and needy. All these things happen when essential goods and services are in scarcity vis-à-vis their demand. As the gap between demand for essential goods & services and its suppy widens, prices and corruption go up too. Illiteracy, ignorance and backwardness perpetuate corruption as these people can not resist the wrongdoers who are clever enough and better united. These ignorant poor people do not know the laws and rules meant for their protection and are totally unaware of their civil and legal rights. They are so gullible and simple that every government official or trader easily exploits them. **Actually, over population in any country and ignorance of its masses are the two sides of the same coin. The degree of ignorance and backwardness varies according to the extent of over population goes ahead of the optimum level.** We have shown in fig. 64A, 64B, 64C, 64D & 64E, a close relationship between the aggregate demand & aggregate supply in an economy and the level of corruption prevailing therein, keeping in view the population level. Now we shall take up these separately;

Fig-64A: This is a situation of the country when it is having an optimum level of population. The goods and services are in reasonably good suppy and can be made available easily as per the demand. Here aggregate demand and supply lines are almost parallel to the x-axis. Prices of essential goods and services are at reasonably low level and every citizen of the country is reasonably satisfied. They maintain harmonious relations with one another. Corruption level is either zero or negligible. Since every family is well educated, adequately prosperous and well-aware of their civil rights and duties with abundance of goods and services, the case for corruption does not arise.

Fig 64 (B): This situation depicts that population of the country has increased and reached at a level where it is around 10 to 15% higher than the optimum level. Here, constraints begin to develop, though very nominally. Aggregate supply line and aggregate demand line slightly move slantingly upward which shows that the aggregate demand level in the economy is on the rise and the corresponding aggregate supply of goods & services are available, though at a higher price-level. This causes the general price level in the economy slightly higher than in the previous case of 64(A), but situation here is not alarming and the level of corruption is still low, though higher in comparison to 64 (A) situation.

Fig 64 (C): Here, the population of the country further grows and reaches at 25 to 30% above the level of optimum number. The economic situation begins to show clear signs of constraints as the scarcity of goods and services raises its head. Production of goods and services lag behind in comparison to growing demand, pushing above the general price-line for all the commodities. General poverty raises its head and compels the government to resort to heavy taxation and mild doses of deficit financing to prop up the poor and downtrodden classes. This impacted the inflationary pressures on the economy and an endless spiral of price-rise, deficit financing, inflation and import-burden start to operate. Underemployment and unemployment show its ugly heads and unscrupulous politicians, rapacious bureaucrats, profit-hungry corporate world, business tycoons and other middlemen start fishing in troubled waters of the economy. Corruption takes a high seat and becomes omnipresent in every branch of economic activity. Kota/permit regime spreads its wings.

Fig 64 (D&E): If population growth of the country continues unhindered, then a time comes when it reaches around 50% or more above the optimum level and economic situation turns more serious. Mounting demand for goods & services and dwindling supplies of the same on account of exploding human population raise the general price-level to a very high position. Common people fail to purchase the essential items to sustain their daily life. Underemployment and unemployment further increases in numbers and common people's real incomes further go downward. Government imposes more heavy taxation (direct & indirect both) to augment its financial resources, still can not cope with the situation in the face of gigantic welfare tasks ahead. Then it resorts to more heavy volume of deficit financing, more public debt and more imports to save its face. This situation lands its economy into an inflationary rise of prices, heavy burden of internal and external debts, a general feeling of unrest among the organised and unorganised workers, farmers and other sections of the society. Now country witnesses strikes, lock-outs, street-violence, crimes and riots, destruction of public property, loss of human lives, increased unproductive expenditure on police and paramilitary forces etc. Economic development and growth takes a back seat for want of resources. Corruption becomes unbearable.

In fig 64 (E), the population figure goes up to more than double of the optimum level, situations become highly explosive. **Total anarchy and lawlessness prevail in the polity, as we have been witnessing in today's India.** Price-rise and inflation become unbearable and out of control, underemployment and unemployment assume very high position, economy falls in the grip of debt-trap, both internal and external, unbound corruption in political and government machinery, percolating down in the general public too, high level of pollution on account of imbecile conspicuous consumption by the rich and powerful, threat to biodiversity and environment are the glaring symptoms of this volatile situation. No government can tackle the situation effectively, where the economy is placed in. **A vicious circle of abject poverty, unemployment/underemployment, high inflation and stagnation both, starts to operate.** The author feels that the economic situation becomes totally untenable and unmanageable, quickly heading towards a black-hole, nobody knows what would be its destination.

No wonder, India remains one of the most corrupt nations of the world. A Transparency International survey has shown that India is more corrupt than three of its BRICS peers _____ China, South Africa and Brazil. According to the list, India has scored 36 points on a scale of 0-100, where 0 means that a country is perceived as highly corrupt and 100 means it is perceived as very clean. The nation's money has been looted by a vast majority of bureaucrats _____ some of them work for State Governments, others with the Union Government and some at Public Sector Units. India has about 1.93 crore babus compared to some 5100 lawmakers.

As shown in fig (40), India's corruption perception index in terms of ranks among the 180 countries of the world has been increasing since Independence. India was at 35th rank in 1995 which went up to 88 in 2005 and now in 2012, it is at 94. This shows that in India, the corruption level is very high and it is regularly increasing with every passing year. In fig (41), a comparison is given among the developed and the developing countries of the world in respect of corruption perception index for the year 2012. While developed countries show a low level of corruption perception index (it ranges from 1 to 19), the developing countries' index is very high, ranging from 54 to 144. It is not a coincidence that all the developing countries of the world today are overpopulated while developed world is having a reasonable level of population. However, it can not be said as to whether they are having optimum level or not. **It clearly demonstrates that the over population and corruption have a co-relation and maintain a symbiotic existence.**

Over population Vs Women Empowerment

Over population of a country like India and its women empowerment are inversely related. When population of a country increases rapidly, it means the rate of birth of babies is very high, may be 4,5 or more per woman which portrays a household picture wherein women are confined to the four walls of their homes and their whole life-time is consumed in child-birth, his/

her rearing and look-after routine, nursing at the time of illness etc. These women have got no time for themselves and their welfare. They remain over-burdened with the household work and children-care. They belong to generally poor families who can not provide them with a healthy and wholesome diet, resulting in their mal-nourished physique and disease prone life. They remain illiterate or semi-literate because of their poverty and social backwardness.

In India, most of the rural and urban slum dwelling women fall under this category. In cities, lower middle class and lower class women join them too. They are all ignorant, socially backward and mostly illiterate or semi-literate. Now with the spread of girl education in India, the picture is slowly changing, but not impressively. Poverty does not allow them to continue their education and they drop-out after primary level or even earlier. Very few girls in urban lower class and rural areas are fortunate enough to go to above primary or higher classes. **Woman empowerment is impossible without a good education, at least up to graduate level.** As shown in table 68-A, drop out rates for girls at primary level in 2004-05 was 36.1% for SCs, 42% for STs and 25.4% for all categories. Similarly, dropout rates for girls at elementary level in 2004-05 were 60% for SCs, 67.1% for STs and 51.3% for all categories. This shows that more than half number of enrolled girls leave the school without completing their elementary education.

Table 68-A
Drop out Rates by Social-Composition (2004-05)

Category	Primary (1-5)			Elementary (1-8)		
	Boys	**Girls**	**Total**	**Boys**	**Girls**	**Total**
SCs	32.7	36.1	34.2	55.2	60	57.3
STs	42.6	42.0	42.3	65.0	67.1	65.9
All	31.8	25.4	29.0	50.5	51.3	50.8

Note- Figures are percentage of total enrolment; **Source-** Ministry of Human Resource Development; Selected Educational Statistics (2004-05 MHRD)

Further in table 68-B below, only 45.28% girls in the country join the secondary education and only 24.46% girls the Higher Secondary education. Out of this population, 63.88% or around 64% girls leave the schools as drop-outs. This figure shows that only around 29% of total eligible girls (around

2.25 crore) in India could pass Secondary level in 2004-05, which comes out as around 75 lakh. Women empowerment can never be achieved with this level of education and literacy. Unless women of India are economically independent, their empowerment shall remain a distant dream. At least education up to graduate level will enable them to acquire a gainful employment which is the only way to achieve women empowerment.

Table 68-B
Drop-out Rates & Secondary Enrolment (2004-05)
Enrolment in Crores

Category	Boys	Girls	Total
1- Secondary (IX-X)	1.42 (57.39%)	1.01 (45.28%)	2.43 (51.65%)
2- Higher Secondary (XI-XII)	0.74 (30.82%)	0.53 (24,46%)	1.27 (27.82%)
3- Secondary & Higher Secondary (IX-XII)	2.16 (44.26%)	1.54 (35.05%)	3.70 (39.91%)
4- Drop-out Rates	60.41%	63.88%	61.92%

Note- Figures in brackets are Gross Enrolment Ratios-percentage of enrolment in the relevant age group 14-18 years for class IX to XII
Source- MHRD, Selected Educational Statistics (2004-05)

As the over population level is growing year after year and Government of India's financial resources are shrinking, we can never expect our education level to go up in the future. However, level of awareness among the young generation is increasing through other means, for example cinema and television/radio etc, which made a great impact on their mindset. First cinema came in bigger cities, then in towns and slowly in small towns and its appeal/impact was much deeper, as it was the only means of entertainment for the general public. Even village people enthusiastically participate in cinema shows by and large. Then came radio/transistor and television, first in big cities, then in tier II and tier III cities and finally got its place in small towns and villages. Battery operated television sets have been made available in non-electrified or electric-scarce villages. This television revolution impacted deeply on the mindset of the general public and enhanced their general awareness vis-à-vis national/socio-economic problems of India. This resulted in adopting to small family norms by many of the young people in cities, towns and villages. Now the rate of population growth has slowed down in India and in 2011 Census, it was calculated as 17.64% only from 21.54% in 2001 Census, 23.87% in 1991 Census and 24.66% in 1981 Census.

But this declining rate of population growth does not impact much on the overall population landscape, because, it has already grown to a dangerous level and we are now more than double of the optimum level. As far as the empowerment of women in concerned, economic independence of women is a necessary condition in India as well as in all the nations of the world. Western women are empowered because they are economically self-dependent. In India, as shown in fig. (42), in 1981, only 23.1% rural women were earning members and only 8.3% urban women were earning members. In 1991, this figure improved to 27.3% and 9.7% respectively and in 2001, this further improved to 31% and 11.6% respectively. A report in The Times of India tells us;

Nearly 160 million women in India, 88% of which are of working age __ that is between 15 to 59 years __ just remain at home doing "household duties", according to Census-2011 data that has just been released. Note that these are women who reported themselves as 'not working'. All the other women who work, whether full time or part time, also do domestic work. But these 16 crore are Great Invisible Workforce, primarily involved in care work and rearing families. The total number of women in the age group 15-59, according to Census data released earlier, is just under 355 million. What the latest data shows is that about 45% of them, or nearly half, are confined solely to domestic duties.

It is clear from these figures that economic independence for most of the women in India is still a far cry, without which their empowerment is unthinkable. It is possible only when Indian government strictly adheres to enforcing 'two-children per couple' norms, which in turn shall strengthen the 'family of four' economically, make it healthier, educated and well aware in all respects.

Problem of Child-Labour in India

The problem of child-labour in India is closely associated with the state of extreme poverty and level of over-population. Cause/effect relationship acts and reacts both ways. Extreme poverty due to over population encourages poor couples to have large number of children so that they, after attaining an age of 08-12 years, start working in retail and repairing shops, in homes as domestic workers, in small & medium industries & enterprises, in agriculture & allied fields etc. These child-laborers earn petty amount on daily or monthly basis which augments their family's income. In this way, they are regarded as 'assets' for their families and never fall under the category of 'liabilities'. But, for society as a whole, they fall under the category of 'liabilities' as they never go to school to get themselves educated, thus remain illiterate or semi-literate and join the large bandwagon of potentially large family segment of population on attaining the marriageable age. **They start the same cycle of having multiple children to augment their monthly income. The vicious cycle of extreme poverty and large family status continues unchecked and these people remain poor and the nation remains over-populated.**

There exists a vicious circle of poverty and over population (fig 43). India has 43.5 lakh labourers in the age group of 5 to 14 years, according to the 2011 Census. Uttar Pradesh has the maximum number of child workers with nearly 9 lakh and a majority of them are in the rural areas. This is followed by Maharashtra with close to 5 lakh. Compared to 2001 Census, there is a drop of 65% in the number of workers in this age group. In the last Census, there were 1.3 crore children aged 5 to 14 working full time in various factories, shops and establishments. A combination of efforts by governments through various legislations, judicial intervention and also by various non-governmental organizations (NGOs) seems to have brought down the number of child labourers in the country. The 2009-10 NSSO survey estimated that there were 49.8 lakh child labourers.

It has been proved beyond reasonable doubt that child labour perpetuates a vicious circle of illiteracy and poverty. Employers prefer children over adults primarily because they do not ask for minimum wages. They work long hours with very little or no pay. Children cannot unionise and raise their voice against exploitation that they face at the hands of their employers. It is important to note that globally, there are 168 million child labourers and around 190 million unemployed adults. Clearly every child works in place of an adult. These children keep on doing repetitive tasks; they miss out on education and grow up to become unskilled individuals with eroded employability, thus remain stuck in poverty.

The Child-labour employment slowed down in India on account of Parliament / States Legislatures enacted laws to declare child-labour employment a cognizable offence, but child labour is still in existence in India. This heinous and inhuman act can never be ceased and obliterated from the landscape of India, till the extreme poverty and over population exist in the nation.

Fig - 44

KNOWN CAUSES OF ANIMAL EXTINCTION
SINCE 1600 A.D.

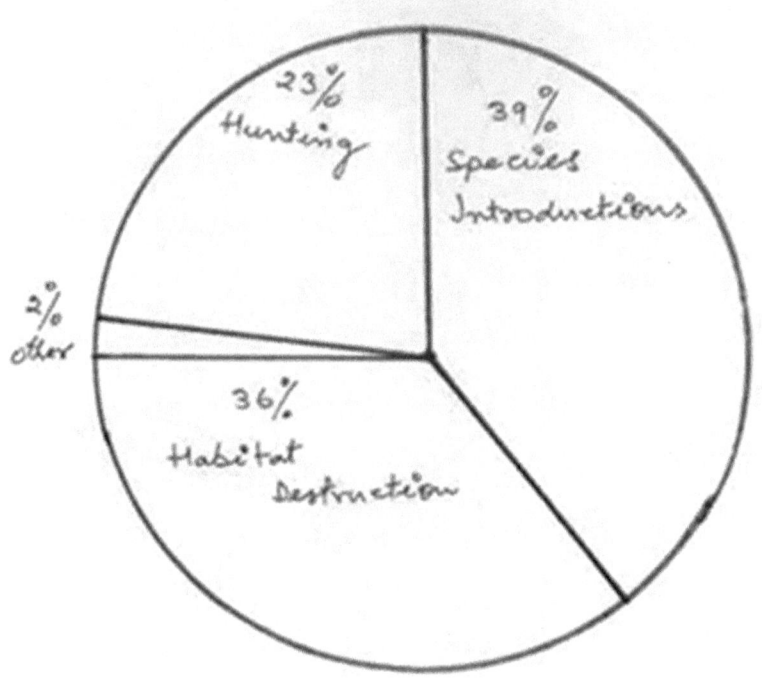

Fig. 46

EXPANSION OF HUMAN SETTLEMENT

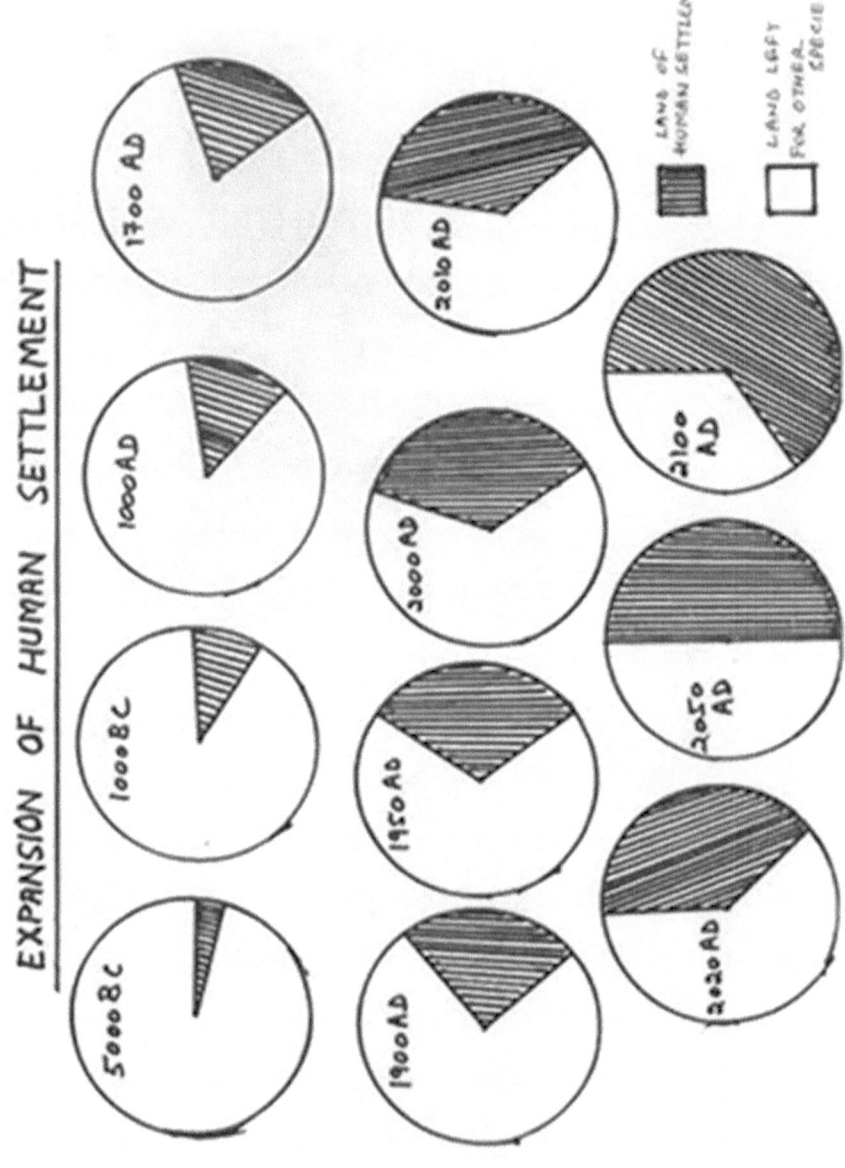

5000 BC

1000 BC

1000 AD

1700 AD

1900 AD

1950 AD

3000 AD

2010 AD

2020 AD

2050 AD

2100 AD

LAND OF HUMAN SETTLEMENT

LAND LEFT FOR OTHER SPECIES

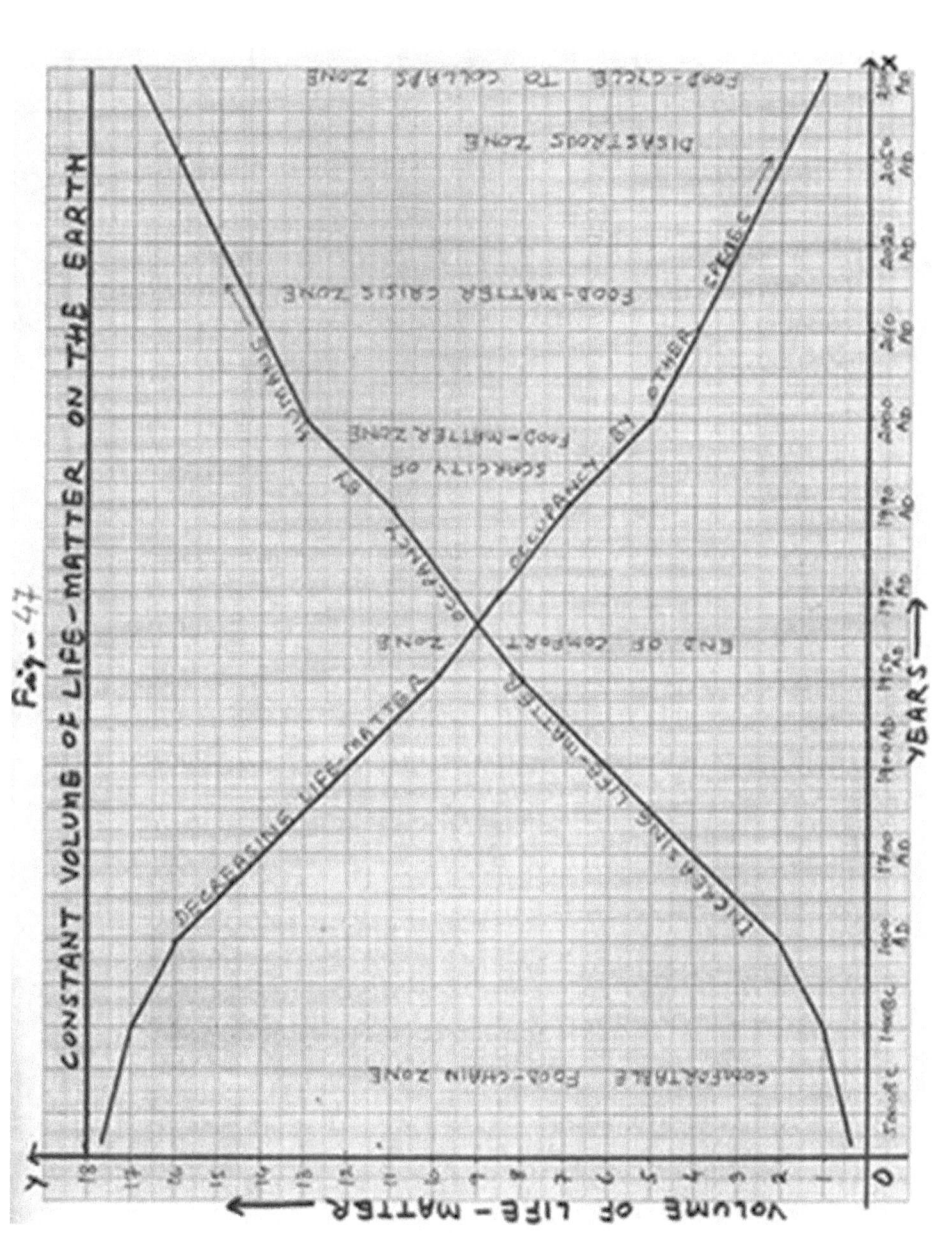

Fig - 47

Fig-48

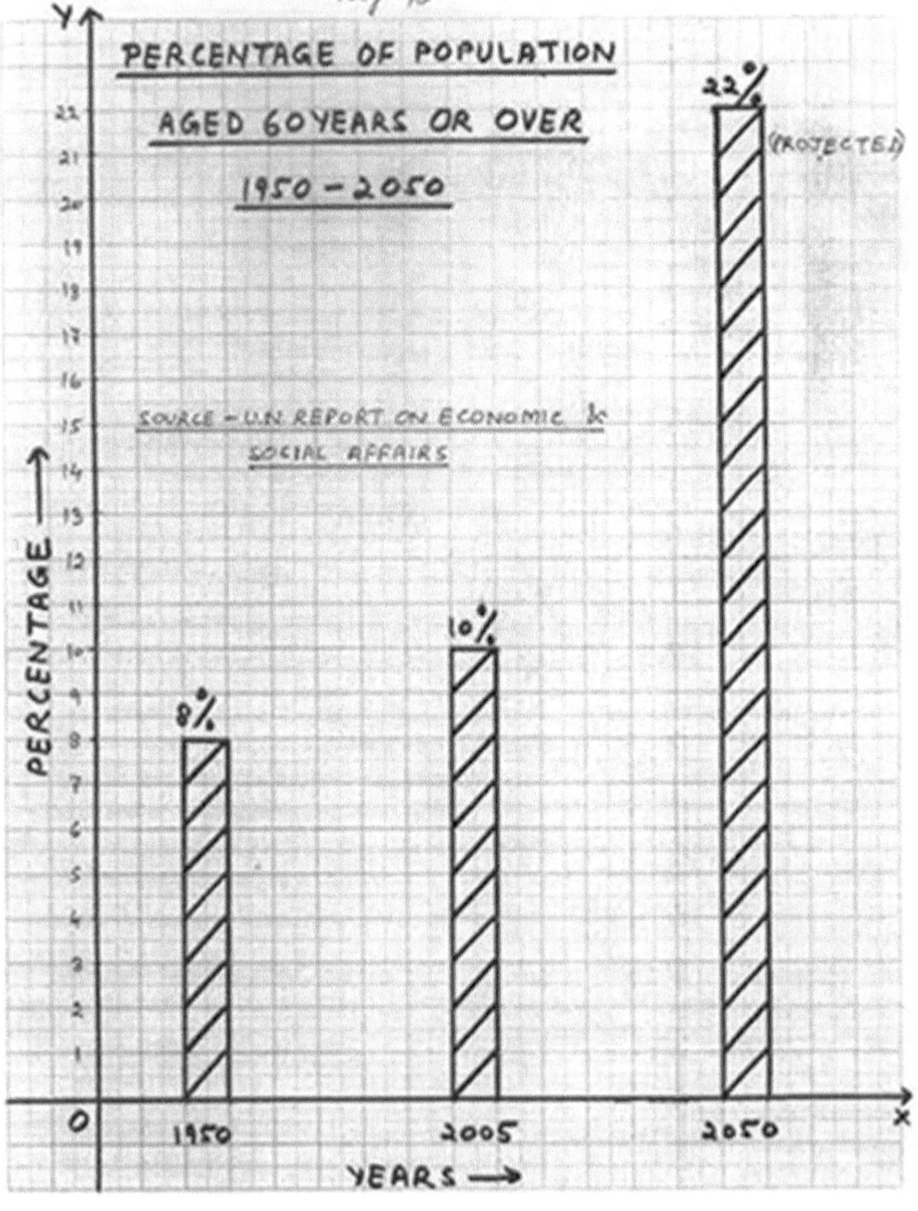
PERCENTAGE OF POPULATION
AGED 60 YEARS OR OVER
1950 - 2050
SOURCE - U.N. REPORT ON ECONOMIC & SOCIAL AFFAIRS
PERCENTAGE
YEARS
8%
10%
22%
(PROJECTED)
1950
2005
2050
Y
X
0

Fig-49

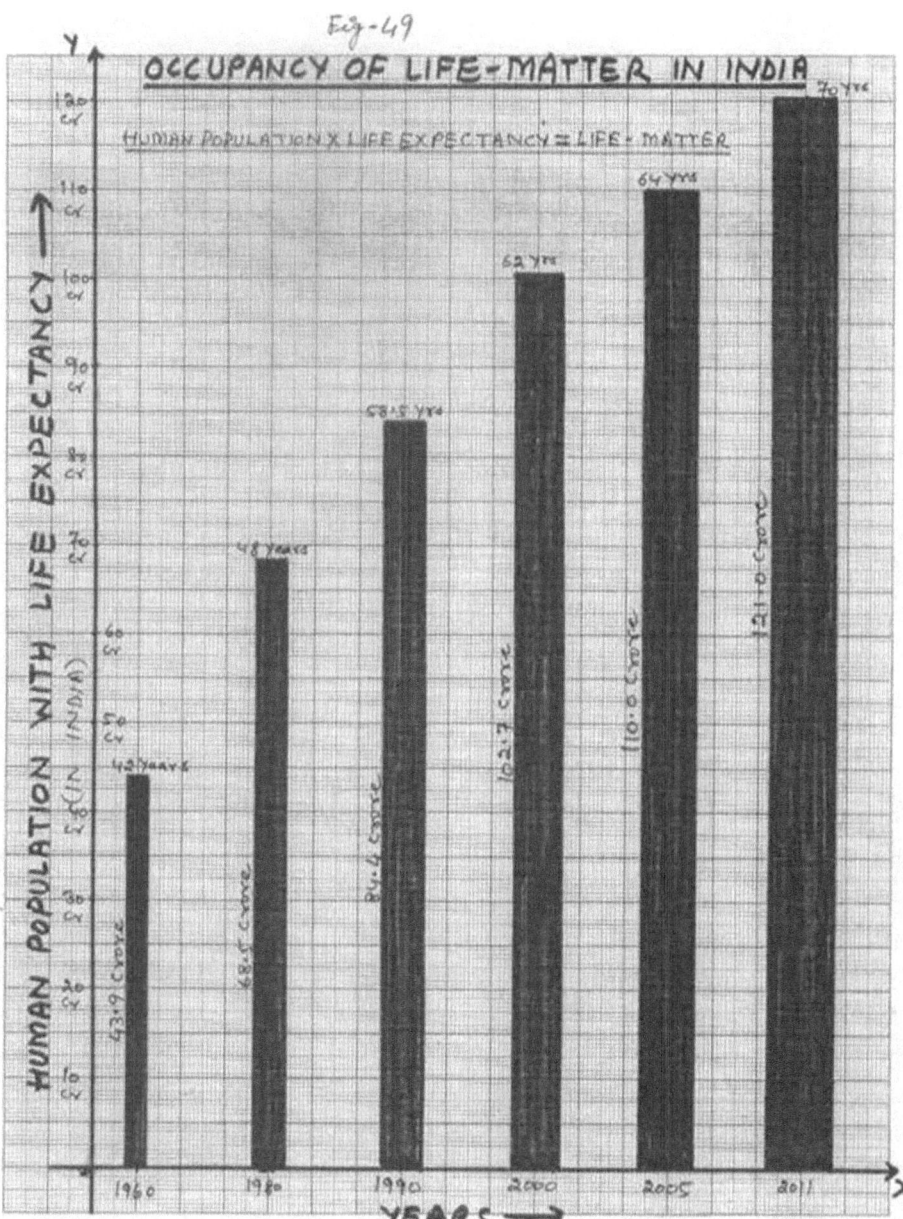

OCCUPANCY OF LIFE-MATTER IN INDIA

HUMAN POPULATION × LIFE EXPECTANCY = LIFE-MATTER

CHAPTER – 9

Threat to Biodiversity

Biodiversity or biological diversity, comprising the variety of all life forms on earth, is essential for our existence. It is a simple concept, but its conservation is a complex issue involving multiple stakeholders across a number of natural resource management and environmental sectors. However, recent concerns on biodiversity loss and reporting requirements of international biodiversity arrangements have called the world's attention to inventorying and monitoring of the wealth of biodiversity. There has been a significant change in the geographical ranges and species composition of India's flora and fauna, and a dramatic change in India's natural eco-systems over the last 100 years. The decline in biodiversity is due to the multitude of actions taken daily by individual land mongers, industries, communities and governments contributing to the loss of native species and their habitat, reducing soil condition and water quality, and modifying ecosystems so that they no longer function as they should. Many of there actions are taken without any real understanding of the long term environmental costs. Although it is recognised that the economic progress and health of ecosystems and biodiversity are intricably linked, the economic forces themselves have become a foremost reason for biodiversity loss in recent times. If mismanaged, it will become impossible to regenerate and replicate these natural resources and ecosystems that harbour unique and varied biodiversity.

Biodiversity is important for the human existence and ecological – balance maintenance. The term biodiversity refers to the totality of genes, species and ecosystems of a region and has many medicinal and economic uses. Genes of wild species are used to confer new properties, such as disease resistance or improved yield in domesticated species. Biodiversity also provides valuable indirect services through natural ecosystem. The total number of species on the earth is estimated to range from 5 to 50 million and average at 14 million, but only about 1.8 million species have so far been known and described, which is fewer than 15% of the total species on the earth. Biodiversity has three levels; (1) genetic biodiversity, (2) species biodiversity and (3) community and ecosystem biodiversity.

Biodiversity increases from poles towards equator and from high elevations to low elevations. Biodiversity has contributed in many ways to the development of human culture, and, in turn, humans have played a major role in shaping the diversity of nature at the genetic, species, and ecological levels. All species contribute some kind of function to the ecosystem. They capture and store energy, produce organic material, decompose organic material, help to cycle water and nutrients throughout the ecosystem, control erosion of pests, fix atmospheric gases, or help regulate climate. Biodiversity also provides us various supports of production, for example, soil fertility, pollinators of plants, predators, decomposition of wastes etc, and various services such as purification of the air and water, stabilization and moderation of the climate, control of flooding, drought and other environmental disasters. These functions are important to an ecosystem and to human survival. Biodiversity provides food; crops, livestock, forestry, fish and several other medicines. Wild plant species have been used for medical purposes since the dawn of human civilization. For example, quinine, a bitter alkaloid extracted from chinchona bark, used in malaria therapy, comes from chinchona tree. Similarly, morphine is extracted from poppy plant for pain relief. According to National Cancer Institute, over 70% of the promising anti – cancer drugs come from plants in the tropical rainforests.

Plants provide fibres for clothing, wood for shelter and warmth. Biodiversity is a source of energy such as biomass. Other important and useful products provided by the biodiversity are; oils, lubricants, perfumes, fragrances, dyes, paper, waxes, rubber, latexes, resins, poisons and cork. Supplies from animals are wool, silk, fur, leather, lubricants etc. Humans use animals as a mode of transportation. In other words, human existence is unthinkable without biodiversity or various forms of flora & fauna, found on the earth. But in modern era, due to insane human actions, species and ecosystems are threatened with destruction to such an extent as rarely seen in earth's history. Since the advent of Industrial Revolution, this destruction of biodiversity and ecosystem has become an easy target owing to large scale demand for goods and services to satisfy the mounting needs of more than 700 crore humans. As the human population crossed 700 crore figure in March 2011, we have transformed, degraded or destroyed roughly half of the world's forests. Humans appropriate roughly half of the world's net primary productivity for their use and appropriated most of the available fresh water for their use. Further, humans harvest virtually all the available productivity of the oceans. The results of all these activities on the part of humans necessitated the disappearance of several species and ecosystems are in danger of destruction. Over hunting has been another significant cause of extinction of hundreds of species and the endangerment of many more, such as whales, loins, tigers and many more large mammals. Most extinctions over the past several hundred years are mainly due to man's lust of over – harvesting the animals for food, fashion, whims and profits. As shown in fig (44), known causes of animal extinctions are; 23% due to hunting, 39% due to species introduction, 36% due to habitat destruction and 2% due to other reasons.

Fast growing population of humans necessitated increased need of land for agriculture and allied activities which have been causing the conversion of forested land into agriculture land for the last 500 year or more. With the discovery of the New World i.e. American continents by Columbus, the destruction of its lowland, seasonal and deciduous forests began on a large scale and caused its disappearance thereafter. They converted these forests into agriculture land which caused its animal assets totally destroyed. Tropical forests are very important, for they harbour at least 50% or more of world's biodiversity. U.N. reports and satellite data show that world's forest cover is fast declining. The original extent of tropical rain forests was 15 million Km^2, which now remained about 7.8 to 8 million Km^2, nearly half is gone. The current rate of loss is estimated at 2% annually. The rate of forest cover loss in the world clearly shows that by the end of the 21st century, the tropical rain forests will be reduced to only 10 to 25% of their original cover, if corrective steps are not taken soon, and with that loss of forest cover, biodiversity too will disappear very fast.

'Enormous growth of human population and its destructive and blind race for economic development together have caused global warming and climate change, which, in turn, is threatening the species and ecosystems both. Climate change may simply affect plants and animals, as they can not easily shift to other suitable regions. Since, they can not adjust abrupt climate change, they will perish. As a consequence of these multiple forces working against the nature, many scientists fear that by the end of twenty first century, around 25% of the existing species will be lost, if immediate corrective measures are not taken. Currently, many environmental groups and governments including the U.N are worried about extinction of species due to human intervention and human expansion which is causing pollution, destruction of habitat, climate change and introduction of new predators. Human expansion or human population growth beyond optimum level is the biggest danger to biodiversity.

Threat to Biodiversity in India

India has been endowed with a very rich biodiversity on account of its vast & varied landscapes from north to south and from east to west. Since Indian subcontinent falls under tropical zone of the world, mother Nature has endowed it with a very good amount of rains due to Monsoon and otherwise. Rains prop-up forests and other plants in a big way which give shelter to our biodiversity and a favourable ecosystems. In India, we have various biodiversity regions, for example, Deccan peninsula, which has the most extension coverage of the Indian landmass (42%), the Western and Eastern Ghats, north – east and the Tarai region, Sub – Himalayan region etc. These bio – geographical regions have several habitats, biotic communities and ecosystems. A large number of species are found in these regions and they are endemic, exclusive to India only. About 33% of the flowering plants found in India are endemic to this country only. In India, we found many endemic fauna, for example, out of the recorded vertebrates, 53% fresh water fish, 60% amphibians, 36% reptiles and 10% mammalian fauna are endemic in nature. These species are concentrated and mainly in north – east, Western Ghats, north – west Himalayalas and Andaman & Nicobar Islands.

In India, we observe the cutting down and clearing of forests and increased pollution of its water – bodies consequent upon its fast growing population have been posing a great threat to its biodiversity and ecosystems. In India, we have a dense forest cover of only 12% of its total land area which was 30% at the time of independence in 1947. This reduction of dense forest cover is due to high demand for land for agriculture to increase food grain production and other consumer items for the abnormally growing human population. While, at the time of independence, India's population was only around 320 million, has now crossed 1250 million in 2013. This four fold jump of human population in India incurs an alarming & devastating impact on our biodiversity's richness. Its water bodies have either been filled – up for residential and industrial uses or turned into polluted entities due to human activities.

At a time when the Green Ministry is trying to speed up clearances of infra projects, the Fifth National Report on Convention of Biodiversity prepared by the Environment Ministry, rings alarm bells over destruction of forest and biodiversity in the country, particularly in the global biodiversity hotspots of Himalayas, Western Ghats, North – East and the Nicobar Islands. The report states that at a conservative estimate, the country has spent approximately Rs 9200 crore in the last financial year on activities that have a direct as well as indirect bearing on conservation of its biodiversity. "Habitat loss, fragmentation and degradation through conversion of land use due to agriculture, urbanization and industrial development, invasive alien species and over exploitation of natural resources, including plants and animals, are among the major threats faced by biodiversity in India," says the report. It further states that mining and quarrying has caused serious habitat loss and degradation, with severe consequences for the ecology of areas such as the Aravalli range and the Western Ghats. According to the report, the Andaman and Nicobar Islands with some of the most pristine island ecosystems of the world is also facing habitat loss and degradation posing major threats to its marine biodiversity.

As far as the biodiversity of Indian region is concerned, it is a homeland of 167 cultivated species and 320 wild relatives of crop plants. It is a centre of diversity of animal species, for example, zebu, Methuen, chicken, water buffalo, camel etc; crop plants, namely, rice, sugarcane, banana, tea, millet; fruit plants and vegetables discourse, alocasia, colocasia; spices and condiments, namely, cardamom, black pepper, ginger, turmeric etc; and bamboos, brassicas and tree cotton. India also represents a secondary centre of domestication for some animals, namely horse, goat, sheep, cattle, yak and donkey; plants, as tobacco, potato and maize.

Destruction of Forest Cover

According to data available, about 21% of the country's geographical area is under forest cover, and every year nearly 35,000 hectares of forest land is diverted for non-forest purposes for construction of dams, mining, roads and other infrastructure projects. In the process, nearly 11,89,294 hectares of forest land has been converted for use in non-forestry purposes after giving approvals to 23,511 proposals since 1980. Of these, maximum approvals have been given to Madhya Pradesh, followed by Chattisgarh and Maharashtra.

In India, the dense forest cover is fast depleting year after year on account of mounting demand for land to establish new industrial units and other institutions apart from demand for residential needs; The Comptroller and Auditor-General of India's (CAG) report on compensatory afforestation has slammed the Union Ministry of Envirmment & Forests for its inefficiency in raising green cover through compensatory afforestation in the country. At a time when forests are depleting faster than the trees being planted, the CAG has also abserved in its report the inability of the Ministry in preventing the violation of Forest (conservation) Act, 1980 and norms by project promoters in various States. According to the report, 1,14,877 hectares of forest land was provided for non-forestry use, and in some cases for mining purposes, in total violation of environmental laws. The user agencies were expected to provide 1, 03, 382 hectares of non-forest land for afforestation between 2006 and 2012. However, the project promoters were allowed to get away with providing only 28, 086 hectares. The CAG also highlighted the free run that corporate houses are having over forest land in States such as Goa and Jharkhand. Yet another issue raised by the CAG report was, regarding the utilization of the Compensatory Afforestation Fund (CAF). The CAF was set up with the objective that where the forest land was allocated for non-forest purposes, the users were required to pay compensation into CAF, which would then be used, for forest regeneration, management, infrastructure development and wildlife protection. However the Funds have remained under – utilised at the expense of ramping up green cover, in spite of the fund increasing substantially over the years. Take for instance, China, which, over the past decades, exhausted its historically – wooded areas. It has embarked on an ambitious venture of afforestation. As part of the initiative, till date, an impressive 47000 sq. km. of afforestation has been achieved. China also ensured that stringent laws were promulgated and implemented to further speed up afforestation. For instance, a law requires every citizen over the age of 11 years to plant a tree an year. Given the population, this law would surely deliver the desired results.

We should afforestate our natural forests, which have been degraded during the past years, for, the nature has provided us forests, deserts, grassland, scrubland, wetland and other habitat, and they all have their natural role to play in preserving our biodiversity. If human will disturb the natural distribution of land use, then biodiversity shall get affected adversely. To be fair, this has pretty much been the philosophy of successive Governments, largely the Congress, which has laid much emphasis on 'greening' deserts, and social forestry, which what is crucial is to protect existing, old growth, bio-diversity, the rich forests, and preserving, natural land-scape, such as deserts, grassland, serub-land, wetland and other habitats that are simply ruled out as 'wasteland' and converted into plantation. There habitat types are rich in bio-diversity and play critical roles in water purification and ground water recharging. **There can be no 'economy' without the ecology.** Even the World Bank estimates that environment degradation is costing around 5.7 per cent of its GDP annually, thereby negating India's 'growth'. (Here see author's fig No-14)

Punjab, India's grain bowl, is afflicted with cancer owing to the intensive and extensive use of pesticides; our water has mercury, the air is loaded with lead, our food is laced with carcinogenics _____ all of which have imperiled public health. India's economic growth has come at a huge environmental cost _____ so much so, that the rate of growth itself is undermined, and questioned. According to a United Nations study, global environmental damage from human activity cost the world \$ 6.6 trillion in 2009 which is roughly about 10% of the global GDP. (See fig-14). **As citizens, we have failed to understand and appreciate that a healthy environment _____ safe, clean drinking water, air, healthy forests and species diversity are the key to not just a better quality of life, but life itself.**

Wild-life & Human Conflicts

Owing to expansion of human settlements all over the world and especially in India, created a situation wherein wild-life has come into conflict with humans, as humans have regularly been encroaching on the areas of wild-life habitat and have been trying to completely destroy it. National highways and railway lines passing through dense forests are regularly destroying the wild-life by way of accidents. The Wildlife Protection Society of India reported that leopard deaths in 2012 had been the highest, where we lost one leopard a day. Last year was also the worst recorded for tiger deaths where we lost over 70 tigers. A change in land-use pattern and encroachment of forest land for plantations and agriculture has only made matters worse. In Gujrat, a shift to sugarcane and mango cultivation on the edge of the Gir forest has been identified as one of the reasons behind conflicts between human beings and lions and leopards. **The human-wildlife conflict is a fight for space and in this push and pull for space, it's not just the villagers who are at the front line. We have smeared our development over forests and rivers and grasslands, with no regard whatsoever. As a result, our forests have railway lines and roads bisecting them, mines and factories outlining them and the once continuous stretch of forest ends up looking more like an incomplete and scattered jigsaw puzzle.** The same situation exists in most of the countries in the tropics where the human needs and pressure on the land are constant and growing. What is happening may be a complex issue to deal with, but it is really quite simple and the result, if only delayed, will be the same. **We have over-populated our land and we need more space, not only to live in, but to feed our millions.**

There is nothing new in the presence of wildlife in rural or even semi-urban landscapes. But the stringent legal protection extended to wildlife coupled with expansion of urban and agricultural landscapes, at the cost of natural habitats, has brought humans and wildlife into increasing proximity. Our major concern of such human wildlife interface is conflict, even fatal conflict, which is so witnessed across the country. In Uttarakhand, over 50 people are reportedly killed by leopards every year, and a greater number of leopards are killed in retaliation.

At the heart of the conflict is the destruction and fragmentation of elephant habitats and corridors by mining, industrialization, infrastructural developments _____ highways, roads, canals _____ and expanding human habitation. All of this leaves the elephants little room and the herds get disoriented in their seasonal migrations in search of food and undisturbed habitat. There is little doubt that it is our people's tolerance, cultural association and indeed veneration for animals that has played a key role in saving wildlife, apart from protectionist laws. But loss and fragmentation of habitats has thrown man and animal into deeper conflict, and coupled with increasing urbanization and consumerism has led to alienation from our roots, and frayed our tolerance.

If we are to grant elephants the basic right of passage, we must secure their habitats and corridor.' Yet the Government is fighting shy of granting legal cover to elephant habitat. Government have bowed to pressure and backed out of creating elephant reserves which overlapped coal and iron ore deposits. According to the Elephant Task Force report, the elephants geographic range has shrunk by 70 per cent since the 1960s. Three out of ten elephants deaths are attributed to illegal killing, train accidents and electrocution.

All the above facts clearly tell us about the human expansion to an unprecedented large territory on the earth surface which has created problems for wildlife and its natural habitats.

Extinction of Species

As we have noticed above, human actions, compelled by the needs of their humongous population growth, have created such a situation on the earth that it has threatened the very existence of several species, even to the level of their extinction altogether. For example, honeybees and other pollinators; they are facing their population decline all over the world and world scientists are very serious about this phenomenon, trying to explain why and where these bees have been disappearing. With no bees and other pollinators, our food supply will get affected. Since approximately one third of the global production volume of food crops is dependent on pollinators, almost 75 per cent of the world's crops would decrease in productivity. A class of pesticide called neonicotinoids has become extremely controversial of late. Unlike traditional pesticides, neonicotinoids were genetically embedded into seeds before planting and were more efficient and longer lasting. A derivative of nicotine, the pesticide targeted the nervous system of insects and seemed to pass all safety and health standards and soon became widespread. Today, one quarter of all global pesticide sales is of neonicotinoids which are now not only used in crops but also in gardens. However, over the years with more research poured into the phenomenon of the colony collapse disorder, the pesticide has now emerged as a prime suspect. India is not far behind nor isolated from this increasingly grim scenario. Pollinators have declined in India as well and this is already resulting in lower vegetable yields.

Similarly frogs are also in the line of extinction due to human activities. Frogs are in trouble all over our adorable planet, and some herpetologists fear that a huge extinction event may be only months away. Why should it matter if a bunch of slippery jumping things goes extinct? For one thing, frogs are an infallible indicator of the health of an ecosystem. Baby frogs are at the bottom of the food chain; only a small percentage will ever make it to adulthood. Even as adults they are prey to a vast range of creatures, from reptiles to birds _____ and other frogs. This too makes them important; if they go extinct, their predators will eventually follow.

The Great Indian Bustard (GIB) is on the brink of extinction and has been put in the category of 'endangered species' by the conservationists across the country. The GIB with the last surviving population of about 200 is now confined to only eight pockets in 6 Indian states _____ Rajasthan, Gujarat, Maharashtra, MP, Karnataka and Andhra Pradesh. The largest population of about 100 birds exists in Rajasthan. The main cause of GIB depletion is degradation of its 'lekking sites'. A 'lekking site' is a traditional place where males gather for competitive display to attract females. If these sites are subjected to disturbance or degradation, GIBs may not be able to breed, and the bird will continue to decline. The critically endangered Great India Bustard with its global population _____ almost exclusively in India __ lesser than 300, though realistic estimates put it at 150. And declining rapidly. The GIBs are besieged by a multitude of threats such as rapid intensification of agriculture, industrialisation, proliferation of wind turbines (ironically touted as 'green energy') encroachments, electric wires, unsound management practices ____ trenching, bunding, etc. _____ problems common in most of the GIB range. Infrastructure like electric poles and wind turbines within Bustard breeding areas can kill birds as flying low to the ground increase the risk of colliding with such man-made structures.

Apart from the GIBs, other prominent species under the critically endangered category include wetland birds _____Baer's Pochard, Siberian crane, and spoon-billed Sandpiper, non-migratory wetland bird the White-bellied Heron. The grassland species include Bengal Florican, Jerdon's Courcer and Sociable Lapwing amongst others. Himalayan Quail and pink-headed Duck are now considered extinct for all practical purposes. Continued destruction of wetlands and riverine habitats has been the cause of decline of these species. Even destruction of forests in the fragile Western Ghats and Himalayas continue to endanger the existence of many other species. Other reasons include incidence of chemical components as diclofenac for decline of vulture species. On a global level, International Union for Conservation of Nature (IUCN) assessed 71576 species for the report and found that 21286 are threatened with extinction. About 799 species were declared extinct, 61 were declared extinct in the wild, and 4286 are listed as critically endangered. The Red List (of IUCN) is considered the most important indicator of both the health of species and the ecosystems in which they live.

The situation of the lesser florican is also of grave concern, with some estimates putting the population to fewer than 2000. The florican was detected in 26 per cent sites during 2010 as opposed to 41 per cent in 1999. Much of the answer lies in the fact that the florican is a creature of the grasslands __ easily the most endangered, ill-managed, misunderstood and undervalued ecosystem in the country ___ even though they support some of our most threatened wildlife including the great India bustard, floricans, wolves, blackbucks, hispid hares, pygmy hog, rhinos, nilgiri tahr, to name a few. A report of the Planning Commission's Task Force, 'Grasslands and deserts are the most neglected ecosystem', stresses the importance of grasslands both from the point of view of biodiversity as well for the rural economy, as these are vital grazing areas for livestock ___ from where half of the fodder for India's 500 million livestock is sourced. It must however be pointed out, that the few remaining grasslands today are threatened by severe grazing pressure, which reduces grass cover. The source of food and concealments to birds when they are vulnerable to hunting, leads to nests and eggs getting trampled by livestock and also spreads invasive weeds like prosopis that eventually take over and drastically reduce available florican habitat. Grasslands also offer intangible, but vital benefits as important catchments for rivers, streams, reservoirs, village ponds, marshes, etc, thus playing a vital role in the hydrological regime. Yet, grasslands are viewed as 'waste land', and are being destroyed, degraded and razed for real estate, industry, roads, canals, agriculture_____ largely cash crops like tobacco, Soya, cotton etc. Another key threat is gross mismanagement; with tree plantation being done on a massive scale to 'green' what has been mistakenly dismissed as 'waste lands', turning grasslands into monoculture, and woodlands with disastrous effects for the species they sustain.

Over-hunting has been another significant factor which causes the extinction of hundreds of species and the endangerment of many more, such as whales and many African large mammals. Most of the extinctions over the past several hundred years have been mainly due to over-harvesting for food, fashion and profit. This is to be strictly prohibited if we want to save our precious biodiversity.

Further, a **fast changing global climate** is also threatening species and their ecosystems. The distribution of species is largely determined by climate, as applicable in the distribution of ecosystems and plant vegetation zones. Climate change may simply shift these distributions but, for a number of reasons, plants and animals may not be able to adjust, and they perish.

As a consequence of these multiple forces, many environment scientists fear that by the next century, perhaps 25% of the existing species on the earth will be lost. We may appreciate the fact that the most effective and efficient mechanism for conserving biodiversity and preventing the extinction of species is to immediate halt further destruction or degradation of habitats by humans. **Humans shall not only have to arrest their own expansion and aggression, but a tactical retreat will have to be staged in order to conserve it as well as to let it flourish.**

Law of Conservation of Life-Matter

This 'law' is similar to the **'law of conservation of energy'.** According to the law of conservation of energy, energy can neither be created nor destroyed; it only changes its form from one set of energy to another. This law of energy is applicable in whole of the universe according to the scientists. On the other hand, the law of conservation of life-matter as propounded by the author of this book, is applicable only for the earth.

According to this law, the total quantity of life matter (both living & non living) on earth's surface, in the air and in water is constant and this quantity can neither be increased nor reduced, in other words it can neither be created nor destroyed; it only changes its form or shape into various living species, both botanical as well as zoological. The total volume of life-matter on the earth remains the same. For example if we observe from the figure (5) which depicts the food-cycle of different species on the earth, we find that one form of species takes its nutrition or food from the other species. I call it life matter as it gives life to others as well as to the species it presently belongs to. This nutrition / life-matter moves from one species to another in the form of food, and a food-chain is formed in our ecological system which sustains life on the earth. This food-chain automatically creates a system of checks & balances in our ecosystem. The population of each species on the earth (this includes air, water & land) remains in control as each one becomes food for others. These food-chains in natural condition never operate as isolated sequences, but are interconnected with each other forming some sort of interlocking pattern which is referred to as food-web or food cycle. Under natural conditions, the linear arrangement of food-chains hardly occurs and these remain indeed interconnected with each other through different types of organisms at different trophic levels. For example, in grazing food-chain of a grassland, in the absence of rabbit, grass may also be eaten by mouse. The mouse in turn may be eaten differently by hawk or by snake first which is then eaten by hawk. Thus in nature, there are found alternatives, which all together constitute some sort of interlocking pattern _____ the food-web.

Here, in this food-web, the 'life-matter' remains constant, and in the shape of food, passes from one species to another, thus changes its form or shape, but contents remain the same. The property of life is--it takes birth, then grows with the help of other species through food, then reproduces itself, then decays and finally becomes dead. This 'dead life' loses the property of the life but not the 'life-matter'. This life matter transforms itself into another form of species, taking energy from the Sun. Existence of Sun-energy is *sine qua non* for all the living 'life-matter'. Thus life matter may be either in the form of living life-matter or dead life-matter, but the sum total of both remains the same on the earth.

Symbolically, we may depict this as;
Total quantity of life matter on the earth =
Total quantity of living life matter +
Total quantity of dead life matter = Constant

Since the total quantity of life-matter remains constant on the earth, if any (A) species, by any reason, multiply itself in numbers, it means, the other species which form food for (A) shall diminish in nature, being eaten away by (A). But (A) is also food for others and shall bear the same fate. **In this way, nature keeps regular checks & balances and any particular species can not grow beyond a certain limit.** But humans are exceptions, though they are part and parcel of the natural food-chain, on account of their conceptual brain – power, they separated themselves from this food – chain, as they have no fear of being eaten away by other carnivores species in general. Humans have been building safe houses for living and invented better weapons and arms to defend themselves from the attacks of other hunting species. Since humans remain in groups, they are successful in defending themselves from the attacks of the non-humans.

This property and behaviour of the humans separate them from other species in the nature and they have been successful in multiplying their number unbridled since long, thus occupying gradually almost all the land area on the earth including water – bodies. In this process humans have been pushing and killing all other species, compelled them to take refuge only in some isolated pockets of the earth, where either humans are unable to enter, or do not want to enter for fear of other humans. As in fig (46), we have shown the expansion of human settlements on the earth surface since 5000 B C, when only four/ five human settlements used to occupy very limited earth's surface for their use and the rest of the vast land and water was left for other non human species. But gradually, by virtue of human brain, their numbers grew rapidly and they began to occupy more and more land surface and water bodies for their use, driving away and killing other species at their will, several of them were eaten away too. In this way, humans developed and expanded themselves by diminishing other species either by eating them away or driving them off into a relatively smaller land and water area.

Now in 2010 AD, human expansion became so high in numbers, crossing 700 crore (7 billion), as to occupy almost 80 per cent of earth-surface, leaving only 20 per cent for other species. This increase of human numbers is still continuing without any check, which will further diminish the space for others. By 2100 AD, it seems that almost entire land surface of the earth would be under human settlement, leaving no room for others, driving them towards extinction. **As shown in fig (47), the number of humans keeps on growing since the dawn of human civilization, while the number of other species goes on diminishing with every passing century.** Now we have reached into a disastrous era, where humans have established themselves all over the globe surface, and the remaining species face extinction for want of space as well as due to human consumption.

Longevity of Humans' Age

Generally, all over the world including India, the average age of the humans has been increasing for the last 50 years due to availability of better diet and an improved medical & health care augmented by increased knowledge in medical science with the help of new technology. In India, we have had an increasing average of life expectancy as shown below.

Year	Life Expectancy
1960	42 years
1980	48 yrs
1990	58.5 yrs
2000	62 yrs
2005	63.9 yrs
2011	69.6 yrs (fig. 49)

Similarly, average age of humans, all over the world, is on the increase, as the population of humans having the age of 60 years or above has been increasing as below;

In 1950 – 8% of the total population
In 2005 – 10% of the total population
In 2050 – 22% of the total population (projected) (fig. 48)

As the twenty first century began, the world population included approximately 600 million older persons (60 years or above), triple the number recorded 50 year earlier. By 2050 AD, the world is expected to have some 2 billion (200 crore) older persons _____ once again, a tripling of the number in that age group within a span of 50 years.

This indicates that, on the one hand, the overall human population in the world is growing fast, the average life – expectancy is also on the increase, on the other. **It means, the total volume of 'life – matter' occupied by the humans all over the world is also increasing, and by the same ratio, the 'life – matter' occupancy with other species is diminishing, assuming the total 'life – matter' on the earth as constant.**

As shown in fig. (49), total human population is not only growing rapidly, but its occupancy-duration of 'life – matter' is also on the increase due to increased life – expectancy. Thus, mathematically we may say that;

Total life matter occupancy by the humans = Total population of the humans in the world x their average age expectancy.

Since this is on the increase, the life – matter occupancy by other species is regularly going down. As shown in fig (47), the volume of life – matter in other species is decreasing during the centuries since the dawn of human civilization around 5000 B.C., as the human population is regularly increasing. Now we have entered into a dangerous era where life-matter occupancy by humans has reached at a very high level, leaving a very small quantity of life – matter for other species. This situation is a disastrous one, for humans totally depend on the life – matter of other species, which they cannot get in sufficient quantity on account of deficiency of life – matter held by other species. Thus, humans, inadvertently, arrived at a destination where they can no longer maintain themselves and their survival is in peril. The sooner humans control their numbers, the better. They shall certainly perish if not corrected by themselves.

Here, I would like to mention a hymn from the 'Geeta', wherein Krishna says to Arjuna, the warrior;

Na jayate mriyate va kadachi-trayam, bhutva bhavita va na bhuyah;
Ajo nityah shashvatoyam purano-na hanyte hunyamane sharire.
The **soul** is neither born, nor does it die;
It neither is, nor will be, nor was;
It is immortal, timeless and age less;
It does not die while the body does;

This is a perfectly correct depiction of the **'law of conservation of life – matter'** if we replace the word **'soul'** by the word **life – matter.** Krisha said this around 5000 years hence, and the people in those days and even today believe that it is the 'soul' which creates life in any body/species. While modern science does not believe in any thing like 'soul', it is the life-matter which creates life in species under certain conditions, like presence of water, Sun-heat, oxygen etc. Hence the existence of 'life – matter' on the earth is a nature's gift which remains constant. It never dies, only changes its shape or form when it transforms itself into other numerous species, all around us. This is the essence of the food-chain manifested into life-cycle and nothing else.

———◆———

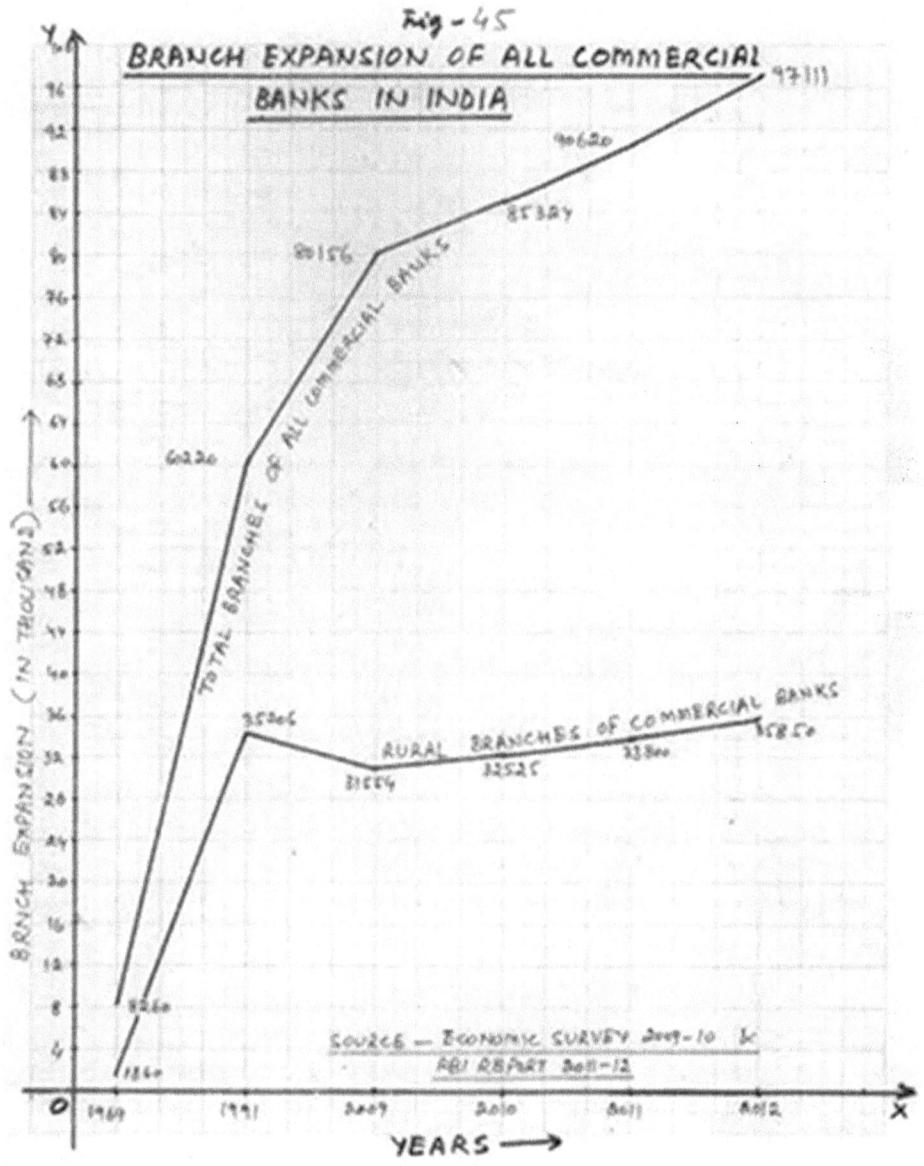

Fig - 45

BRANCH EXPANSION OF ALL COMMERCIAL BANKS IN INDIA

SOURCE — ECONOMIC SURVEY 2009-10 &
RBI REPORT 2011-12

YEARS ⟶

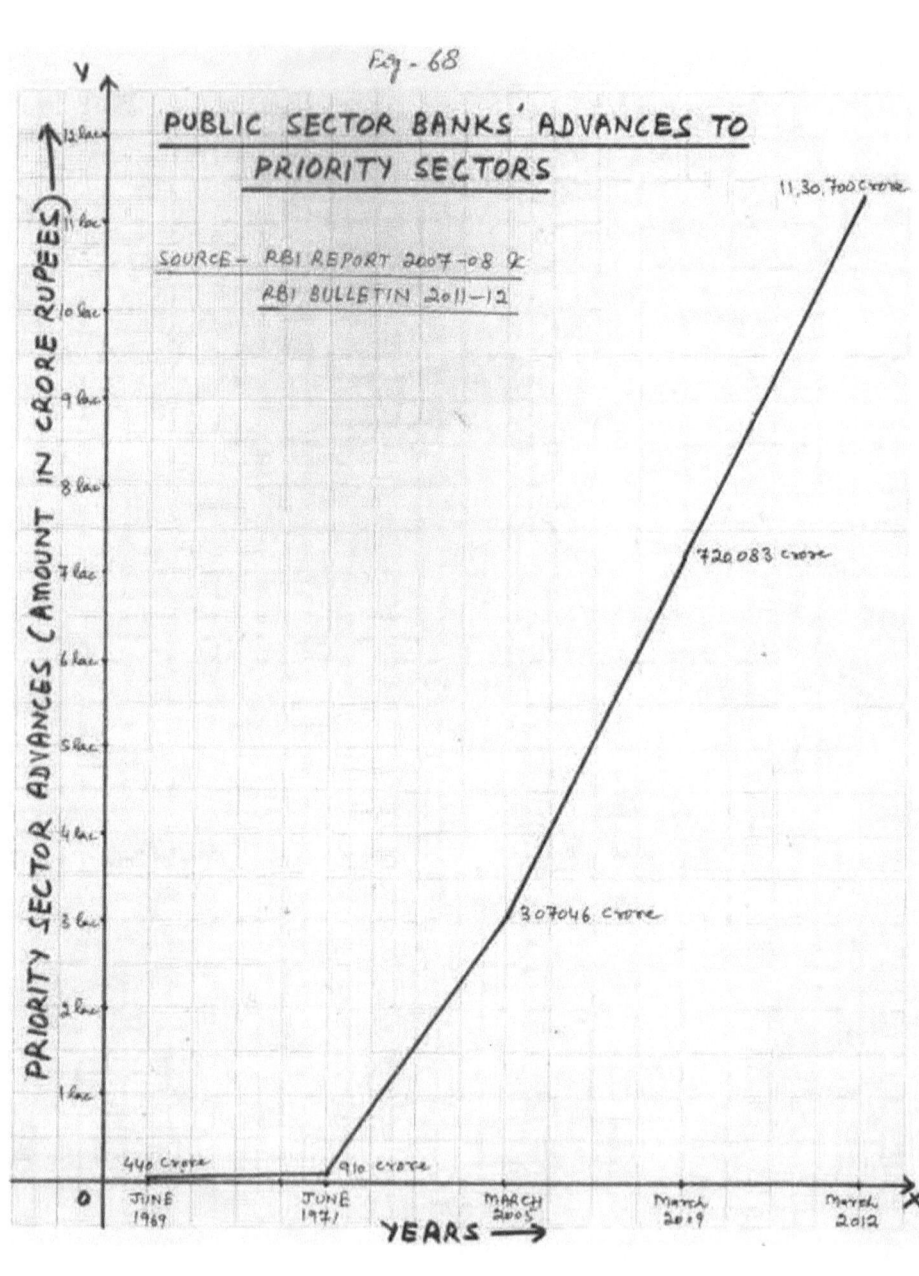

Fig - 68

PUBLIC SECTOR BANKS' ADVANCES TO PRIORITY SECTORS

SOURCE- RBI REPORT 2007-08 &
RBI BULLETIN 2011-12

CHAPTER – 10

Over Population & Banking Sector

Pre – Nationalization Period

The Indian Banking system witnessed a turbulent period during the first half of the 20th century. During the British rule, organized banking was confined only to big cities and towns, whereas small towns and rural India were totally without banking unlike in the present days. In small towns and villages, the indigenous bankers had been performing the role of banking in the form of family or individual business. The indigenous bankers have been called differently, as, Shroffs, Seths, Sahukars, Mahajans, Chettis, and so on, in different parts of the country. They vary in their sizes from petty money – lenders to substantial shroffs who carry on large and specialised business which at times exceeds that of the scheduled banks. The business of the indigenous bankers has been generally a family affair. They used to employ their own or family's working capital and they accept deposits from their friends and relatives. They do not get deposits from the general public as do the joint stock banks. They grant loans against all kinds of securities such as gold, jewellery, land, promissory notes, *hundis* etc. They also lend against the personal credit of the borrowers. They also buy and sell remittances and discount *hundis*. They even finance the movement of crops from the villages to the inland trade centers and ports. According to the committee on Finance for the Private Sector, known as Shroff Committee 1954, these indigenous bankers were performing between 75 to 90 per cent of total banking trade of the country during the pre – nationalization era in India.

These indigenous bankers have been working on profit motive and they used to charge very high rate of interest from their borrowers, that is why, they are called usurers. It has been very difficult for the debtors to repay their debt on account of very high interest rates and it happens usually that the debtor loses his security in the form of jewellery or land. Many farmers lost their jewellery and land on account of indigenous banker's usury. They turned poorer and poorer while indigenous bankers have been cornering huge profits.

As commercial banks have been covering only 10 to 25 percent business in different parts of the country during the pre-nationalization era, the indigenous bankers had a big field to operate. In was felt necessary to expand commercial banks in small towns and villages, but the commercial banks were owned by big business or industrial houses and they did not move towards small towns and villages for fear of losing profits. In 1950-51, there were 430 commercial banks but the number of banks declined rapidly due to RBI's policy of mergers and amalgamations of small banks with big banks as a measure of strengthening the banking system. In 1960-61, there were as many as 256 small non-scheduled commercial banks; the rest of them were merged with bigger banks or had become large banks themselves.

Post – Nationalization Era

As 90 percent population of India was residing in small towns and villages, it could not avail the benefits of organized modern banking facilities and these people were at the mercy of usurious indigenous bankers. Govt. of India felt the need of nationalizing big 14 private commercial banks in July 1969. Thus, nationalization was done on the ground that the private commercial banks did not play or refused to play its required social role in the planned development of India. Entire commercial banking system was controlled by a coterie of industrialists and business magnets who had been using bank funds (pubic money) to build up their own industrial and business empires. Small industry, small business, agriculture and allied sector, capital-starve entrepreneurs etc. were totally left unfinanced by these banks with the exception of State Bank of India which had had its branches only in big cities and some district headquarters. Even bank funds were used to support anti-social and illegal activities against the interest of the general public. Owing to these drawbacks, the Govt. of India had decided to nationalize 14 major commercial banks of

India, having deposits of Rs 50 crore or more in July 1969. Further, in 1980, Govt. of India again nationalized another 6 major commercial banks to expand the base of social banking. Now, there were 20 nationalized banks beside State Bank of India and its associate banks in 'Public Sector' in 1980. Later, New Bank of India, had been merged with Punjab National Bank, thus reducing the number of nationalized banks to 19.

Having nationalized 14 major commercial banks in July 1969, the Govt. of India instructed these banks to open their branches in small towns and villages. As shown in fig (45), total number of bank branches in 1969 in India were only 8260, covering an average population of 63800 persons per branch. In 1991, these figures were; 60220 total branches, 35206 rural branches and coverage of 14150 persons per branch. Now, in 2012, there were total 97111 branches all over India which include 35850 rural branches and a coverage of 12600 persons per branch. While in 1950-51, total deposit and credit of all the scheduled commercial banks in India were only Rs 820 crore and Rs 580 crore respectively, it rose to mountainous heights of Rs 59,09,082 crore and Rs 46,11,852 crore in 2011-12.

With the expansion of commercial bank branches all over India, the deposits of these banks also grew rapidly. Planned economic development, deficit financing and increase in currency volume, apart from development of banking habits among people at large, have led to a mountainous growth of bank deposits. While in 1950-51, the deposits of all scheduled commercial banks in India were only Rs 820 crore, it grew to Rs 9,62,620 crore in 2000-01, and further grew upto Rs 59,09.082 crore in 2011-12. Similarly credits (loans & advances) of all the scheduled commercial banks in India also grew mani-fold during the last 60 years. While total credit in 1950-51 was only Rs 580 crore, it went up to Rs 5, 11, 430 crore in 2000-01 and further jumped to Rs 46,11,852 crore in 2011-12.

Priority Sector Lending

Credit to agriculture & allied sector, small scale industries, small business enterprises, retail traders, small transport operators, professionals and self employed persons, housing and education sectors etc. were bracketed under the head of 'Priority Sector', for, these sectors were to be given priority over all others in order to benefit hitherto neglected sections, as they were in urgent need of funds. Before the nationalization in 1969, these commercial banks had been largely neglecting agriculture & allied sector on the ground that rural credit was to be undertaken by Cooperative Credit Societies and Cooperative Banks. Consequently, they remained largely indifferent to the credit needs of farmers for agricultural operations and other allied works etc. Since, pre-nationalization commercial banks were owned by private big business houses, they only looked after the credit needs of industrial/ big business houses. Even, small scale sector too remained neglected. After the nationalization, the nationalized banks and other public sector banks were asked to pay their attention towards the urgent credit needs of the priority sector of the economy.

Gross neglect of priority sector lending was one of the causes for nationalization of the top 14 commercial banks in July 1969. However, it was one of the Working Group on the Priority Sector Lending and the 20-Point Economic Programme, chaired by Dr. K.S.Krishnaswami, which clearly spelt out the concept.

"The concept of priority sector lending is mainly intended to ensure that assistance from the banking sector flows in an increasing manner to those sectors of the economy which, though accounting for a significant proportion of the national product, has not received adequate support of institutional finance in the past."

In 1980, RBI issued certain directives to banks, especially public sector banks regarding priority sector lending, these were;

1- Priority sector advances should constitute 40 per cent of aggregate bank credit;
2- Out of total priority sector advances, at least 40 per cent should be provided to agriculture;
3- Direct advances to weaker sections in agriculture and allied activities in rural areas should form at least 50 per cent of the total direct lending to agriculture;
4- Bank credit to rural artisans, village craftsmen and cottage industries should at least be 12.5 per cent of the total advances to small scale industries;
5- About 12 per cent of bank credit should go to exports, and
6- At least 1% of the priority sector advance should go to very weak sections at 4 per cent interest under DRI scheme.

Thus, priority sector lending was directed towards the upliftment of economically weaker sections of the society at concessional rate of interest with liberal norms, not insisting on collateral security very much. The commercial banking system and especially the public sector banks, under the influence of Finance Ministry and the ruling party politicians, took to priority sector lending enthusiastically. As a result of it, whereas in June 1969, the priority sector lending was only Rs 440 crore, constituting only 12 per cent of total bank credit, it grew to Rs 307046 crore in March 2005, constituting 42.8 per cent of the total bank credit, which further went up to Rs 11,30,700 crore in March 2012, constituting 37.5 per cent of total bank credit. (see fig. 68) Initially, the priority sector lending went well, but after a lapse of 10 years, its short-comings and problems began to emerge. Since this lending was made to weaker sections, whose number was large and amount advanced was relatively small, proper follow-up and recovery could not be adhered to due to shortage of bank staff on the one hand and forced lending on the other. In their anxiety to reach the assigned target of 40 per cent, the banks went in for indiscriminate lending. There was also political pressure too on the banking sector to lend to weaker sections liberally.

The commercial public sector banks were subjected to squeez in two ways. On the one hand, they were forced to keep a high proportion of their deposits ____ as much as 53.3 per cent in liquid reserves till 1992 under CRR (15%) and SLR (38.5%) provisions; thus leaving only 46.5% of their deposits as lendable resources. On the other, even out of these limited lendable funds, banks were to allocate 40 per cent of this for priority sector lending, leaving only 60 per cent funds for other profitable investments/advances. Since priority sector lending was mostly on concessional rate of interest i.e. below the cost of funds, it resulted in losses to banks. **Only 60 per cent lendable funds were to be financed at commercially profitable rate of interest, which could not cover the losses under priority sector lending plus bank's establishment costs.**

Debt Waiver Measures

Even lending to priority sector segments on low rate of interest, capital subsidy and liberal loan distribution did not work and recovery of bank loans turned either very poor or zero in several cases. Loans granted under various government schemes, for example IRDP, SCP, SEEUY, SEPUP, crop loans etc turned sticky and banks resorted to legal and administrative steps to recover the loans. They issued recovery certificates (RCs) under the provisions of Public Money Recovery Act and Rural Credit Recovery Act, which caused much resentment among the rural people and urban poor. **The abject poverty of the borrowers forced them to utilize the borrowed funds for consumption purposes and after 4/5 years, they were on the same level of poverty as before. Hence recovery certificates and other coercive methods brought their economic and social downfall beyond limit.**

The ruling party at the Central level and economists of the country now felt the need of debt-waiving schemes in order to protecting banks from losses and giving a helping hand to the poor borrowers as well. Thus, in 1990, the then finance minister, Mr. Madhu Dandawate, announced in Parliament the 'Agricultural and Rural Debt Relief Scheme', also called Loan – Waiver Scheme. The scheme provided loan-relief up to Rs 10,000/- to the borrowers of the public sector banks and RRBs. The borrowers include those engaged in agriculture and allied activities and artisans engaged in any activity of rural development relating to cottage and village industries, handicrafts, weaving etc. A scheme on similar patterns was framed and put into operation by the State Governments and applied to banks in the cooperative sector. According to Government estimate, the total debt relief burden was to the tune of Rs 2840 crore, and according to independent estimates, the total debt relief burden on the Central and State Governments was to the tune of Rs 14,000 crore.

After this, it was decided again to start the same lending process to help these poor of rural and urban dwelling. The same old schemes, like IRDP, SCP, SEEUY, SEPUP, Crop loan under Credit Card scheme etc. again launched vigorously entitled as 'second dose'. The 'first dose' went futile, hence 'second dose', this time with enhanced loan amount and capital subsidy. The 'second dose' lending process continued for another 16/17 years and the problem of bad-debts and recovery of loans reappeared in greater volume in terms of amount involved as well as the number of loanees. It was again felt that these debts did not improve the economic conditions of the poor loanees, instead, they utilized it again for their consumption purposes. **Hence again a debt-waiver and debt relief scheme should be launched.**

In the year 2008, in the budget speech for 2008-09, the then Finance Minster Mr. Chidambaram indicated one time debt waiver for all marginal and small farmers holding up to 2 hectares of land. The total financial burden on the Government was Rs 65,000 crore which was to be reimbursed to the banks through public exchequer in two installments. These schemes of debt-waiver and debt-relief for the poor rural masses indicate that mere cheap loan and capital subsidy is not going to help them in their poverty eradication any more. The problem lies somewhere else, which is being ignored deliberately or otherwise. **The problem is extreme over – population with no check on it and its byproduct, the extreme poverty which consumed and absorved the meager financial help in the shape of cheap loans and capital subsidy. It did not improve their economic conditions a bit. 81 crore people of India still do not have even the food-security is a real proof of this phenomenon.** The story did not end here. The demonstration effect of these debt-waiver and debt-relief schemes of the Government impacted negatively on the other bankable schemes due to which the recovery process of the banks has become faulty and cumbersome. The honest borrowes felt cheated, and they too wanted not to pay their loans in the hope of a future waiver. The problem of non-performing assets or NPAs is on the rise partly due to these debt –waiver schemes and partly due to prevailing economic slowdown in the country encompassing extreme poverty & mass unemployment /underemployment.

Non-Performing Assets

A major problem confronting these days by the public sector banks especially and all the commercial banks in general is the acute growth of Non – Performing Assets or bad loans. When a loan or advance given to an individual or firm is not repaid to the bank as per its terms of agreement, it falls under the category of bad loan or non performing asset. As we have already mentioned above that rural and agricultural credit system of banks have been facing problems in respect of repayment on the part of its borrowers and our Government has had to resort to debt-waiver & debt-relief schemes to lessen the burden of rural folk and farmers on the one hand and to save bankers from incurring losses on account of non-payment of their loans, accumulated in their books as bad loans or NPAs on the other, by reimbursing the NPAs fully or partly through public exchequer. **But this is not a permanent solution as the money doled out from public exchequer is nothing but taxes collected from the people of India out of their hard-earned incomes.** This also encourages willful default on the part of the borrowers and discourages honest borrowers' will to pay regularly. **In fact, debt-waiver and debt-relief steps pollute the whole financial atmosphere of the country.** Since the implementation of first debt relief scheme of 1990, the number of willful defaulters has increased in banks' books, especially in rural and agricultural sector and our Government has again resorted to the same debt-waiver/debt-relief scheme in 2008, after 18 years of the first. Since them, bad debts/NPAs are on the increase in numbers and amount and now posing a great challenge to their capital base and profitability.

In the SBI, the decline of profit (for the years 2013-14) was due to higher provisioning for bad loans and future wage revision. The total provisioning for the full year stood at Rs 7587 crore, 70.06 per cent higher than Rs 4461 crore in the previous year (2012-13). The stressed sectors of the bank were engineering, textiles, pharmaceuticals and services. Net interest margin declined from 3.34 per cent in March 2013 to 3.17 per cent in March 2014. Regarding asset quality, SBI's gross NPA (bad debts) rose from Rs 51,189 crore in March 2013 to Rs 61605 crore in March 2014, reflecting a rise of 20.3 per cent. SBI's gross nonperforming assets (NPAs or bad loans) as a percentage of total loan rose to 4.95 per cent or Rs 61605.35 crore during the quarter from 4.75 per cent or Rs 51.189.39 crore. The Bank's net profit tanked to Rs 10891.17 crore in 2013-14 from Rs 14104.98 crore in the previous financial year.

The NPA is the real indicator of the state of the economy. It demonstrates that more and more people, corporates and entrepreneurs are unable to repay the money the banks have lent them. It is telling heavily on the financial health of the banks as well as of the economy at large. Listed banks had gross NPAs to the tune of Rs 2.3 lakh crore at the end of September 2013, which was nearly 25% higher than the level seen in March 2013.The record restructuring proposals point to the building stress on the banking system with several companies finding it tough to repay the loans that they had taken over the past few years. While the economic slowdown has taken a toll, there are several companies that are highly leveraged as projects have either failed to take off or their cash flow arithmetic has gone hay wire.

From 2003 to 2008, the Indian economy grew at a spectacular 8-10%. That was then. Now, the irrepressible Indian economy jugarnaut is struggling to maintain even a 5% GDP growth rate. Indeed, the optimism which typified India's growth story has vanished. Economists now consider the current grim growth rates as "the new normal". The heady days of India's growth story seem over; it's now all doom and gloom. **Indian corporate sector (and by consequence the banking sector) is sitting on a debt time bomb.** Bank loans to infrastructure sector have grown over 100 fold in the last 13 years to almost Rs 8,00,000 crore. The cumulative impact of sluggish growth across sectors is increasingly felt by the common man as employment outlook remains bleak. Even if you disregard statistics, industry sentiment is that of despair and gloom.

Banks' inability to recover large volume of NPAs compelled them to write-off the amount out of their profits. This figure was Rs 6446 crore in 2001, Rs 8711 crore in 2002, Rs 12021 crore in 2003, Rs 13559 crore in 2004, Rs 10823 crore in 2005, Rs 11657 crore in 2006, 11621 crore in 2007, Rs 11653 crore in 2008, Rs 15996 crore in 2009, Rs 25019 crore in 2010, Rs 23896 crore in 2011 and Rs 20892 crore in 2012. This year (2013), when economic indicators have been plummeting and national growth has come to a near standstill, the write-off figure has touched an all time high of Rs 32,218 crore. RBI numbers showed that as the gross domestic product (GDP) was rising, banks added Rs 4,94,836 crore to their bad loans between 2007 and 2013. **In other words, the gain in terms of economic indicators was actually a gross loss for the banking sector.**

As per Basel-3 norms, banks are compelled to maintain a 100% provision for their gross NPAs, which means Rs 4, 94, 836 crore amount is to be kept as provisions out of their profits as potential loss. In this way, the total funds of the Banks locked in NPAs plus provision are to the tune of around Rs10, 00, 000 crore, which Indian banks are not in a position to bear. Further, they can not book interest on NPA amount which will further reduce their profit margins. In fact, the NPAs and writing-off of bad-debts brought Indian commercial banks in the position of big capital loss. Slowly, they have been eroding their entire capital base and looking towards the Government to re-capitalize them from the public exchequer, which is nothing but tax-money of the Indian people. Government is already very much hard pressed on account of mounting subsidy amount meant for several welfare measures like food security bill, right to education bill, mounting unproductive expenditure and other planned developmental expenditures / works. For the current year (2014-15), the government has provided Rs 11200 crore for bank capitalization and is asking banks to tap the capital markets to raise more equity.

This new burden of recapitalization of the commercial public sector banks shall further deteriorate the fiscal deficit of the Government's exchequer; a situation of total collapse of the economy is in the offing. Banking, unlike other industries, requires capital every year. Banking, if you have to grow their business even, to take one step forward, you need additional capital because there are provisioning requirements, capital requirement. Therefore, banking is a very special business where additional capital is required every year and therefore boards of banks, employees of banks must recognize that a significant part of their earning must be put aside as cash.

Recapitalization of banks will lag the real economy. Given that credit is expected to grow by 15%, and the stress that is already there on bank balance-sheets, the system would need between Rs 3.5 lakh crore to Rs 4 lakh crore in the next three-four years. One of the big issues the new government will have to face is capitalization of the banking system.

Thus, economic slowdown, growing NPAs, unprofitable priority sector lending, rising establishment costs, all are contributing into pushing the Indian public commercial banking system towards total bankruptcy and failure. **This is a very dangerous situation for Indian polity, the root-cause of which lies in the humongous growth of human over-population, more than twice of the optimum level. Unless our planners address this problem on war-footing, first and foremost, all others can not be subdued and India's economic system shall collapse.**

Resurgent China: Full of Confidence

China's clever and farsighted leadership clearly envisioned the importance and indispensability of urgent population control measures in China as soon as it got independence in 1949. But this movement for population control could not get sufficient momentum on account of over emphasis on 'Cultural Revolution' launched by Mao Tse Tung, the unchallenged Communist leader of that era. After the death of Mao in 1976, the next leadership of China, headed by Teng Hsio Peng took keen interest in this direction and set a target of total population of 1.2 billion (120crore) by the year 2000, and to achieve this target, they set 'one child norm' for every chinese couple.

In 1956, following the 1953 census, the Government of China announced a policy of promoting late marriage and birth limitation. This was replaced by ideological polemics against population control during the 'Great Leap Forward', which started in 1958. Attempts were made to reintroduce the birth planning programme in the early 1960s, but the contraceptive services were disrupted during the early years of the Cultural Revolution (1966-69). Throughout this period, the progress was justified principally in terms of contribution to maternal and child health.

In the early 1970s, however a new birth control campaign began in earnest. Birth planning was more closely linked to the national objectives of economic development and modernization. The Government endorsed a specific set of norms with respect to child bearing, embodied in the slogan of "later-longer-fewer" _____ late marriage and child birth spacing (of at least four years) between children, and a smaller total number of children per couple. **With its adoption of the notion that reproduction is a concern not only to the family, but also of the society, was specifically endorsed for the first time in China. The current of population policy is to limit total population to 1.2 billion in the year 2000.**

In 1979, the Chinese Government initiated a campaign to promote the one-child family. Its purpose is to reduce family size in the next decades enough to bring the birth rate down still farther, even in the face of the continuing increase in the proportion of the population entering child bearing years. Finally, there are economic incentives and disincentives to discourage births, and more recently in particular to promote the one-child family. Incentives have existed since the early 1970s when the Central Government instituted a schedule of benefits in the form of vacation days, for women undergoing various types of planned birth operations. The possibility of additional incentives specially to promote the one-child family was raised in August 1979. For example, to provide for a five-year monthly subsidy to one-child families (8% of the average worker's wage) until the child is 14 years old. The child will have priority in admission to schools and in obtaining a factory job. In rural areas in Hunan, one-child parents are to receive an annual bonus of 400 workpoints until their child is 14 years old and private plots and housing lots of a two-child standard. Disincentives apply to the birth of third child; they include deductions of wages or work -points (amounting to 5% in Hunan and 10% in Tianjin and Shanghai), payment by parents of all medical expenses for a third child and the exclusion of that child from cooperative medical schemes.

In a February 1980 radio broadcast and an editorial in the 'People's Daily', the Chinese called attention to the role of education and persuasion in inducing couples to have only one child, rather than any direct financial incentives. Perhaps the motivation was the financial burden demographic success would impose. For most of the world, birth and death rates are closely associated with per capita income. In general, the higher a country's per capita income, the lower its birth and death rates. Among developing countries, those of sub-Sahara Africa and the Indian subcontinent (Bangladesh, India, Pakistan) have the highest levels of fertility and mortality and the lowest incomes; the developed countries have the lowest levels of fertility and mortality and the highest incomes. China is a striking exception to this rule. China's fertility lies well below the value expected for its income.

Health Care in China

Several other factors associated with low fertility across countries undoubtedly helped set the stage for the rapid fertility decline of the 1970s in China. The first is the significant gains in life expectancy achieved in 1950s and 1960s and the probable drops in infant mortality that occurred throughout this period and that contributed to increased life expectancy. Infant mortality for China as a whole in 1973-75 ranged between 53 and 63 per thousand, which compared favourably with a rate of 37 per thousand in Korea, 68 in Thailand

and 62 in Brazil. A point related to that of general heath improvement is that the creation of an extensive health care delivery system in the 1960s provided the structure within which intensification of birth planning programs could be implemented in 1970s. **Few other developing countries could not so easily launch a birth planning program of the magnitude of China's, simply because comparable health service delivery systems are not in place.**

Education in China

A second factor is current relatively widespread access to basic education and in particular the increase in female enrollment rates in the post revolution period. The enrollment ratio in primary schools has risen from 25% to 93%. Of primary school age girls, 84% are now enrolled, compared to an average among all developing countries of 56%. Girls education in the 1950s and 1960s are now in their childbearing years. Secondary and higher education encourage reduced fertility because they broaden female opportunities beyond family and child bearing; but very few adult women in China have received more than primary education. However, even a few years of schooling are likely to improve the effectiveness of contraceptive use; it is in this regard that China is probably now reaping the benefits, in terms of reduced fertility, of widespread basic education. In China, a higher proportion of women now in their twenties have received some primary education than in most other low-income developing countries.

Further, human resource development has been treated as a priority area since the 1980s. Science and technology manpower has constantly increased from 0.425 million in 1952 to 5.276 million in 1980 to 28.48 million in 2002. The corresponding figure for India as of 2000 is 7.664 million. In China, over recent years, Research & Development expenditure has increased over 10 times from U.S. $ 3.45 billion in 1995 to more than U S $ 38 billion in 2006. The corresponding figures for India are U.S. $ 1.55 billion in 1995 to only U.S $ 6.62 billion in 2006.

China's Economic Development

China's emphasis on population control and simultaneous expansion of education and health facilities paid her rich dividends in her commendable economic development. She has a land area which is three times that of India and her population at present is 136 crore (1360 million) while India's population is 125 crore (1250 million). **When we compare the population of China and India in relation to land area they occupy, the population of China comes out only as 45.33 crore (136/3), which is very close to her optimum population level, while India is 70 crore above her optimum level (125-55). Here lies the crux of the matter.** China is marching ahead on the road of rapid economic development whereas we Indians are lagging behind in every sphere and heading towards an economic collapse.

When we speak of India and China, we are really talking about David and Goliath, except that David has no slingshot. In absolute size, China's industry is 6.5 time that of India. One indication of this is infrastructure development. In 2006, India's coal based power production capacity was 80,000 M.W. and overall capacity was 1,20,000 M.W. China's coal-based power capacity was 4,84,000 M.W., i.e. over 5 times India's. Since 2006, China has added a further 90,000 M.W. In short, the increase that year in China's generation capacity in thermal power exceeded the whole of India's thermal power generating capacity. It is this infrastructure heavy investment that has made it possible for China to attract every company that wants to lower its cost of production. Chinese exports have actually grown between 2001 and 2006 by 400 per cent. This was because it was in this period that leading Asian economies such as Taiwan and Korea began to run out of labour (and not merely cheap labour) and were compelled to move their last stage manufacture into China. They went to China not only because it was close but also because the required infrastructure was already there, and was excellent. In contrast, India has invested virtually nothing in infrastructure. Capital investment, whether in the maintenance of existing infrastructure or new infrastructure is on more than Rs.5000 crore or US$ 1 billion. The equivalent figure for China is US $ 500 billion.

Thus, initial and timely efforts by Chinese political leadership in the direction of population control along with judicious investment in mass education and mass health improvement proved highly beneficial and now paying rich dividends. China is now considered a big power at par with the U.S.A, the U.K, Russia and France and got a permanent place in the U.N. Security Council. At the same time, China's economic upsurge and mass awakening shall certainly pave the way for a more democratic liberal polity which hitherto is illusive.

India, on the other hand did not pay any serious attention to control her booming human population effectively and its cumulative ill effects are there to be seen by everybody. A large chunk of our scarce resources are being diverted to prop-up the ever increasing poor population of the country along with a huge problem of unemployment and underemployment has arisen like a Himalayan mountain. A small country like Israil, which gained independence at almost the same time as India, and with a population less than 1% of India's, today accounts for 10% of total global defense exports. China which until 2006 was the largest importer of defence goods, is today the fifth largest defence equipment exporter. Paradoxically India, with its huge pool of technically qualified, globally competitive manpower, in dire need for employment for its population, has emerged as the largest importer.

Indian nation is on the verge of a great implosion, only to be watched keenly by economic and political scholars. As a columnist in The Pioneer writes;

A matter which Mr. Narendra Modi's Government (newly elected PM for 16th Lok Sabha) needs to treat as an urgent priority is India's rapidly growing population. It is now 1.27 billion (2014) against China's 1.36 billion. In 2040, it is expected to rise to 1.52 billion, outstripping China's 1.45 billion, and, in 2050, it is expected to be 1.69 billion against China's 1.31 billion. If this does not worry the country, one wonders what will. The first question is: How will the country feed this gargantuan mass now that the green revolution has lost its momentum? Even if the green revolution has a second coming, the question of land water availability remains. On an average, it takes 1000 tonnes of water to produce one tonne of foodgrain. India now has 17per cent of the world's population and only about two per cent of the globe's land area. Besides hunger, malnutrition and death _____ and India is no stranger to any one of them _____ foodgrain shortages fuel inflation as well. A rise in foodgrain prices is often the driving force behind a general price rise, the consequences of which need hardly be spelt out both in terms of developmental activity and political stability. The latter indeed, the country's democratic system itself can be seriously threatened by a growing army of unemployed youngsters whose anger and frustration is all the greater because they are in the midst of a glittering and expanding world of consumer goods and services open to only those with sufficient income.

Here, I would like to reproduce the under noted very popular couplet of Hindi;

Ekai sadhe sab sadhai, sab sadhe sab jay;
Jo tu sinchai mool ko, foolai falay aghai.

(If you tackle the main problem, it will solve all others automatically; As you water the roots of a plant, it shall grow, blossom and give delicious fruits in abundance.)

———◆———

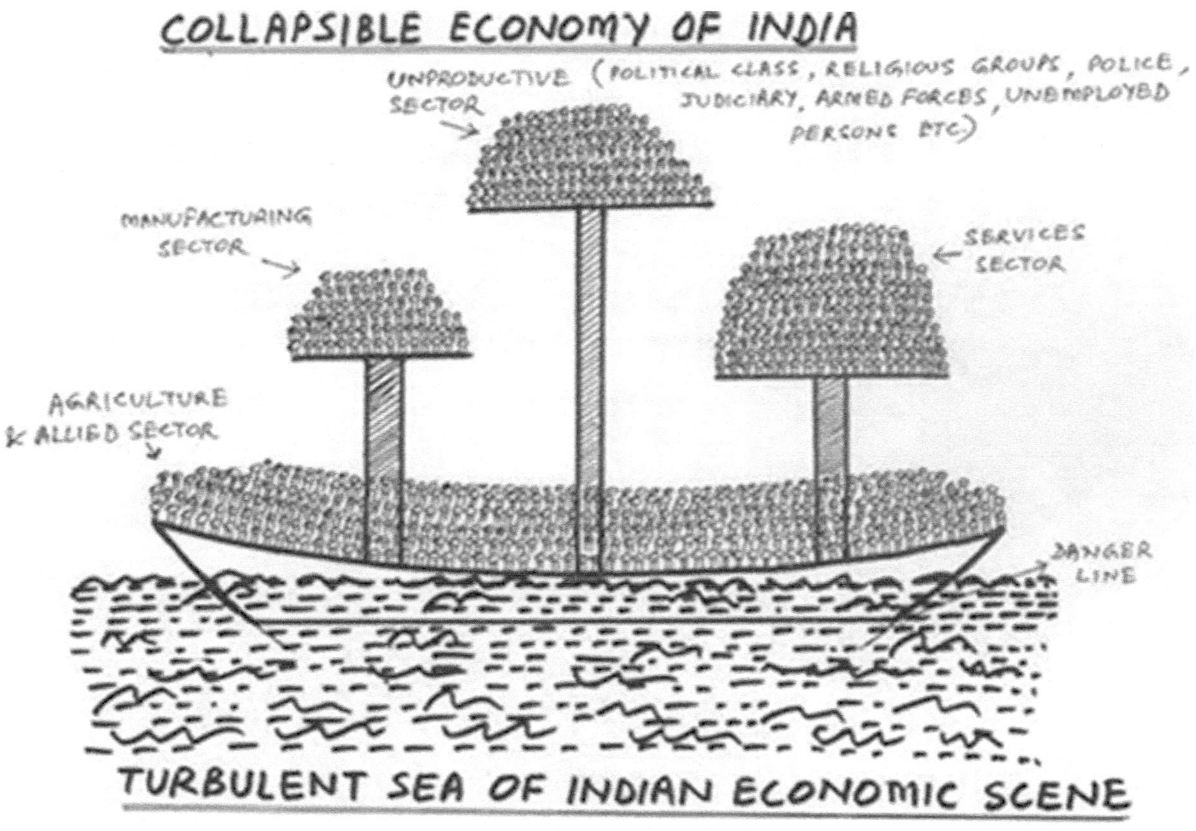

COLLAPSIBLE ECONOMY OF INDIA

UNPRODUCTIVE (POLITICAL CLASS, RELIGIOUS GROUPS, POLICE, JUDICIARY, ARMED FORCES, UNEMPLOYED PERSONS ETC) SECTOR →

← SERVICES SECTOR

MANUFACTURING SECTOR →

AGRICULTURE & ALLIED SECTOR ↓

DANGER LINE

TURBULENT SEA OF INDIAN ECONOMIC SCENE

Fig. 50

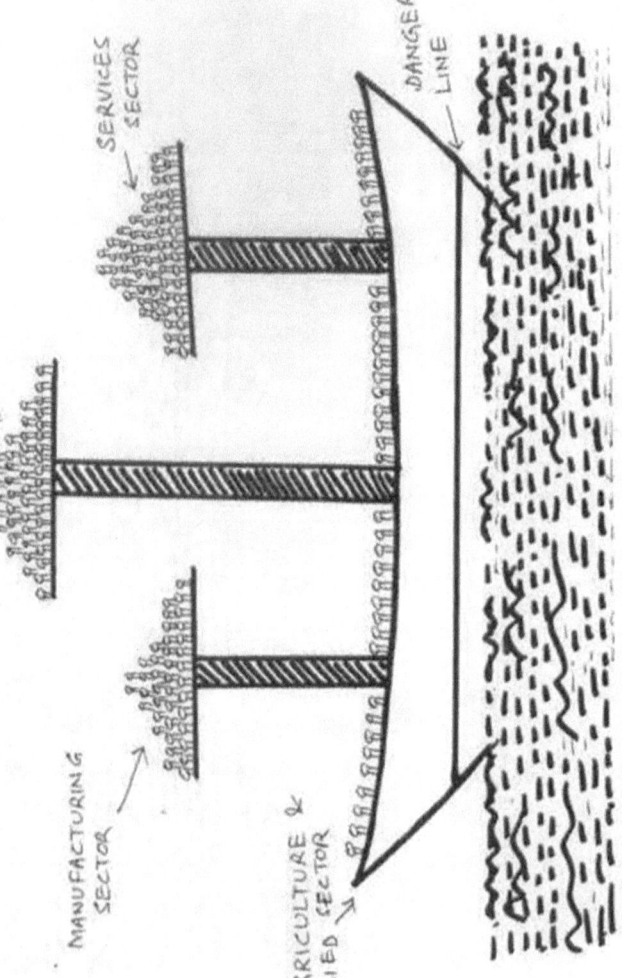

EASY-GOING INDIAN ECONOMY

UNPRODUCTIVE SECTOR

SERVICES SECTOR

MANUFACTURING SECTOR

AGRICULTURE & ALLIED SECTOR

DANGER LINE

TURBULENT SEA OF INDIAN ECONOMIC SCENE

Fig SI

Fig. 52

FOODSTUFFS & POPULATION IN INDIA

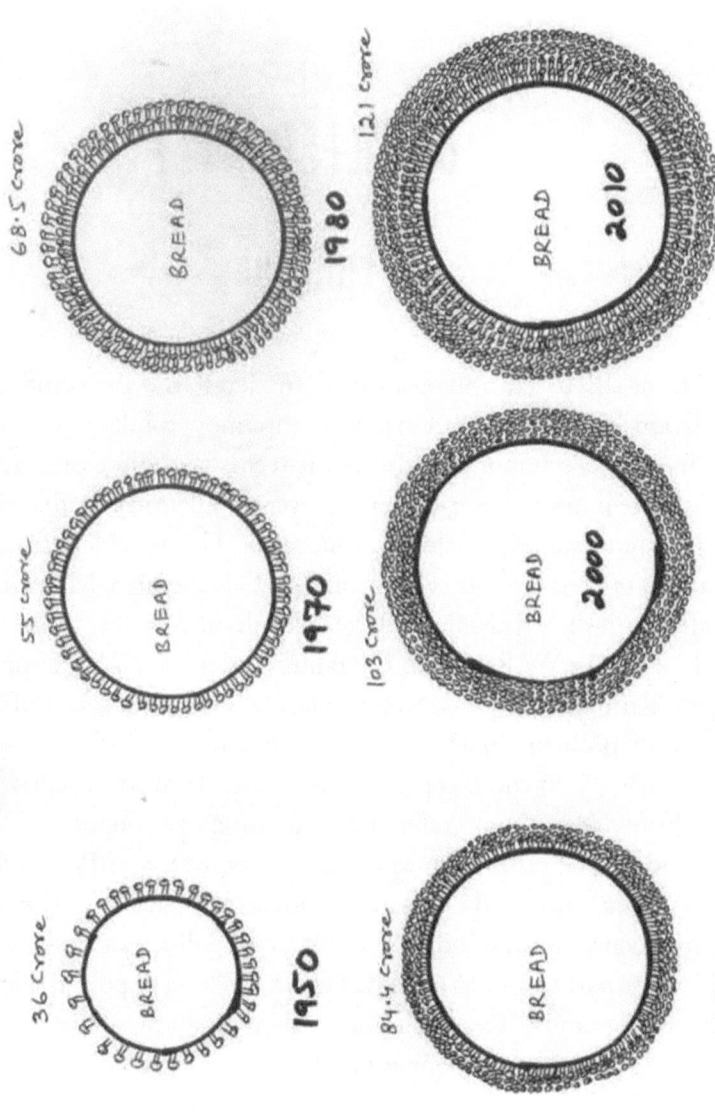

36 Crore
BREAD
1950

55 Crore
BREAD
1970

68.5 Crore
BREAD
1980

84.4 Crore
BREAD
1990

103 Crore
BREAD
2000

12.1 Crore
BREAD
2010

CHAPTER – 11

Epilogue

We have discussed and examined in detail the pros and cons of over-population in India which have been an almost totally neglected dimension in India's socio-economic landscape. It seems that discussing and examining seriously the impact of ever-increasing over-population of India on its economic growth is not a subject matter of economists. This is evident from the fact that India's top ranked economists like messers C.Rangrajan, Montek S.Ahluwalia, Bimal Jalan, Vijay L.Kelkar, Rakesh Mohan, Shankar Acharya, V.S.Vyas, N.A.Majumdar, Y.V.Reddy, C.H.Hanumantha Rao, S.S.Tarapore, K.C.Pant, Nagesh Kumar and Uma Kepila have'nt even touched India's exploding population problem in their essays, published in 'India's Economy in the 21st century'. With the exception of Mr. K.C. Pant in his essay 'Planning for Agriculture', where some references regarding over-population of India have been made, none other even touched it. Even Mr. K.C.Pant did no scientific analysis to examine and evaluate the adverse impact of over-population, and its consequences on the Indian economy and polity, nor has any attempt been made on his part to ascertain India's optimum level of population in relation to its natural resources. Keeping highest regard for all the above top economists of India, the author wishes to mention Dr. Pant's essay 'Planning for Agriculture';

Here in this essay, Dr. Pant has expressed his concern regarding food shortage and shrinkage of agricultural land in the face of growing population's needs, but he did not offer any solution or remedy to cope with it, nor any concept of optimum population did exist in his line of thinking. Similarly, the population policy of the Indian Government never attempted at evaluating an optimum level of human population to be targeted, keeping in view India's natural resources and its level of development. Though, the government of independent India, from the very beginning i.e. since 1947, emphasized the need of small family and population control, it never consider it a major challenging problem, growing with the time. Even Nehru, the first Prime Minister of free India and a statesman who was the main architect of nation's policies, never took it seriously. Among those who supported family planning, there were few who agreed with the solution of our economic problems lies in radical reduction of the population. Nehru, while supporting the policy of restricting population growth felt that the population growth by itself was not responsible for under – development. There were also serious differences on methods to be adopted for family limitations. It is reported that Gandhiji agreed that birth control was desirable but disapproved of contraceptives. He recommended self control and abstinence to build up the moral strength.

An expert panel of the U.N. Population policy Commission says that ultimate goal of population policies is to improve the general wellbeing of the population, and not only to improve per capita income. A population policy must form an integral part of over-all development policy and be explicitly related to such goals as better education, full employment, and rationalization of reproductive behaviors. There is a two-way relationship between variables in question and socio-economic development. For example, the rates of population growth have significant effect on levels of education and housing but these levels also tend to have a significant effect on population growth.

Here, we find that from the very beginning, the population policy of the Govt. of India has been a passive one instead of an active policy. The population planners of India accepted the growing population as a cause of poverty and backwardness, but also considered poverty and backwardness a cause of population growth. Thus they have attempted at diluting the movement of any effective measures to control the population. Instead, they emphasized to remove poverty and illiteracy first, which would eventually restrict the growth of population. This was a utopian concept which failed to control India's unabated growth of human population, thereby, defeated all the efforts of eradicating poverty, backwardness and illiteracy from the landscape of India for want of adequate resources. A nation, starved of resources can never and should never pursue this policy of population control. Here lies the main factor responsible for the total failure of population control in India, while our neighbour China has got success in the same. The socio-economic condition of China and India were nearly the same and so the population level. China very actively moved into population control measures and adopted 'one-child' per family norm strictly from the very beginning along with her efforts to remove her people's illiteracy and poverty on the one hand and improvement in education and health on the other. These combined efforts of the Chinese planners have had a remarkable and visible impact on her population quality in general and improved its general awareness which put in an enthusiasm in life. For the Chinese poor people, now life was no longer a burden, but a fountain of several niceties to achieve. Bright hope and fervour enlightened their life and they participated in nation building with full force and energy.

The reverse situation developed in India. Here, our planners and political leaders did not visualize an active role of their's in controlling the population menace and left it on the development plank. Since, the majority of population was illiterate, backward, thoroughly superstitious and deeply poor, whatever dividends it received from the State, it consumed it without any hesitation, presuming that these were in their rights from their own government after a prolong loot and exploitation by the British. They continued to follow their old life-style of having large families with a view to gaining economically in short span, but in the long run, this proved disastrous and ill-conceived, when their resources got fragmented and lessened with every passing year. Unemployment and underemployment prevailed all over the economy and subsidized food, fertilizer, medicines & medical help, children's education, transport, housing and clothing and several other articles of necessity became indispensable to maintain the poor and downtrodden, both urban and rural.

India's Central and State Governments both increasingly resorted to heavy taxation, huge public debt and then large volume of deficit financing to garner their incomes in order to prop-up a large poor population. Now, even after 67 years of Independence, 81 crore (810 million) people of our country do not have the basic security of food and our Central Government recently passed a Food Security Bill in Parliament to ensure food-security to these poor people of India. How strange! This is very deplorable and frustrating situation for nation's well-wishers.

It is often said in academic and political circles that China is ruled by an authoritarian ruling class represented by the Communist Party of China, where democratic freedom and independent thinking is not allowed to prevail and

Chinese people have had no choice except to accept the will of the ruling class. That is why the rule of 'one-child' norm for a Chinese family became operative successfully in China, as none dared to raise any dissenting voice. Here, it is correct that Chinese polity, after the communist revolution in 1949, has been an authoritarian one and people's democratic rights and liberties have largely been curtailed to a substantial level, even then the Chinese ruling class did successfully manage the various socio-economic problems of Chinese people and confidently catapulted China as a super power, capable of facing challenges of the modern times vigorously. Now China enjoys a status of equality vis-à-vis other super powers of the world. Even the U.S.A, the strongest super power of the world, could not match the economic power of China when we cast an eye on her favorable balance of trade position with that of the U.S.A. Currently, the U.S.A.'s economy is gratefully utilizing Chinese trade surpluses amount as Chinese investments on their land, thanks to a highly favorable trade-balance of China. This remarkable and qualitative economic development could not have been possible without the inclusive and vigorous participation of the Chinese people.

It is very likely that China has overtaken the U.S. to become the world's largest trading nation, a spokesman for China's customs administration, said while announcing that the county's imports and exports totalled $ 4.16 trillion last year. U.S. trade came to $ 3.5 trillion in the first 11 months of 2013, and there is little possibility that it would cross China's level in the first month. China may become the top trader for the first time and stay ahead of the U.S. in total foreign trade by $ 250 billion once Washington releases full data for 2013, sources said. China continued to buy less than it sold resulting in a 12.8 per cent rise in trade surplus to $ 259.75 billion, according to Customs data released on 10/01/14.

China's foreign exchange reserves, the largest in the world, reached a record $ 3.95 trillion in March and it plans to invest around $ 500 billion overseas in the next five years, a large share of which is expected to find India's way.

Mere authoritarian rule can not deliver quality and skill, unless a genuine and honest endeavour is there to improve the lot of the people. The Chinese government has had a strong will and clear direction to pull their polity towards a prosperous destination with full and vigorous participation of its people.

In 1980 China initiated a tough new drive on births with a goal of lowering the annual birthrate to 1 per cent during the decade. Among other measures, a financial disincentive program was started which included a provision that salaries of those workers who have a third child are reduced 10 per cent until that child reaches the age of 14. The child is also denied free education and medical care. Women are not permitted to marry before age 23 while the minimum age of marriage for men was raised to 26. Additional incentives include housing priorities for couple with no more than two children, job preference for the children of small families, the allocation of private garden plots to those with small families and finally, increased pension benefits scaled inversely to the number of children a retiree has had.

On the other hand, in India, we see that Indian ruling class, though democratic in its out-look and behaviour, never paid any serious and honest thinking for the well-being of its people and always took them 'for granted'. Had they taken seriously the problem of growing population and its all-round backwardness, they would have taken the timely steps in this direction by enacting a law in Indian Parliament as early as in 1951-52, just after the first general elections wherein the ruling Congress Party under Nehru's leadership had got an overwhelming majority, winning 364 seats out of 489 in the Lok Sabha (the lower house) and the Congress Party had formed ministries in all the states (provinces). This was the most favourable situation when a 'two-children' norm for a family might be got enacted and an optimum level of population should have been targeted. But, this could not happen in India, as the Indian leaders were totally oblivious of the impending menace of over-population going to loom large over India.

Later, in the year 1975-76, when Emergency had been imposed on India, some attention was paid to this problem of over population and some steps had been taken to control the population. But its implementation was so faulty and irrational that the scheme turned into a disgrace and dreadful in the eyes of the Indian people who disdainfully rejected it. Excesses were committed on the people and tyrannical methods were adopted to achieve birth control targets which proved counter-productive. People began to hate the ruling Congress Party, especially Mr. Sanjay Gandhi, the younger son of Mrs. Indira Gandhi, who was the master-mind of the scheme and its implementation. Indian people, en masse, rejected the Congress Party in the general elections of 1977 when Emergency had been lifted. **Paying no attention towards population**

control for almost 30 years since Independence and then all of a sudden implementing population control measures in a faulty, high handed and bureaucratic manner, both were equally harmful and disastrous. But as the dictum goes 'blessings in disguise', the educated and prudent people of India began to feel the importance and significance of small family norms. The educated middle and upper class people began to adopt 'two-children' norms as they saw economic prosperity into it. As a result, India's economic development since 1991 has taken a good lead and all sectors of the economy, especially manufacturing sector grew at a rapid rate due to increased demand for domestic goods, for example, televisions, refrigerators, home-furniture, cars and motorcycles/scooters, mobile phones, iron & cement and other housing materials, clothes and several other consumable articles etc. The boost in demand for these goods was purely due to the generation of income-surpluses with the middle class people who adopted small family norms (maximum two-children). A general awareness regarding small family took over in the minds of these people which eventually convalesced our ailing economy. But this awareness did not reach to lower classes who continued to increase their population as usual. India's population growth rate has come down during the last three decades, but in absolute terms, it is still growing rapidly.

Perhaps the least understood aspect of population growth is its tendency to continue even after birthrates may have declined substantially. Population growth has a built-in tendency to continue, a powerful momentum which, like a speeding automobile when brakes are applied tends to keep going for some time before coming to a stop. In the case of population growth this momentum can persist for decades after birthrates drop.

In India, the vehicle of population growth is also running very fast and, though the brakes have been applied very late & half-heartedly, a great momentum is still persisting, keeping chances of collision very imminent. In India, the talk of decreasing growth rate population is meaningless and ludicrous, as it has already grew too much above the level of optimum figure and becoming unmanageable. Now our economy is fast moving towards the threshold of collapse. (see figs. 50&51)

Role of the United Nations

The role of the United Nations should be of a friend, philosopher and guide for all the countries of the world, especially for the developing countries. The problem of over-population is not confined to India only, but most of the developing world is facing the same problem. In this way, this is an international problem and should be addressed at international macro level. The United Nations Organisation aims at the all round development of its member nations. The Department of Economic and Social Affairs of the Unites Nations Secretariat is a vital interface between global policies in the economic, social and environmental spheres and national action. The Department works in three main interlinked areas as:

1- It compiles, generates and analyses a wide range of economic, social and environmental data and information on which States Members of the United Nations draw to review common problems and to take stock of policy options;

2- It facilitates the negotiations of Member States in many intergovernmental bodies on joint course of action to address ongoing or emerging global challenges; and

3- It advises interested governments on the ways and means of translating policy frameworks developed in United Nations conferences and summits into programmes at the county level and through technical assistance, helps build national capacities.

It is clear from the above that the role of the United Nations is a vital one and it is doing its job well on the above said objectives. As far as, the issue of over-population is concerned, the U.N. has organised several conferences on this problem. The International Conference on Population and Development (ICPD) held at Cairo, Egypt in 1994 was one of such conferences organized by the U.N. The conference adopted a Programme of Action, according to which, the key development goal for the international community is to achieve sustainable development as a means to ensure human well-being, equitably shared by all people today and in the future. According to the Programme of Action, the achievement of sustainable development requires that **the interrelationship between population, resources, the environment and development be fully recognized, properly managed and brought into**

a harmonious, dynamic balance. Consequently, the Programme of Action calls for the formulation of development strategies that realistically reflect the short-term, medium term and long term implications of population dynamics by integrating population into development and environment programmes that take into account patterns of production and consumption and seek to bring about population trends consistent with the achievement of sustainable development and the improvement of quality of life.

It is clear from the above 'Programme of Action' on the part of the U.N. that it recognizes and underlines the need to have an interrelationship between population, resources (natural), the environment and development (inclusive) which should be managed in such a fashion that a balance of harmonious existence of humans with the mother nature is sustained. This is nothing but the very concept of maintaining an optimum level of human population in every country which the author of the book is advocating before the economists, politicians, academics and all the well-wishers of environment and humankind, including the United Nations. Unless an optimum level of human population is adhered to for every individual nation vis-à-vis its natural resources and environmental endowment and sustainability, real, eco-friendly and inclusive development is not possible. Even world peace and security is directly related to the maintenance of optimum population for every country. When real and inclusive development takes place for every country of the world, wars and revolutions shall cease and world peace shall descend on the earth. **Today, when there is general recession in the Western economies, the war industry is still flourishing.** Stockholm International Peace Research Institute's recent report mentions that despite the financial crisis of 2007-08, the global arms trade has been recession-proof. Military spending across the globe has been steady, and countries last year spent in excess of U.S. $ 1.7 trillion on their armed forces.

In is to be observed that global war industry and armed sale shall prosper as nations of the world go higher and higher from the level of optimum human population, for the simple reason, that they can not provide gainful jobs to their growing number of young people on the one hand and are bound to face the shortage of food grains and other edibles on the other, pushing their prices upward & the agricultural holdings towards uneconomic units. All these things raise the discontent level of the society and governments resort to oppressive methods to keep polity going. External conflicts and aggression also take place to grab other country's natural resources. Thus wars and conflicts can be very much controlled if all the polities of the world move towards maintaining an optimum level of human population. The demographic experts of the United Nations should come forward to ascertain and calculate the optimum level of population for all the individual nations of the world, keeping their natural resources in view. This can be done by the U.N. only. But the U.N. has not done this hitherto. **It has occasionally expressed concern over population explosion in the Third World developing countries, but never focussed its attention on calculating the optimum population of its individual member nations in order of facilitate them to target the same to achieve.** This should immediately be done by the U.N if we want to save our mother earth from a certain catastrophe. Once this is done, all the member nations of the United Nations may be persuaded to limit their respective human population around optimum level. Only then the future of earth as well as that of humankind is safe and healthy. Already, world human population is facing food shortage. Several studies had shown that global crop production needed to double by the middle of this century to meet the demands from an increasing human population, more meat and dairy consumption driven by growing afluence and more biofuels use as well to provide food security to millions who were chronically undernourished, observed Deepak K. Ray and his colleagues at the University of Minnesota's Institute on the Environment in the U.S. The researchers used a newly-developed crop yield and area harvested database to examine yield changes across the globe in maize, rice, wheat and soyabean, focussing on trends in the recent two decades. Yields of there crops needed to grow at about 2.4 per cent annually to double production by 2050. But the global average yield increase was only 1.6 per cent a year for maize, one per cent for rice, 0.9 per cent for wheat and 1.3 per cent for soybean. At there rates, global production of the four crops would be far below what is needed to meet projected demands by 2050. **Clearly, the world faces a looming and growing agricultural crisis. A portion of the production shortfall could be met by expanding croplands, but at a high environmental cost.**

The recent political disruptions like 'Arab Spring' and instability across the world clearly show that unemployment and underemployment, which are the legitimate babies of over-population, are the main driving forces behind all this.

More eye-catching has been the political revolutions, popular uprisings and protests in emerging markets. This spans June's demonstrations in Brazil (the largest in the country for two decades); through to the remarkable developments in North Africa and the Middle East, including the civil war in Syria which now occupies much international attention; revolutionary changes of power in Egypt, Tunisia and Libya; transfer of power in Yemen; plus demonstrations and uprisings in Turkey, Iran, Algeria, Bahrain, Jordan, Morocco and Oman. Thus unrest in the Middle East has often stemmed from deep-seated political and socio-economic discontent that pre-dates the financial crisis. Post-2008, however, factors including liquidity crunches, increased food prices and unemployment spikes have exacerbated these longer standing grievances. Even if the worst of the financial crisis has now passed, its consequences endure, especially for the young. People aged 15-24 constitute 17% of the global population, but 40% of the unemployed, a figure the International Labour Organisation forecasts will grow. This puts many at risk of long-term damage to their earnings potential and job prospects, fuelling discontent. In the EU, around 5.6 million people aged 15-24 are unable to find work (a record 24.4%) as career opportunity structures have been swept away for many. This has given rise to concern, including from German Chancellor Angela Markel about a "lost generation" especially in Greece and Spain where youth unemployment now tops a staggering 50%. As in Europe, youth unemployment in numerous Middle Eastern and North African Countries is above 50%, and it is estimated that the regions average rate could reach 30% within five years. **In the Middle East, the problem is acute because it has the world's biggest youth bulge comprising increasingly educated people. Indeed, overall political instability may decline if the world economy enters a sustained recovery phase.**

The big question is; will the world economy ever enter into a sustained recovery phase without controlling enormous population growth beyond the level of optimum numbers? Will that era ever come or not? **The author keeps a firm conviction that world economists and social-scientists shall certainly pay their immediate attention towards this unavoidable problem where everything is at stake.**

From Rapacious Capitalism To Social Capitalism

With the collapse of the Soviet Union and its East European allies during the nineties of the last century, the era of Marxist Socialism ended and it became clear that capitalism, in its transformed attire and insinuations, is the arbiter of the modern world. The innovative urge with competitive edge has been the hallmark of capitalism and profit earning its soul since its birth at the time of the Industrial Revolution in England. Since then, capitalism has faced several periods of crisis and wild accusations, but it emerged victorious after all. The great crisis of 1930s and then the collapse of imperialism after the Second Word War, the capitalism not only emerged triumphant, but gave a tremendous push to new discoveries and inventions in every sphere of knowledge and technology. **It successfully demonstrated that only capitalism has had the capacity and vigour to bring in and sustain progress with innovations.** The rapid development of the U.S.A., the U.K. and other Western European countries took place under the shadow of capitalism and free enterprise. Most of the newly freed Third World Countries initially pursued the path of mixed economy which contained the features of capitalism and socialism both wherein the concept of welfare economics found a central position. But this did not yield desired results and problems of abject poverty, massive unemployment and underemployment and staggered growth emerged. They all became indebted heavily to foreign aid burden and internal high inflation. Collapse of the Soviet Union and its Block pushed these developing countries towards the U.S.A. Block and under compulsion or otherwise, they gradually shifted towards free market economy with liberal policy framework. This further accentuated their problems as their economic growth turned almost into jobless growth and a large scale corruption with crony capitalism found its notorious place in the system. Concentration of wealth and vast inequalities are visible everywhere in capitalist world.

Seven out of the ten people in the world live in countries where inequality has increased over the past three decades. The richest 85 people in the world own the same amount of wealth as the bottom half of the world's population. In the U.S., inequality is back to where it was before the Great Depression, and the richest 1 per cent captured 95 per cent of all income gains since 2009, while the bottom 90 per cent got poorer. In India, the net worth of the billionaire community increased twelve fold in 15 years, enough to eliminate absolute poverty in this country twice over. Nevertheless, we need to get to grips with it, and make sure that inclusion is given as much weight as 'growth' in the design of policies. Yes, we need inclusive growth. More inclusion and opportunity in the economic life also means less cronyism and corruption.

Inequalities of very high level give birth to discontentment and strife between individuals as well as between nations. World peace always faces dangers when high level of inequalities exists in any society, within the nation or internationally. Thus maintenance of optimum population is the only **necessary** condition (but not a **sufficient** one) for a peaceful social order. Well educated people with a high awareness level, exercising their rights & duties vigilantly in a democratic set-up, are another equally important condition for a just and peaceful human existence. But the starting point is the attainment of optimum level of human population for any country including India and the rest shall follow afterwards *ipso facto*.

Thus a rapacious capitalism shall have to give way to **social capitalism**, wherein economic growth is not only eco-friendly and environment preserving, but human-friendly too. Wasteful expenditure incurred on advertisements for sales-promotion to outpace the rivals of the field is nothing but a hidden tax on the consumers, as its cost is included in the price of the commodity or service. Further, resources employed by those who lagged behind in the race of competition go waste and these companies resort to retrenchment of their employees. **Job security is as important as profits.** Mad-race for production and profits turns the capitalist class as an inhuman and anti-environment entity who is willing to go to any extent, least caring for environment or biodiversity. Today, world capitalist class is least bothered about environmental degradation, loss of biodiversity and global warming or over population. It's only concern is profit and capturing of markets. **This shall have to be changed into a new social-capitalism which cares for environment, ecology, protection of biodiversity and a sustainable economic development, keeping humans at the centre.**

As the great British economist John Maynard Keyens had said;

'**The political problem of mankind is to combine three things: economic efficiency, social justice and individual liberty.**'

This is possible only when rapacious capitalism is replaced by **social capitalism.** Since ideology is taking a back seat even in the erstwhile communist societies, there is a convergence that is taking place in all political systems in the world. Nationalization or privatisation is being viewed as the means and not the ends in themselves. **The question that is relevant is not to use the state or the market, but to use the state and the market and strike a balance, which fulfils the three objectives outlined by Keynes above.** This means that 'man' shall have to be a focus of wellbeing rather than mere a 'customer', who is a source of profit, though treated as 'sovereign' apparently in modern capitalist world. In today's world, wellbeing of man is totally absent from the market/profit oriented capitalism; its only concern is to extract profit out of its 'sovereign' customer's pocket. Once its objective is achieved, it no longer cares for him. The concept of 'social capitalism' introduces the element of humans' wellbeing in its totality and not in isolated boundaries. For example, when a country's electricity generation growth is very nicely achieved through thermo-electric methods, it means its air pollution growth is also very high and general public health is deteriorating too in the same proportion, making health and medical expenditure on a higher graph through increase in hospitals, doctors, nurses and other staff, stocks of medicines and other paraphernalia. Under this growth scenario, while people in general might be getting 24x7 electric supply, they are now having a poor health (asthma & cancer) and often resort to the services of doctors/hospitals, thus creating a loss of work-hours for the economy as a whole, apart from people's own expenses thereon. This model of growth and development has got no meaning in social capitalism wherein the electricity generation is to be done in such a fashion that it does not create any environmental problem. **In other words, people should get 24x7 electric supply without losing their health.**

Concluding Remarks

Here, I would like to reproduce a cartoon (see fig.73) developed by the author himself. In this cartoon, a dexterous T.V mechanic of repute has been shown as unscrewing his customer's T.V. set to search out a fault, but could not find any with the set. All of a sudden, his apprentice boy happened to see the disconnect of electric supply wire from the socket, done inadvertently by some one in the family, which his over-confident master could not notice. As soon as the electric supply has been restored, T.V. proved to be all right, without any fault. **The problem was absence of electric supply/current.**

Similar is the story of India's economic machinery. There is no major fault in the economy, only **the current of optimum population** is absent from the system, and if this deficiency is removed, Indian economy will flourish and furnish happy results. Unless this is done, no efforts would succeed, how much dedicated and prudent they are. They all go in waste and condition of the economy will deteriorate, instead of improving. We should stop forthwith treating the symptoms of the malady and concentrate our efforts on obliterating the malady itself, if we want to save our earth, its ecology and human existence thereon.

To conclude the book, I would like to say that there is still time to correct our path, before it is too late.

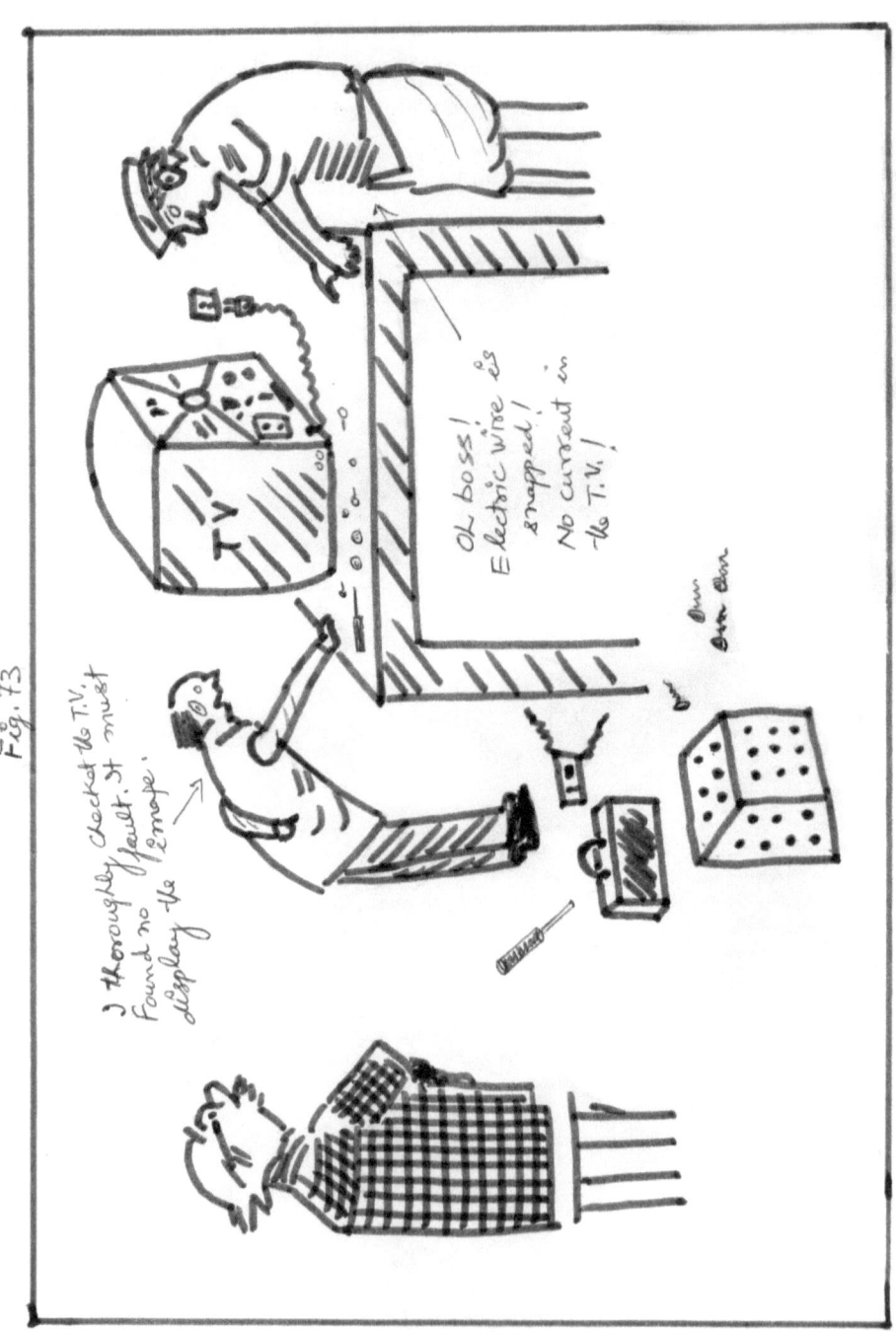

THE END

BIBLIOGRAPHY

1) Glimpses of World History: Jawahar Lal Nehru
2) A People's History of the World: Chris Harman
3) The Communist Manifesto: Marx & Angels
4) An Illustrated History of the Great October Socialist Revolution: Albert Nenarokov
5) Twentieth Century Britain: Kenneth O. Morgan
6) The Discovery of India: Jawahar Lal Nehru
7) Economic Development in the Third World: Michael P. Todaro
8) The Geeta: Ved Vyas
9) India's Economy in 21st Century: Raj Kapila & Uma Kapila
10) Population Policy: Col. B.L.Raina
11) Population Challenges and Development Goals: A United Nation's Publication
12) China: Socialist Economic Development Vol. III: A World Bank Study
13) China--Economy & Environment: Edited by M. Rasgotra
14) The Science Reporter – July 2013
15) Kurukshetra: A Journal On Rural Development
16) An Autobiography by Jawahar Lal Nehru
17) Demography: Measuring & Modeling population by Samuel Preston & Patrick Heubeline
18) A History of India (vol.two) by Percival Spear;
19) Population Growth and Economic Development in Low Income Countries: Coale and Hoover;
20) Problems of Capital Formation in Under-developed Countries: Ragnar Narkse;
21) Deficit Financing and Economic Development: R. G. Kulkarni;

22) The General Theory of Employment, Interest & Money: J. M. Keynes
23) Ecological Economocs for Sustainable Development: Edited by Raj Kapila & Uma Kapila
24) The Dominant Animal : Human Evolution and the Environment by Paul R Ehlrich & Anne H Ehlrich
25) Poverty and Famines by Anartya Sen

www.ingramcontent.com/pod-product-compliance
Lightning Source LLC
Chambersburg PA
CBHW030423290526
45786CB00001B/114